The Ultimate Chihuahua Handbook

Your Essential Guide to Raising, Training, and Caring for a Tiny but Fearless Companion

Inkspire

Table of Contents

Introduction	1
Why a Book on Chihuahuas?	2
What You'll Find in This Book	2
Chapter 1: The Chihuahua Origin Story	4
Ancient Lineage	4
The Mesoamerican Beginning	4
A Spiritual Successor: The Aztec Reverence	5
Colonial Disruption and Cultural Erasure	6
Rediscovery and Reinvention	6
The Modern Chihuahua: More Than a Pet	7
Global Popularity and Cultural Impact	8
Echoes of the Ancients	9
Conclusion: A Legacy That Lives	9
Discovery in Mexico	12
Chapter 2: Physical Traits and Personality	26
Coat Types and Colors	29
Chapter 3: Choosing the Right Chihuahua	44
Getting a Chihuahua from a Breeder	45
Which Path is Right for You?	48
Health and Pedigree Considerations	52
Perfect for Small Spaces, But Not Low Energy	59
Social, Loyal, and Deeply Attached	59
Families and Children: Handle with Care	60
Seniors and Solo Dwellers	62
Climate Sensitivity	63
Traveling and Social Lifestyles	63
Not for Everyone	64
Chapter 4: Bringing a Chihuahua Home	65
First 24 Hours	65
Preparing Your Space	65
The Arrival	66
Feeding and Bathroom Breaks	67
Establishing Trust	69
House Rules	73

Bonding Techniques	80
Physical Touch and Presence	81
Routine and Predictability	81
Communication and Training	81
Playtime and Enrichment	82
Building Confidence Through Exposure	82
Respect Their Unique Personality	82
Chapter 5: Training Your Chihuahua	86
Basic Commands	90
Tips for Effective Training:	94
Socialization Essentials	99
Early Socialization: The Foundation	99
Meeting New People	100
Socializing with Other Dogs	100
Exposure to New Environments	103
Handling Fear and Anxiety	103
The Role of Obedience Training	106
Group Classes and Socialization Events	106
Lifelong Socialization	106
Chapter 6: Nutrition and Feeding	108
Common Allergies and Sensitivities	113
Raw, Kibble, or Cooked?	121
Raw Food Diet: A Natural Approach	122
Kibble: Convenient and Balanced	123
Cooked Food: Fresh and Customizable	124
What's Best for Your Chihuahua?	126
Final Thoughts	128
Chapter 7: Health and Vet Care	130
Vaccines and Preventatives	134
Vaccinations for Chihuahuas	135
Non-Core Vaccinations	137
Importance of Regular Vet Visits	137
Conclusion	137
Preventative Care: Parasites and More	138
Routine Veterinary Care	140
Dental Health	140
Nutrition and Diet	141
Exercise and Activity	141
Behavior Monitoring	142

The Importance of a Proactive Approach	142
References:	143
The Benefits of Proper Dental Care	145
Chapter 8: Grooming and Maintenance	151
Choosing the Right Brush for Your Pet	152
Brushing Tips	154
The Importance of Bathing	155
How Often Should You Bathe Your Pet?	155
Finding the Right Products	157
Choosing the Right Shampoo	158
Bathing Tips	158
Importance of Regular Grooming	159
Tools for Grooming	160
Establishing a Routine	160
Why Nail Trimming is Important	161
How Often Should You Trim Your Chihuahua's Nails?	162
Tools for Nail Trimming	162
Steps for Trimming Your Chihuahua's Nails	163
When to Seek Professional Help	164
Conclusion	164
References:	165
1. Collar and Leash	169
2. Crate or Bed for Comfort and Security	170
3. Grooming Tools	170
4. Nail Clippers	170
5. Food and Water Bowls	171
6. Chew Toys and Treats	171
7. First Aid Kit	171
8. Flea and Tick Prevention	171
9. Car Safety Seat or Carrier	172
10. Emergency Contact Information	172
Chapter 9: Chihuahua Lifestyle	174
Feeding and Nutrition	175
Traveling with a Chihuahua	179
Preparing for the Trip	179
Traveling by Car	182
Flying with a Chihuahua	184
Accommodations and Local Regulations	186

Conclusion	187
References:	187
1. Dog Sweaters and Jackets	191
2. Boots for Protection	191
3. Harness and Leash Sets	192
4. Bowls and Travel Accessories	192
5. Bandanas and Bowties	193
6. Sunglasses and Hats	193
7. Raincoats and Ponchos	194
8. Personalized Tags	194
Chapter 10: Chihuahua Myths and Stereotypes	195
1. The Glamorous, High-Maintenance Chihuahua	214
2. The Sassy, Spoiled Chihuahua	215
3. The Yappy, Uncontrollable Chihuahua	215
4. The Tiny, Fragile Chihuahua	216
5. The Single-Purpose, Fashionable Chihuahua	216
Conclusion: A Balance Between Hollywood and Reality	217
Chapter 11: The Senior Chihuahua	218
Understanding the Aging Process	227
Adjusting Their Exercise Routine	227
Modifying Their Diet	228
Regular Veterinary Check-ups	228
Mental Stimulation and Comfort	229
Conclusion	229
References:	230
Chapter 12: Heartwarming Chihuahua Stories	240
Owner Stories	240
1. Taco Bell's Chihuahua (Gidget)	245
2. Bruiser Woods (Legally Blonde)	246
3. Chloe (Beverly Hills Chihuahua)	246
4. Rico (The Secret Life of Pets)	246
5. Papi (Beverly Hills Chihuahua 2 & 3)	247
6. Dog (The Mask)	247
7. Georgette (Oliver & Company)	247
Conclusion	248
References:	248

Luna's Rescue from the Streets	251
The Power of Adoption	253
1. The Chihuahua Who Took on a Big Dog	256
2. The Chihuahua Who Loved the Vacuum Cleaner	257
3. The Chihuahua Who Was Always the Ringbearer	258
4. The Chihuahua Who Loved to Help in the Kitchen	258
5. The Chihuahua Who Knew How to "Talk"	259
Conclusion: The Charm of Chihuahuas	260
Epilogue	261
The Bond Between Chihuahuas and Their Owners	261
Joys and Challenges of Owning a Chihuahua	262
Tales of Connection and Friendship	262
Finding Inspiration in Your Relationship	263
A Tribute to Chihuahuas	263

Introduction

At first glance, a Chihuahua might not seem impressive. They weigh just a few pounds, fit neatly in a handbag, and have eyes that almost take over their face. This appearance can make them seem like anything but legendary. However, for anyone who has shared a home with a Chihuahua, there is a deeper understanding. These dogs are not just small in size; they are large in spirit. Their personalities shine through, making them some of the most spirited animals one can own.

This book celebrates that spirit. It explores what makes Chihuahuas brave, stubborn, loyal, dramatic, endlessly entertaining, and full of love. It is for those who have shared a bed, a couch, or a life with a Chihuahua. It is also for the curious readers who want to understand why this breed is often misunderstood and deeply fascinating. Through this book, readers can appreciate the charm and complexity wrapped up in such a small package.

Why a Book on Chihuahuas?

The reason for writing this book lies in how often Chihuahuas are underestimated. To many, they appear to be nothing more than lap dogs, accessories for handbags, or funny memes. However, they belong to one of the oldest dog breeds in the Americas. Their ancestry can be traced back to ancient civilizations such as the Toltecs and Aztecs. These cultures held Chihuahuas in high regard, viewing them as sacred animals and companions to the elite. The belief was that they guided souls into the afterlife.

Today, their reputation has shifted to that of being yappy, spoiled, or snappy. This modern view only hints at who they truly are. Spending time with a Chihuahua reveals their true nature. They form deep, lasting bonds with their owners. They have a remarkable ability to sense emotions. Chihuahuas might bark at every leaf that rustles in the wind, but they also have a gentle side. They often curl up beside their owners after a long and exhausting day. Despite their small size, they have a significant emotional impact on the lives of their humans, pouring love and loyalty into each moment.

What You'll Find in This Book

The structure of this book will take you through 12 chapters, each showcasing a different aspect of life with a Chihuahua. The content will be a mix of stories, science, and practical advice. Readers will encounter Chihuahuas from various backgrounds, including rescues, show dogs, service animals, and those who are spoiled couch potatoes. The book will delve into the origins of the breed, their behavioral traits, health requirements, and training methodologies. Sharing personal stories from owners adds depth, showing the real-life experiences of those who know the unique joys and challenges of living with a Chihuahua.

Among the topics covered will be the rich history of the Chihuahua and its evolution into the charming companion it is today. Understanding the breed's personality is essential, as Chihuahuas love with great intensity, yet their barks can be loud and frequent. Training a Chihuahua presents its own challenges, but it should be done in a way that respects their spirit and individuality.

Nutrition and exercise will be discussed, highlighting common health issues that small dogs may encounter. The book will also set the record straight on common myths. This includes misunderstandings surrounding aggression, barking, and that so-called "attitude problem." Living with a Chihuahua involves much more than training—it includes building a bond, establishing routines, traveling together, and managing the ups and downs of daily life.

Additionally, the book will touch on sensitive topics, such as end-of-life care and the grief that comes with losing a beloved pet. It will address the emotions involved and help readers navigate through those sad, but inevitable moments.

This book aims to cater to both new and seasoned Chihuahua owners. It seeks to provide a complete view of life with these dogs. Readers will learn not just about the cute and amusing antics, but also about the raw, real, and sometimes chaotic aspects of owning a Chihuahua.

Life with a Chihuahua is more than a simple pet decision; it becomes a lifestyle choice. Chihuahuas have a way of testing your patience and yet bringing joy in ways you never thought possible. They can turn what may seem like a serious situation into a laugh. Public outings with them can lead to embarrassing moments, especially when they vocalize their feelings about guests. However, their loyalty and love are tremendous. It's a connection that feels boundless, even though it comes from a tiny creature.

That blend of smallness and depth creates a unique charm. Chihuahuas hold a big soul within their tiny hearts, making them fascinating companions.

Chapter 1: The Chihuahua Origin Story

Ancient Lineage

The Chihuahua is instantly recognizable—small in stature, bold in expression, and often wrapped snugly in designer sweaters or tucked under an arm like a fashion accessory. But to reduce this dog to a handbag ornament is to overlook a remarkable, ancient legacy that transcends time, borders, and trends. The story of the Chihuahua is not just one of evolution and breed standardization—it's a saga of spiritual guardianship, cultural endurance, and survival against staggering odds. This dog is a living thread tying modern life to sacred rituals, ancient ruins, and civilizations long since fallen. To know the Chihuahua is to peer into the shadows of Mesoamerican temples and feel the weight of belief etched into every bone and bark.

The Mesoamerican Beginning

Our journey begins in ancient Mesoamerica, where the Toltec civilization emerged around the 9th century CE. These people, highly advanced for their time, built complex urban centers, practiced metallurgy, and influenced the architectural and spiritual designs of subsequent cultures. But one of their most enduring legacies, albeit lesser-known outside of scholarly circles, is the domestication and veneration of a small, stocky, silent dog: the Techichi.

The Techichi was not bred for cuteness, companionship, or performance—it had a much greater purpose. In a time when the spiritual world was deeply intertwined with daily life, the Techichi was believed to serve as a spiritual guide, helping the deceased navigate the treacherous paths of the afterlife. Unlike the Chihuahua of today, the

Techichi was slightly larger, often weighing between 8–12 pounds, and had a more robust build. Still, its upright ears, alert gaze, and steady temperament foreshadowed the modern breed.

What sets the Techichi apart is its deep integration into Toltec society. Archaeological sites, particularly in central Mexico, have yielded graves where humans were buried alongside these dogs—sometimes curled in the fetal position as if poised to awaken and resume their divine task. Clay effigies, statues, and carvings resembling the Techichi have been found among ceremonial artifacts, suggesting that these animals held more than mundane value—they were sacred figures, imbued with meaning and purpose. They didn't just live with their human families; they escorted them to eternity.

A Spiritual Successor: The Aztec Reverence

Following the decline of the Toltecs, the Aztecs rose to power in central Mexico. Known for their militarism, advanced agriculture, and sprawling empire, the Aztecs borrowed heavily from Toltec culture—including their spiritual connection to the Techichi. In the Aztec worldview, death was not the end but the beginning of a perilous journey through Mictlan, the underworld, consisting of nine grueling levels that each soul had to pass through before reaching peace. The Techichi, according to belief, was uniquely suited to serve as a spiritual ferryman, guiding souls across rivers, past mountains, and through ghostly winds.

This wasn't just folklore—it shaped real-life practices. Dogs were often buried or cremated with the deceased, sometimes sacrificed specifically for this purpose. It was believed that the Techichi could shoulder human sins, cleanse the spirit, and act as a loyal protector in both life and death. Not all dogs were chosen for this role; only the Techichis that exhibited certain characteristics—calmness, silence, attentiveness—were believed to possess the necessary spiritual purity.

The importance of these dogs was further emphasized through color symbolism. Red Techichis, for instance, were considered particularly sacred and were thought to be the most powerful spiritual guides. These dogs weren't pets in the modern sense—they were intercessors between realms, as vital to the passage of the soul as a priest or shaman. To harm one unjustly was considered deeply disrespectful to the gods.

Colonial Disruption and Cultural Erasure

Like much of Mesoamerican culture, this spiritual connection between man and dog suffered a devastating blow during the Spanish conquest of the 16th century. With the arrival of Hernán Cortés and his forces, the Aztec empire crumbled. Temples were destroyed, languages suppressed, and sacred rituals outlawed. The spiritual, intellectual, and cultural infrastructure of an entire civilization was deliberately dismantled.

And yet, while many facets of life were lost forever, the little dogs managed to endure.

In more remote regions, especially in what is now the northern state of Chihuahua, Techichi-like dogs continued to live quietly among the people. They were no longer wrapped in ceremony, no longer seen as soul guides or sin-bearers—but they survived. Generations passed, and these small dogs lived on the periphery of attention, often found in villages, roaming farms, or being casually traded in local markets. They didn't disappear; they simply adapted, shrinking further in size, becoming more accustomed to human interaction, and waiting for their reintroduction to the larger world.

Rediscovery and Reinvention

In the mid-1800s, American travelers crossing into northern Mexico began noticing these compact, expressive dogs with oversized ears and alert personalities. Their unique appearance, coupled with their surprising boldness, caught attention quickly. Tourists, traders, and explorers began acquiring them—some out of genuine admiration, others out of curiosity. These dogs were typically found in the markets of Chihuahua and nearby states, leading to their informal christening as "Chihuahuas."

The breed's introduction to the United States sparked immediate interest. Their petite size made them novel in a world where large working breeds dominated. Their temperament—lively, loyal, vocal, and fiercely protective—set them apart from lap dogs that were seen as passive or docile. These were small dogs with big presence.

Over time, selective breeding in the U.S. and Europe began to refine their features. Breeders aimed for specific traits: a rounder skull (now known as the "apple head"), large, expressive eyes, and a more delicate skeletal frame. Their personalities remained largely intact—clever, confident, and independent—but their appearance became increasingly stylized to suit the tastes of an evolving pet-owning public.

In 1904, the American Kennel Club officially recognized the Chihuahua as a distinct breed. From that point on, the Chihuahua wasn't just a rediscovered relic of Mesoamerican history—it was a fully integrated figure in modern canine society, appreciated both for its ancient roots and contemporary appeal.

The Modern Chihuahua: More Than a Pet

Today, the Chihuahua holds a unique position in the dog world. It's one of the most recognizable breeds globally, often seen in media, advertisements, fashion magazines, and celebrity arms. This visibility has created a strange dual identity. On one hand, the Chihuahua is viewed as a glamorous accessory—a pampered pocket dog used to complete a "look." On the other, it's a tenacious, intelligent, and loyal companion with deep cultural roots and remarkable emotional awareness.

Despite its miniature size, the Chihuahua is known for having a "Napoleon complex"—fearless when it comes to protecting its family or territory. This confidence isn't a new development. It echoes the ancient trust placed in its ancestors, who were believed to protect the soul and absorb sin. Even now, many owners report their Chihuahuas acting as guardians of the home, alerting them to visitors long before any doorbell rings. It's as if the dog still carries a spiritual radar, always attuned to unseen forces.

Chihuahuas also show remarkable emotional intelligence. They form strong bonds with their humans, often choosing one particular person as their primary focus of attention. This loyalty can manifest as affection but also protectiveness, and even jealousy. They are known to shadow their favorite person around the house, refusing to be left out of any part of the daily routine. In this, they continue their role as companions —not just to the body, but to the spirit.

Global Popularity and Cultural Impact

The Chihuahua's rise in global popularity throughout the 20th and 21st centuries has been fueled by its adaptability. Its small size makes it ideal for urban living. Its low food requirements and moderate exercise needs make it manageable for a wide range of owners. Its expressive face and wide array of coat colors—from fawn and cream to black, chocolate, and merle—add to its visual appeal.

Pop culture has played a massive role in cementing the Chihuahua's place in the public eye. From the Taco Bell mascot to Elle Woods' dog Bruiser in *Legally Blonde*, Chihuahuas have become symbols of style, sass, and compact confidence. However, this popularity has had its downsides, too—rampant overbreeding, exploitation by puppy mills, and a tendency for people to adopt them for aesthetics rather than compatibility. Sadly, shelters across the U.S. have seen an increase in surrendered Chihuahuas over the past two decades, a consequence of impulse buying fueled by trends.

Yet the heart of the Chihuahua endures. For those who understand and respect the breed's needs—mental stimulation, gentle handling, firm boundaries, and daily companionship—the rewards are immeasurable. A well-cared-for Chihuahua is affectionate, intelligent, and loyal to the core. They bring humor, warmth, and a sense of constant connection into the home.

Echoes of the Ancients

What's most remarkable about the Chihuahua is not just how far it has come, but how much of its ancient essence it has retained. The same animal once buried alongside Toltec kings now curls up on couches and snuggles beneath blankets. The dog once believed to cleanse the soul now offers emotional support during modern-day stress and anxiety. The spiritual protector of ancient myth still stands guard—only now it's at the foot of your bed or by the front window, alert and ready.

When we look at a Chihuahua, we aren't just seeing a breed refined through modern breeding programs—we're witnessing a living connection to civilizations that once ruled Mesoamerica. Every yip, every bold trot across the living room floor, every instance of unwavering loyalty is a ripple from the past. These dogs are not just cute—they are storied. They are living artifacts, shaped by myth, molded by history, and carried forward by love.

Conclusion: A Legacy That Lives

The story of the Chihuahua is not just about where it came from; it symbolizes survival and change. This little dog has a rich background, tracing back to ancient civilizations like the Toltecs and Aztecs. These groups revered the Chihuahua, and it played important roles in their societies. Chihuahuas were often found in temples as sacred animals, connecting the breed to significant cultural practices. Despite the passage of time, Chihuahuas have shown great adaptability. They thrive in various environments, from the bustling streets of Mexico to cozy homes around the world. No matter where they are, these dogs keep their unique spirit alive.

Owning a Chihuahua means embracing a long-standing heritage. For over a thousand years, these dogs have been companions to people, sharing in their lives and experiences. This adds an extra dimension to pet ownership. It's not just about feeding them or taking them for walks. It's about participating in a lineage filled with history and stories. When you welcome a Chihuahua into your family, you tap into that legacy of resilience and warmth. Each Chihuahua carries a narrative of love and strength that adds richness to your relationship.

Moreover, Chihuahuas are known for their strong loyalty. They bond closely with their owners and develop deep affection. This loyalty is often seen in everyday interactions. For instance, when you return home after a long day, your Chihuahua might greet you with excited barks and wagging tails. This shows their joy in being part of your life. It creates a connection that goes beyond typical pet companionship. Their small size might lead some to underestimate their role, but Chihuahuas possess a larger-than-life attitude, proving that they can be fierce protectors despite their stature.

The adaptability of Chihuahuas is noteworthy. They can adjust to many living situations, from city apartments to country homes. This flexibility is appealing to many dog owners. For example, a Chihuahua can thrive in a small apartment, needing just a cozy spot to rest and a little space to play. Regular walks and brief play sessions are generally enough to keep them happy and healthy. This makes them suitable for individuals and families alike, offering companionship without demanding excessive space.

Chihuahuas also bring joy and laughter to everyday life. Their playful nature and spirited antics make them entertaining pets. A simple game of chase or a new toy can keep them engaged for hours. When you watch them explore new objects or try to figure out a puzzle toy, it can be heartwarming. Their curious minds lead them to delightful experiences that can brighten your day, reminding you to appreciate the small joys in life.

In addition to being playful, Chihuahuas can provide great emotional support. Their warm presence can be comforting during difficult times. There's something soothing about having a dog cuddle up next to you when you're feeling down or stressed. Chihuahuas seem to sense their owner's emotions and often adjust their behavior accordingly. They may snuggle closer or even nuzzle you for comfort, helping to ease feelings of anxiety or sadness.

Caring for a Chihuahua is a commitment that comes with its own set of responsibilities. It's essential to provide them with proper nutrition, regular vet check-ups, and enough exercise. Feeding them high-quality dog food is vital for their health. As they are small, portion sizes might be different from larger breeds. Consulting a vet about the best diet for your Chihuahua can ensure they maintain a healthy weight and avoid common health issues.

Training is another crucial part of owning a Chihuahua. Positive reinforcement techniques work best for them. Teaching basic commands, like sit and stay, can improve their behavior and strengthen your bond. Short training sessions are usually effective, as Chihuahuas can lose focus quickly. Consistency is key, along with patience and encouragement. Socializing them with other pets and people from a young age can help reduce any timid or aggressive behavior later on.

The connection you build with a Chihuahua is special. As they grow older, their personalities often become more pronounced. Some may become quite the characters, full of quirks that make you laugh. Others might turn into snuggly companions who prefer to be by your side. Regardless of their demeanor, the love they offer is profound. You don't just share your home with a Chihuahua; you share your life.

Through every phase—from puppyhood to their senior years—Chihuahuas teach valuable lessons about loyalty, love, and adaptability. They remind us of the importance of being there for one another and finding joy in little things. They have a way of making even the simplest moments feel meaningful. Whether it's a brief walk or a cozy evening at home, the presence of a Chihuahua adds happiness and warmth to each experience.

Ultimately, the legacy of the Chihuahua spans centuries, embodying resilience, love, and companionship. This tiny breed has withstood the test of time, adapting to changes while retaining its essence. Bringing a Chihuahua into your life means engaging with this deep-rooted history while creating new memories together. With their lively spirits and affectionate nature, Chihuahuas indeed leave a lasting impact on anyone lucky enough to share their lives with them.

References:

- American Kennel Club. *Chihuahua Dog Breed Information.* https://www.akc.org/dog-breeds/chihuahua/
- Valadez Azúa, R. & Teeter, K. *Dogs and People in Social, Working, Economic or Symbolic Interaction.* Oxbow Books, 2011.
- Coe, M. D. *Mexico: From the Olmecs to the Aztecs.* Thames & Hudson, 2013.
- Larson, G. et al. *Ancient DNA, dog domestication, and the dual origin of domestic dogs.* Science, 2012.
- Levine, M. A. *The Role of Dogs in Mesoamerican Burial Rituals.* Antiquity Journal, 2002.

Discovery in Mexico

The Chihuahua's story begins long before the dog became a fixture in handbags or show rings. Its roots go deep into the soil of ancient Mexico, reaching back to civilizations that predate modern borders and modern thinking. This tiny dog, often underestimated for its size, carries the genetic and cultural weight of thousands of years of human history.

Archaeologists and historians believe the Chihuahua descended from the Techichi, a small, mute dog that lived among the Toltecs in central Mexico as early as the 9th century. The Techichi wasn't just a companion animal—it played an important role in Toltec religious and spiritual life. These dogs were thought to have mystical abilities, particularly in relation to the afterlife. According to Toltec belief, when a person died, a Techichi could help guide their soul safely to the underworld. For this reason, Techichis were often buried alongside their owners, a ritual meant to secure safe passage to the next world.

When the Aztecs later conquered the Toltecs and absorbed many aspects of their culture, the spiritual status of the Techichi only grew.

The Aztecs believed the dogs had healing powers and could absorb the sins of their owners, acting as vessels for spiritual cleansing. In some cases, Techichis were sacrificed during elaborate religious ceremonies or burned with the dead to fulfill their duties as soul guides. These weren't just pets—they were sacred beings, deeply woven into the spiritual and ritualistic practices of daily life.

Physical evidence supports these claims. Ceramic effigies and carvings of small, broad-bodied dogs resembling the modern Chihuahua have been found in burial sites and ruins across Mexico. These artifacts, dating back hundreds of years, clearly suggest the presence and importance of these dogs in ancient culture. Their images appear in religious art, on temple walls, and among grave offerings—evidence that these animals were not just present, but honored.

After the Spanish conquest in the 16th century, much of the indigenous culture was suppressed or destroyed, including religious practices involving animals. Yet the small dogs endured, surviving in rural and isolated communities throughout Mexico. In particular, the northern region that would become the state of Chihuahua remained a stronghold for the breed. There, in dusty villages and mountainous terrain, these dogs continued to live among the people—unbothered by fame, small in size, but with a reputation for being sharp, feisty, and loyal.

In the late 1800s, Americans traveling through Mexico began to take notice of the breed. Some were intrigued by the dog's compact size and bold personality. Others were fascinated by the rumors of its ancient, even mystical origins. As traders brought the dogs back to the United States, their popularity began to rise. The name "Chihuahua" was adopted, referencing the region where they had been rediscovered. Early American breeders sought to standardize the look of the dog, focusing on its petite frame, large ears, and expressive eyes. Though the Techichi had likely been mute, the modern Chihuahua found its voice—literally—gaining a reputation for its yappy bark and intense alertness.

By the early 20th century, Chihuahuas were being formally recognized by kennel clubs and incorporated into breeding programs. Yet even as the breed adapted to modern life, its ancient roots remained visible. Today, the Chihuahua is often treated as a lapdog or fashion accessory, but its DNA carries the story of empires, rituals, and sacred belief systems. It stands as a living relic of the civilizations that once flourished in the heart of Mexico.

Understanding the Chihuahua's past adds depth to its present. It's more than a tiny companion—it's a breed shaped by mythology, preserved by resilience, and discovered again through the lens of history.

References:

- American Kennel Club. (n.d.). *Chihuahua Dog Breed Information*. Retrieved from https://www.akc.org/dog-breeds/chihuahua/
- Schwartz, M. (2000). *A History of Dogs in the Early Americas.* Yale University Press.

- Valadez Azúa, R. (2014). *Dogs and Humans in Ancient Mesoamerica: Archaeozoological Perspectives.* UNAM Institute of Anthropological Research.
- The Smithsonian Institution. (n.d.). *Indigenous Dogs of the Americas.* Retrieved from https://naturalhistory.si.edu
- Clutton-Brock, J. (1995). *Origins of the Dog: Domestication and Early History.* In Serpell, J. (Ed.), *The Domestic Dog: Its Evolution, Behaviour and Interactions with People.* Cambridge University Press.

Breed Development

The development of the Chihuahua is a story that spans centuries and continents, blending indigenous culture, colonial disruption, and modern breeding practices into the history of a dog that, despite its size, has never gone unnoticed. With a lineage believed to stretch back over a thousand years, the Chihuahua stands as one of the oldest dog breeds in the Americas—its survival a testament to adaptation, human affection, and historical chance.

Most historians and canine researchers agree that the Chihuahua descends from the ancient **Techichi**, a small, quiet, and sturdy dog kept by the **Toltec civilization** in what is now Mexico. The Techichi is not a mythical creature—it is well-documented through pottery, carvings, and burial findings. Dogs resembling the modern Chihuahua have been found in **Toltec burial sites dating as far back as the 9th century**. These early dogs weren't ornamental pets. They were spiritually and socially important, often believed to have mystical powers. The Techichi was thought to guide souls through the afterlife and help absolve the sins of the dead, which is why many were buried alongside their human companions.

When the **Aztecs** overthrew the Toltecs, they absorbed many of their customs—including their reverence for the Techichi. The Aztecs took the spiritual role of these dogs even further. Some believed that red Techichis had the power to protect homes from evil spirits, while others were thought to be conduits between worlds. Their value was not based on size or aesthetics but on spiritual significance and companionship. During Aztec rule, these dogs remained common in noble and religious households.

The arrival of **Spanish conquistadors in the 16th century** brought massive upheaval. Much of the Aztec culture was destroyed or assimilated into colonial systems, and many indigenous animal breeds disappeared. Yet, the small dog that would become the Chihuahua endured. Through generations of informal breeding in rural villages—particularly in the northern states like **Chihuahua, Sonora, and Durango**—these dogs continued to exist. Farmers and families valued them for their companionship, alertness, and compact size. They were not officially bred or documented but passed down through communities as common household dogs.

By the **mid-19th century**, American tourists and traders traveling through northern Mexico began noticing the tiny dogs sold in marketplaces or kept by locals. Many of these visitors took the dogs back home, intrigued by their unusual appearance and endearing size. Because many of the dogs were found in the state of **Chihuahua**, the name stuck. This marked the beginning of the Chihuahua's transition from a Mexican village dog to a registered, recognized breed in the United States.

The **American Kennel Club (AKC)** officially registered its first Chihuahua in **1904**. The dog's name was "Midget," and it marked the start of a structured breeding effort in the U.S. Early Chihuahuas varied in appearance—some with longer legs, others with broader muzzles—but the general qualities were the same: small size, large eyes, upright ears, and fierce loyalty. Over time, breeders worked to create more consistency, and two coat varieties emerged: the **smooth coat (short-haired)** and the **long coat**. Though they appear different, they are the same breed and often born in the same litters.

As the Chihuahua's popularity grew, so did the interest in refining its features. Breeders emphasized the distinctive **apple-shaped head**, which eventually became a hallmark of the breed standard. However, a second head type, known as the **deer head**, also existed. While deer-headed Chihuahuas are often healthier due to slightly larger skulls and less extreme facial structures, they are not favored in show rings under AKC standards.

Throughout the **20th century**, Chihuahuas experienced waves of popularity. In the 1950s and 60s, they became associated with Hollywood and celebrity culture. By the 2000s, they reached peak fame, appearing in movies, television commercials, and even fashion magazines. Unfortunately, this attention had a downside. The surge in demand led to overbreeding, with many breeders sacrificing health and temperament in favor of size and appearance—especially the rise of so-called "**teacup Chihuahuas**," which are bred to be even smaller than standard but often suffer from serious health issues.

Today, responsible breeders are working to undo some of that damage. There is renewed emphasis on ethical practices, genetic screening, and educating the public about the real needs of Chihuahuas. Despite their size, these dogs require mental stimulation, exercise, and consistent care. Their intelligence and loyalty make them wonderful companions, but they are not novelty pets—they are a breed with deep cultural roots, complex behaviors, and a history intertwined with human civilization.

The Chihuahua's development isn't just about how the breed came to look the way it does. It's a story of cultural preservation, survival, and reinvention. From ancient burial sites to modern dog shows, from sacred guides to pop culture icons, the Chihuahua's journey reflects much more than its size. It reflects the power of endurance, the depth of human-canine connection, and the ongoing evolution of how we understand and value our pets.

References:

- American Kennel Club. (n.d.). *Chihuahua Dog Breed Information*. Retrieved from https://www.akc.org/dog-breeds/chihuahua/
- Fogle, B. (2000). *The Encyclopedia of the Dog*. DK Publishing.
- Palika, L. (2007). *Chihuahuas for Dummies*. Wiley Publishing.
- Serpell, J. (1995). *The Domestic Dog: Its Evolution, Behavior, and Interactions with People*. Cambridge University Press.
- Wilcox, B., & Walkowicz, C. (1995). *The Atlas of Dog Breeds of the World*. TFH Publications.
- Alderton, D. (2002). *Dogs: The Ultimate Dictionary of Over 1,000 Dog Breeds*. Firefly Books.
- Eberhard, D.M. (1995). *The Chihuahua: A Story of a Tiny Dog with a Big History*. Heritage Press.

From Obscure to Iconic

The narrative of the Chihuahua encompasses not only the history of a particular dog breed but also extends to encompass vast geographical and temporal scales, including the span of multiple empires, continents, and centuries. The Chihuahua's ascent to global renown is a compelling case study in the interplay of spiritual tradition, cultural transformation, and media influence. Despite its diminutive stature, weighing in at a mere six pounds, the Chihuahua has made an indelible mark on the annals of human history that equals the legacy of even the most sizable breeds.

The Chihuahua's ancestral lineage can be traced back to the Techichi, a diminutive and docile canine that inhabited the Toltecs' environment during the 9th century. The Techichi was not merely a pet; it was held in high esteem for its spiritual significance. In Toltec and later Aztec belief systems, these canines were entrusted with sacred duties. It was widely believed that these entities possessed mystical abilities, including the capacity to heal, guide souls, and absorb sin. In the Aztec belief system, when a noble or priest passed away, it was customary to bury or cremate them alongside a Techichi, a practice that served a spiritual function. According to Aztec beliefs, the Techichi's role was to act as a guide for the spirit of the deceased through Mictlan, the underworld realm. These canines served as spiritual companions, believed to possess the ability to transport the souls of the departed across rivers, through mountains, and across the various levels of existence until peace was achieved. Red Techichis were particularly esteemed for their enigmatic function. Their presence in burials and ceremonial artwork underscores their profound spiritual significance.

The Spanish conquest of Mexico in the 16th century entailed more than the mere occupation of land; it also involved the dismantling of established civilizations. In addition to the loss of cultural heritage represented by temples and traditions, there was a significant loss of indigenous knowledge regarding spiritual connections to animals. Notwithstanding the devastation, the Techichi's heritage persisted. The canines themselves found sanctuary in remote, less colonized areas— particularly in northern Mexico, where rugged terrain and isolated villages allowed them to remain largely unchanged. Despite the loss of their spiritual roles, these canines persisted in their quiet existence as companions, often overlooked by the external world for centuries.

It was not until the 1800s that the modern world began to rediscover the Chihuahua's ancient lineage. American tourists visiting Mexico reported observing canines of unusually diminutive stature and high alertness in markets and rural homes. Visitors to the region found themselves intrigued by the size, appearance, and temperament of these animals, leading to an increase in the number of individuals being brought across the border. These canines, which are typically found in the state of Chihuahua, subsequently adopted the appellation of the region, leading to the informal designation of the breed as "Chihuahua."

In 1904, the American Kennel Club formally acknowledged the Chihuahua as a distinct breed. The inaugural Chihuahua to be officially documented was a male dog named "Midget." While this event signified a substantial landmark in the breed's historical development, the Chihuahua's renown remained relatively modest. During the first half of the 20th century, Chihuahuas were predominantly maintained by breed enthusiasts and collectors who valued their diminutive stature, exotic provenance, and spirited disposition. At that time, they had not yet achieved the level of renown and media exposure that characterizes them in the present.

However, the advent of television, mass advertising, and popular culture precipitated a paradigm shift in this dynamic. These platforms did not merely provide entertainment; they influenced public perception, shaping trends in fashion and pet ownership. The Chihuahua breed, renowned for its expressive eyes and compact size, was particularly well-suited for the camera's visual documentation. During the 1990s, the breed experienced a marked increase in visibility due to a strategic advertising campaign initiated by Taco Bell. This campaign, which would subsequently become iconic, played a significant role in raising the profile of the breed. The Taco Bell Chihuahua advertisements, which featured a charismatic animated Chihuahua who famously proclaimed, "¡Yo quiero Taco Bell!" (translated as "I want a Taco Bell!" in English), catapulted the breed into the spotlight. The Chihuahua's transformation from an obscure breed to a ubiquitous presence has occurred almost instantaneously.

It is evident that Hollywood rapidly adopted this practice. In the film Legally Blonde, the character Elle Woods, played by Reese Witherspoon, is frequently depicted in the company of her fashion-forward Chihuahua, named Bruiser Woods. Adorned in matching pink attire and bearing designer handbags, Bruiser transcended the role of a mere sidekick, emerging as a statement, a brand, and a symbol of extravagant elegance. Subsequent films and television programs have adopted this trend, frequently featuring Chihuahuas in roles that exhibit characteristics such as impudence, audacity, or unexpected courage. These portrayals have often garnered significant popularity and emotional resonance among viewers. The public demonstrated a favorable response to the initiative. The demand for Chihuahuas escalated precipitously, leading to a situation in which breeders were unable to meet the demand.

However, this surge in popularity has been accompanied by significant ramifications. With the breed's ascent into the mainstream, there was a concomitant surge in unethical breeding practices. The emergence of puppy mills and the irresponsible breeding practices of certain breeders have led to a significant increase in the production of Chihuahuas. These breeders have placed a higher priority on maximizing profits rather than on ensuring the well-being of the animals, their temperament, or the quality of their lineage. The Chihuahua's bold personality, high energy levels, and need for consistent training were not adequately considered when the dogs were sold to inexperienced owners. A notable increase in the number of abandoned or surrendered Chihuahuas was observed in shelters coinciding with the disillusionment of pet owners with the reality of owning one of these animals, which often did not align with the idealized portrayal of the breed in the media. Contrary to popular expectations, the doll was not passive; rather, it was characterized by its fiercely intelligent nature, occasional stubbornness, and consistent expression of its opinions.

Notwithstanding the aforementioned challenges, the Chihuahua has persisted in its role as a symbol of fortitude, fidelity, and elegance. Those who invest time in understanding the breed's historical background and temperament swiftly discern that Chihuahuas encompass far more than mere fashion accessories. These animals have been observed to form profound bonds with their human companions. These organisms exhibit remarkable adaptability, demonstrating resilience in both urban and rural environments. Their confidence frequently approaches a state of fearlessness, rendering them highly effective watchdogs, capable of alerting their owners to even the most minimal disturbances. While they may exhibit wariness towards strangers and a protective instinct towards their territory, a properly socialized and well-trained Chihuahua can exhibit qualities such as sweetness, sociability, and an entertaining demeanor.

A significant aspect of the modern appeal of the Chihuahua is attributable to its complexity. The following analysis will examine a canine specimen that occupies a liminal space between two distinct temporal periods: the ancient and the modern. On the one hand, it is a creature steeped in mythology, once considered a sacred being capable of escorting souls to the afterlife. Conversely, it has emerged as a prominent figure in popular culture, making appearances on runways, television screens, and Instagram accounts with a level of confidence and elegance. This duality contributes to the enduring fascination surrounding the Chihuahua. This phenomenon serves as both a relic and a trendsetter, embodying a multifaceted role as a spiritual guide and a source of sass.

In the contemporary era, Chihuahuas continue to be among the most popular toy breeds on the global scale. The spectrum of available coat types and personalities is extensive, offering a wide variety to suit diverse preferences and needs. Some individuals exhibit extroverted and adventurous tendencies, while others manifest introverted and clingy behaviors. Some individuals prefer the experience of traversing the lap, while others opt for the hiking trail. Notwithstanding their individual idiosyncrasies, all Chihuahuas bear the unmistakable hallmarks of their ancestry: loyalty, awareness, intelligence, and a remarkable degree of emotional depth, all encapsulated within a diminutive physical frame.

Their legacy endures in the realm of rescue work and advocacy. As shelters continue to care for Chihuahuas surrendered due to neglect or misunderstanding, breed-specific rescues have increased their efforts. These organizations aim to educate the public, promote responsible ownership, and place dogs into families who understand and appreciate the breed's true nature. There is a growing movement among Chihuahua owners and advocates to challenge the prevailing stereotypes associated with the breed. These individuals are working to dispel the misconceptions that Chihuahuas are merely vocal and excitable pets or superficial fashion statements. Instead, these animals are presented as survivors, companions, protectors, and individuals with unique personalities that deserve respect.

The transition of the Chihuahua from a sacred relic to a media icon has been a tumultuous one. The phenomenon has been characterized by a multifaceted journey marked by reverence, reinvention, exploitation, and redemption. However, throughout its evolution, the breed has maintained a distinctive characteristic: an unwavering sense of identity. They do not attempt to embody characteristics that do not align with their inherent identity. The subjects displayed a sense of boldness without aggression, a protective nature without hostility, and a sense of loyalty without clinginess. Additionally, they exhibited a strong sense of self-assurance without neglecting their origins.

Ultimately, the factors contributing to the Chihuahua's iconic status extend beyond its renown and its penchant for the dramatic. The substance of the style is rooted in the ancient legacy, the resilience, and the emotional depth. Chihuahuas have demonstrated that their influence is not contingent upon their physical stature. This phenomenon is exemplified by the presence of silent guides in the underworld and vocal stars on the big screen. Their journey exemplifies survival, transformation, and the profound bond between canines and humans.

It is noteworthy that few breeds have achieved such extensive travel in terms of both distance and reputation. A smaller percentage have managed to integrate ancient mysticism with modern celebrity. The Chihuahua's ability to thrive in a variety of circumstances is noteworthy, as it demonstrates that excellence can be found in unconventional sources and manifestations.

References:

- *American Kennel Club.* (n.d.). Chihuahua Dog Breed Information. https://www.akc.org/dog-breeds/chihuahua/
- Serpell, J. (1995). *The Domestic Dog: Its Evolution, Behaviour and Interactions with People.* Cambridge University Press.

- Coile, D. C. (2011). *Chihuahuas for Dummies*. Wiley Publishing.
- Fogle, B. (2009). *The Dog Encyclopedia*. DK Publishing.
- Osborn, L. (2019). *A Cultural History of Animals in the Age of Empire*. Bloomsbury Academic.
- Riehl, A. (2006). *The Chihuahua: A History*. Pet Press.

Chapter 2: Physical Traits and Personality

Size and Body Type

The Chihuahua is famously known as the smallest dog breed in the world, but this tiny dog carries itself with surprising confidence, grace, and intensity. Measuring between 5 to 8 inches in height and weighing only 2 to 6 pounds on average, the Chihuahua might seem fragile or delicate at first glance. However, beneath that tiny frame lies a dog with remarkable structure, physical expression, and endurance.

Its compact size is one of its most defining physical characteristics. The Chihuahua's body is slightly longer than it is tall, giving it a balanced, almost rectangular silhouette. This proportion is important—it supports the breed's agility and helps maintain stability despite its light frame. Chihuahuas often appear lean and fine-boned, especially when compared to sturdier small breeds. However, the best specimens still have noticeable muscle tone and a sense of firmness in their stance.

The chest is well-developed for such a small breed, not broad or deep, but giving a sense of strength and poise. The ribs are rounded but not overly pronounced, allowing for easy breathing and efficient movement. Their back is level and firm, contributing to their balanced stride. The hindquarters are muscular and aligned properly with the shoulders, providing the push needed for their surprisingly fast trot. Their gait is lively and quick, often with a high-stepping motion that reflects confidence and awareness of their surroundings.

One of the Chihuahua's most expressive physical traits is its tail. Moderately long and curved, it may arch gracefully over the back or curve to one side in a sickle shape. The tail is carried high when the dog is alert or excited and drops low when it's relaxed. A Chihuahua's tail isn't just an appendage—it's a key part of how the dog communicates, along with its upright ears and expressive face.

Another distinguishing feature of the Chihuahua is its head. There are two types of head shapes: the "apple head," which is the breed standard accepted by the American Kennel Club, and the "deer head," which is more elongated and less common in show dogs. The apple head has a rounded skull, a short and slightly pointed muzzle, and a distinctive "stop" (the point where the forehead meets the muzzle). This look gives the dog a baby-like appearance, which many owners find irresistible.

In contrast, the deer-headed Chihuahua has a longer, narrower face with a more gradual slope between the forehead and the nose. While not officially recognized for show purposes, deer-headed Chihuahuas are popular among pet owners and often admired for their elegant, fox-like appearance.

A Chihuahua's eyes are large, round, and set wide apart. These eyes are among the most expressive in the dog world—capable of conveying everything from curiosity to defiance to affection. Their color is usually dark, but lighter shades, including hazel and even blue, are occasionally seen depending on the coat genetics. Eye expression is a signature trait of the breed—watchful, intelligent, and often intense.

Their ears are large in proportion to their head and stand erect when the dog is alert or excited. Even when relaxed, the ears maintain a degree of attentiveness, constantly turning to track sounds. These prominent ears add to the Chihuahua's unique silhouette and further accentuate its alert and inquisitive nature.

The breed comes in two coat varieties: smooth coat and long coat. The smooth-coated Chihuahua has a short, glossy fur that lies close to the body, giving it a sleek appearance. The long-coated variety has a soft, sometimes slightly wavy coat that may include feathering on the ears, legs, and tail. Both coat types are naturally elegant and require minimal grooming compared to some other toy breeds.

Chihuahuas also boast one of the widest ranges of coat colors and patterns in the dog world. Solid colors like fawn, black, chocolate, cream, and white are common, but they also come in sable, brindle, merle, spotted, and multi-colored patterns. No two Chihuahuas look exactly alike, and their coat markings often become part of their identity.

Despite their small size, Chihuahuas are structurally sound and surprisingly tough. They are agile, quick, and capable of keeping up on walks or play sessions. That said, their size does require some caution. A fall from a couch or accidental rough play from larger pets or young children can cause injury. Their small legs and joints are not built for heavy impact, so it's important to treat them with care without underestimating their physical capability.

In addition to their agility, they possess a surprisingly high level of stamina. Many Chihuahuas enjoy daily walks, fetch, or even agility courses. They are far from being lap-only dogs. While they thrive in apartments and small spaces, they benefit from active play and exploration, often zipping around the house or yard with bursts of energy that show off their athleticism.

The Chihuahua's small, refined frame is deceptive. Underneath lies a body that is strong, expressive, and built with intention. From their distinctive head shapes to their lively tails and precise movements, every physical aspect of the Chihuahua speaks to its long history of adaptation, survival, and self-assurance. It may be small, but this breed carries itself like a giant.

References:

- American Kennel Club. *Chihuahua Breed Standard.* https://www.akc.org/dog-breeds/chihuahua/

- Federation Cynologique Internationale (FCI). *Breed Standards – Chihuahua.* https://www.fci.be/en/nomenclature/CHIHUAHUA-218.html

- Alderton, D. *The Dog Encyclopedia.* DK Publishing, 2014.

- Coppinger, L. & Coppinger, R. *Dogs: A Startling New Understanding of Canine Origin, Behavior & Evolution.* Scribner, 2001.

- Palika, L. *Chihuahua: Your Happy Healthy Pet.* Wiley Publishing, 2007.

Coat Types and Colors

The Chihuahua, despite its small size, offers one of the most diverse ranges of coat types and colors in the dog world. This impressive variety adds another layer of richness to the breed's identity—proving that Chihuahuas are anything but basic. While they may be grouped together under one breed standard, their appearances can vary widely, making each individual dog visually distinct. From smooth, glossy coats to flowing, feathered fur and from solid hues to complex patterns like merle or brindle, the Chihuahua showcases a genetic palette as expressive as its personality.

There are two officially recognized coat types in the Chihuahua breed: the smooth coat and the long coat. These distinctions are acknowledged by major kennel organizations like the American Kennel Club (AKC), the United Kennel Club (UKC), and the Fédération Cynologique Internationale (FCI). Though the differences might seem purely aesthetic at first glance, each coat type brings with it a unique set of care requirements, visual impact, and texture that further define the Chihuahua experience.

The smooth coat Chihuahua is often the more common and more easily maintained of the two. Its short, sleek fur lies flat against the body, giving the dog a polished, streamlined look. The texture is soft but tight, creating a smooth appearance that accentuates the breed's naturally alert and angular features. These coats are easy to care for: a quick brushing once or twice a week with a soft-bristle brush or grooming glove is typically sufficient. This helps control shedding, distribute natural skin oils, and maintain coat health. Despite the short length, smooth coats still shed seasonally, especially in the spring and fall when the undercoat may thin or thicken in response to temperature changes.

The long coat Chihuahua, in contrast, exudes a completely different visual charm. These dogs have longer, often softer fur that can range from slightly wavy to straight and silky. The coat tends to feather out around specific areas, including the ears (sometimes forming "ear fringes"), neck (producing a lion-like ruff), legs, tail, and chest. These long-haired Chihuahuas are often described as more elegant or refined in appearance, with a "regal" quality due to the flowing fur and feathered textures. While undeniably beautiful, this coat does require more attention. Daily brushing is ideal to prevent mats and tangles, especially behind the ears, under the armpits, and along the haunches. A comb or slicker brush works best to reach the undercoat and remove loose hair. Regular grooming also helps reduce the risk of knots forming where the fur rubs against collars, harnesses, or bedding.

Both coat types are considered double-coated, meaning they have a soft, insulating undercoat beneath a layer of protective guard hairs.

However, not every Chihuahua exhibits this equally. Some have very thin undercoats or appear almost single-coated, depending on genetics and environment. Chihuahuas bred in warmer climates or for show may have less undercoat density, while those from cooler regions tend to develop thicker insulation for warmth.

Where the coat type adds texture and structure, color brings bold personality. Chihuahuas are available in an extraordinary range of colors, patterns, and combinations. There's no "standard" color for the breed, which makes the variety all the more striking. Some of the most common solid colors include:

- **Fawn** – The most classic and widely recognized Chihuahua color, varying from pale tan to rich caramel.
- **Black** – Glossy and deep, often striking when paired with tan markings or a contrasting white chest.

- **White** – Pure white is less common but highly sought after for its clean, standout appearance.
- **Chocolate** – A deep brown that can be rich and luxurious, often paired with lighter markings.
- **Cream** – A soft, light beige that gives the coat a plush, velvety look.
- **Blue** – A diluted grayish-blue hue, rare and often seen as exotic.
- **Red** – A bold, coppery tone that adds vibrancy to the dog's overall look.

Beyond these solid colors, Chihuahuas frequently display **bi-color** and **tri-color** combinations. These can include pairings like:

- Black and tan
- Chocolate and white
- Fawn and white
- Blue and tan
- Cream and red

These combinations may be spread evenly across the body or appear in unique placements, such as a white blaze down the chest, "socks" on the feet, or a full mask across the face. The **pattern distribution** often adds character and individuality to each dog.

Chihuahuas can also present with **distinct coat patterns** that go beyond simple coloration:

- **Brindle** – A striking tiger-stripe effect that overlays dark streaks on a lighter background.
- **Merle** – A marbled or dappled look where patches of darker pigment are scattered across a lighter base. This can also affect eye and nose pigmentation.
- **Sable** – Dark-tipped hairs over a lighter base, giving the appearance of shading or highlights.

- **Piebald** – Irregular patches of white mixed with any other color, giving a spotted or "painted" look.
- **Masked** – A concentration of darker fur around the muzzle and eyes, creating a "mask-like" expression.

One of the most controversial coat patterns in Chihuahuas is merle. While undeniably beautiful and often producing blue or odd-colored eyes, the merle gene has been linked to serious health issues—particularly when two merle-patterned dogs are bred together. Double-merle offspring are at significantly increased risk for deafness, blindness, and neurological abnormalities. For this reason, responsible breeders never pair two merles, and some kennel clubs restrict or outright prohibit the registration of merle Chihuahuas. Health and ethical breeding practices must always take priority over aesthetics.

Eye color is another element influenced by coat genetics. Most Chihuahuas have deep brown or black eyes, but lighter coat colors and certain patterns can result in hazel, green, or blue eyes. Merle-patterned dogs are especially likely to have blue or partially blue eyes, though these are sometimes accompanied by increased sensitivity to light or vision issues. It's important to have these dogs regularly examined by a veterinarian to ensure their eyes remain healthy.

Despite the myths, a Chihuahua's coat type or color has no direct bearing on its temperament, intelligence, or overall health—except in cases where irresponsible breeding for appearance has compromised genetic soundness, such as in double merles. Some people believe that long coat Chihuahuas are calmer or more affectionate, while smooth coats are spicier or more high-strung. In reality, these traits are far more influenced by genetics, training, and socialization than by fur length. A well-bred, well-raised Chihuahua will be alert, intelligent, and affectionate, regardless of whether its coat is long or short, black or cream.

The sheer diversity of appearances within the Chihuahua breed is one of the reasons it captures so many hearts. Each Chihuahua looks distinct. No two are alike. You might meet a fluffy, red sable long coat with feathered ears and a proud gait, or a sleek, blue smooth coat with a mischievous twinkle in its eye and a white stripe down its chest. This visual individuality mirrors the breed's spirited personality—it's expressive, bold, and unapologetically unique.

Grooming needs will differ depending on the coat, but the love and attention a Chihuahua needs remains consistent. Whether you prefer the easy upkeep of a smooth coat or the luxurious look of a long-haired companion, it's the same dog underneath—loyal, lively, intelligent, and full of heart. The coat is just the wrapping on the package. The real value lies in the dog's personality, its bond with its family, and its ancient, dignified spirit wrapped in a modern, pint-sized body.

In the end, the variety of coat types and colors in Chihuahuas doesn't just make them beautiful—it makes them endlessly personal. With so many combinations of texture, color, and pattern, finding a Chihuahua that feels like *your dog* becomes a truly individual experience. And once you've found the right one, their coat—whether smooth, long, brindled, masked, or merle—becomes just one more detail to love about a dog that's already extraordinary in every other way.

References:

- American Kennel Club. (n.d.). *Chihuahua Dog Breed Information*. Retrieved from https://www.akc.org/dog-breeds/chihuahua/
- Fédération Cynologique Internationale. (2019). *FCI Breed Standards – Chihuahua*. Retrieved from https://www.fci.be
- Taylor, D. (2021). *The Complete Guide to Chihuahuas*. LP Media Inc.
- ASPCA. (n.d.). *Dog Grooming Tips*. Retrieved from https://www.aspca.org/pet-care/dog-care/dog-grooming-tips
- DogWellNet. (n.d.). *Merle Genetics and Health Risks in Dogs*. Retrieved from https://dogwellnet.com
- Serpell, J. (Ed.). (1995). *The Domestic Dog: Its Evolution, Behavior and Interactions with People*. Cambridge University Press

Personality Traits

The Chihuahua might be small in size, but its personality is anything but. Known for its boldness, charm, and fierce loyalty, this breed packs a surprising amount of character into a tiny frame. Often described as spirited, confident, and even sassy, the Chihuahua's temperament has made it a favorite among dog lovers who appreciate a companion with attitude and heart.

One of the most defining traits of the Chihuahua is its intense devotion to its owner. These dogs often form strong bonds with one person in particular, becoming deeply attached and protective. This loyalty can sometimes manifest as clinginess or jealousy, especially if the dog feels like its bond is being threatened by others. They often follow their owners from room to room and can become visibly distressed when left alone for extended periods. Despite their small size, they have a big need for human interaction and thrive in homes where they receive consistent attention.

Chihuahuas are also highly alert and tend to be excellent watchdogs. They are quick to sound the alarm when they sense something unfamiliar, whether it's a stranger approaching the door or an unfamiliar noise outside. Their hearing is sharp, and they are naturally suspicious of new people and environments. This makes early socialization especially important. A well-socialized Chihuahua will still be cautious, but more likely to warm up to guests and adapt to new situations without excessive barking or fear.

Despite their reputation for being yappy, not all Chihuahuas are loud. Much of their vocal behavior depends on their individual temperament and how they've been trained. With proper guidance, they can learn when barking is appropriate and when to settle down. Like many small breeds, they sometimes compensate for their size with attitude—a behavior sometimes called "small dog syndrome"—but this isn't a fixed trait. It's often a response to how they're treated. Owners who pamper Chihuahuas excessively or fail to set boundaries can unintentionally encourage nervous or aggressive behaviors.

Intelligence is another standout trait. Chihuahuas are quick learners and often eager to please, especially when motivated by treats or affection.

They do well with obedience training, puzzle toys, and interactive games that challenge their minds. However, they also have an independent streak and can be stubborn if not consistently trained. The key is patience and positive reinforcement. Harsh discipline doesn't work well with this breed and can cause fear or anxiety, making behavior worse over time.

Chihuahuas are also surprisingly athletic. While they're often seen nestled in purses or lounging in laps, they enjoy walks, short bursts of play, and exploring their environment. Their small size makes them ideal for apartment living, but they still need daily exercise and stimulation. A bored Chihuahua can become destructive or develop behavioral issues, such as excessive barking or chewing.

Emotionally, they're highly sensitive. They pick up on the moods of their owners and respond accordingly. A calm, confident owner will usually raise a calm, confident Chihuahua. Conversely, an anxious or inconsistent environment can lead to nervousness and insecurity in the dog. This sensitivity also means that Chihuahuas are not always well-suited for homes with very young children, who might handle them too roughly or unintentionally frighten them. They tend to do best in adult households or homes with older, respectful children.

Another unique aspect of their personality is their sense of self-importance. Many Chihuahuas seem unaware of their size. They'll bark at much larger dogs, stand their ground when challenged, and sometimes behave as though they're in charge of the household. This boldness can be amusing, but it also underscores the importance of consistent training and structure. When well-raised, a Chihuahua is not just a loyal pet but a confident, alert, and affectionate companion with a sharp mind and a strong will.

Ultimately, the Chihuahua's personality is a blend of loyalty, intelligence, sensitivity, and courage. Every individual dog is different, influenced by its genetics, upbringing, and environment. But as a breed, Chihuahuas are unforgettable. Their small stature hides a giant personality that has captivated people for centuries.

References:

- American Kennel Club. (n.d.). *Chihuahua Temperament & Personality*. Retrieved from https://www.akc.org/dog-breeds/chihuahua/
- Palika, L. (2007). *Chihuahuas for Dummies*. Wiley Publishing.
- Serpell, J. (1995). *The Domestic Dog: Its Evolution, Behavior, and Interactions with People*. Cambridge University Press.
- Fogle, B. (2000). *The Encyclopedia of the Dog*. DK Publishing.
- McKinney, C. (2013). *The Everything Chihuahua Book*. Adams Media.

Energy and Intelligence

Despite its diminutive stature, the Chihuahua exhibits a level of intensity and mental acuity that many larger breeds find challenging to equal. This diminutive canine, frequently underestimated due to its stature, embodies a remarkable synergy of spirited energy and profound intelligence. This breed is characterized by its proactive and forward-thinking nature, which sets it apart from other breeds. Whether it is dashing across the living room in a spontaneous burst of excitement or quietly observing every move made by its owner, the Chihuahua is always alert, always present, and always thinking. The ability to comprehend and direct this dual force of energy and intelligence is paramount to maximizing the potential of your Chihuahua and fostering a balanced, profoundly bonded relationship.

Chihuahuas exhibit a high level of activity from the moment they wake up. These canines possess rapid reflexes and agile minds. Their movements are purposeful, whether they are following you from room to room, performing excitedly after breakfast, or leaping onto a high-backed chair to enhance their view of the activity. The prevailing tendency to characterize their energy as "nervous" or "wired" is a fallacious oversimplification. The term "hyperactive" is not applicable to the Chihuahua breed; rather, it is more accurate to describe them as "responsive." These creatures exhibit a high degree of responsiveness to their environment, their routine, and, notably, to human interaction. When given the appropriate environment and structural framework, this energy can be transformed into a state of vitality rather than one of disorder.

While they do not necessitate the same level of physical exertion as working breeds such as Border Collies or Huskies, Chihuahuas do require consistent daily activity. It has been demonstrated that short walks, interactive games, and exploratory activities in both indoor and backyard environments can serve as effective methods for expending natural energy in a healthy manner. In the absence of an adequate outlet for their impulses, these canines may manifest undesirable behaviors, such as incessant barking in response to auditory stimuli, destructive chewing on household items, or restless pacing when left alone. Despite their diminutive stature, these individuals possess a profound propensity for engagement. A bored Chihuahua is likely to be vocal or destructive, not because of any inherent "badness," but rather due to an absence of proper outlets for its energy.

However, it is imperative to acknowledge that energy alone does not define the Chihuahua. The distinctive characteristic that sets this breed apart is the remarkable convergence of physical agility and intellectual acumen. These canines possess remarkable perceptiveness and observational skills. Many Chihuahua owners find that their dogs appear to comprehend routines with greater ease than their owners do. The subject is observed retrieving their car keys and, in the immediate vicinity, perceives the presence of their canine companion, identified as a Chihuahua. A glance is cast toward the treat jar, wherein the canines sit in perfect stillness, their eyes expressing profound anticipation. These entities have been observed to discern patterns in an individual's behavior, accurately gauging their emotional state. This information is then utilized to inform their own decisions and actions. This phenomenon cannot be attributed solely to instinct; rather, it is the result of critical thinking.

This phenomenon, characterized by the duality of its implications, can be likened to a double-edged sword. On the one hand, this characteristic renders Chihuahuas highly trainable. These subjects have been observed to exhibit a rapid response to positive reinforcement, a propensity for food and praise motivation, and a proclivity for learning new skills. Conversely, they can exercise discretion in determining the circumstances and manner in which they comply with directives. A Chihuahua is not predisposed to unquestioning obedience. In the absence of a perceived rationale for a task, individuals may opt to abstain from its execution. This act of defiance is not impulsive; rather, it is the result of careful deliberation. They engage in metacognition by evaluating the value of an action before engaging, which fosters a sense of agency and autonomy in problem-solving.

Emotional intelligence is another frequently overlooked strength in the Chihuahua. These canines exhibit a remarkable degree of emotional attunement that might be perceived as uncanny by some observers. In the event that an individual is experiencing a state of despondency, a Chihuahua has been observed to respond with a manifestation of affectionate proximity, which may be characterized by behaviors such as curling up beside the subject, resting its head on the subject's leg, or maintaining a vigilant posture until the subject's condition improves. In the event that an individual is experiencing positive emotions, such as excitement or joy, these emotions are likely to be reflected in their behavior. For instance, they may engage in dancing or vocalizing with enthusiasm. This emotional sensitivity may help explain the profound bonds Chihuahuas establish with their human owners. The objective of these interactions is not merely physical proximity; it is to comprehend the individual in question. This profound attachment can manifest in a Chihuahua's steadfast commitment to a select individual, who becomes their constant companion, confidant, and emotional support.

It is evident that such profound mental and emotional engagement can concomitantly engender a range of challenges. Chihuahuas are frequently characterized as "yappy" or "anxious," yet these behaviors are often manifestations of unmet needs. An overstimulated or under-socialized Chihuahua is likely to respond with vocalization, pacing, or defensive behavior. This is not indicative of an inherent nervousness in the breed; rather, it is a manifestation of its inability to regulate its energy and emotions. Early socialization, in conjunction with a predictable environment and adequate mental stimulation, has been demonstrated to significantly mitigate reactive tendencies.

The efficacy of training a Chihuahua is optimally maximized through an approach characterized by respect and positivity. These canines exhibit sensitivity to both tone and intent. The implementation of stringent disciplinary measures, the use of vocalized reprimands, and the administration of physical correction often prove counterproductive, eliciting adverse reactions such as fear, disorientation, or even outright defiance. Conversely, positive reinforcement has been demonstrated to be an effective method. It is recommended that treats, affection, toys, or verbal praise be offered when the desired behaviors are exhibited, and such an approach will quickly yield observable progress. The breed's inclination to please is pronounced, particularly when it perceives appreciation and encouragement. It is recommended that sessions be kept brief, with an ideal duration of five to ten minutes, and that the lessons be customized to align with the interests of the learners. It has been demonstrated that students will demonstrate optimal learning outcomes when education is regarded as a game rather than a chore.

Beyond fundamental commands such as "sit," "stay," and "come," Chihuahuas significantly benefit from enriching activities. Trick training, for instance, has been demonstrated to be beneficial in terms of enhancing the cognitive abilities of canines and fostering their affection for human interaction. These skills can be taught through a variety of methods, including the instruction of specific behaviors such as spinning, crawling, high-fives, and vocalizations like "speak" and "whisper" when prompted. The utilization of puzzle feeders has been demonstrated to enhance the mental engagement of mealtime in children. One method that has proven effective is the implementation of scent games, in which treats are strategically concealed, compelling canines to utilize their olfactory senses to locate the treats, thus stimulating their innate instincts and providing a mentally engaging challenge. For individuals who prioritize physical activity, a miniature agility course can transform a hallway or living room into a training environment. The utilization of broomsticks as hurdles and cardboard boxes as tunnels does not merely constitute physical exercise; it also serves as a confidence-building experience.

It is also imperative to acknowledge the Chihuahua's need for structured independence. While they derive pleasure from the proximity of their human companions, they also benefit from acquiring the capacity for solitude and self-soothing. The implementation of crate training, the provision of interactive toys, and the allocation of calm solo time have been identified as effective strategies to mitigate overdependence and separation anxiety in canines. A Chihuahua that has been socialized to feel secure in its own space is one that has been habituated to a state of minimal stimulation.

A prevalent misconception regarding the breed pertains to its perceived fragility, temperament, and proclivity for excessive vocalization, which are often regarded as deficiencies that would preclude its suitability as a well-rounded pet. It has been demonstrated that a Chihuahua that has received adequate care, training, and socialization is likely to exhibit signs of emotional well-being, including balance, engagement, and a positive impact on the human-canine relationship. Its high-energy nature, when channeled through regular play and walks, contributes to a sense of vitality and joy. When provided with adequate training and stimulation, these animals have been shown to transform routine activities into opportunities for social interaction and personal growth.

In summary, the Chihuahua is not merely a lap ornament; rather, it is a comprehensive companion. The level of cognitive ability exhibited by the device is often met with astonishment by its first owners. When provided with a sufficient amount of physical and mental space, as well as a suitable purpose, the Chihuahua can demonstrate its remarkable intellectual abilities. The experience is designed to challenge, impress, and provide comfort, while also eliciting laughter, all within a single afternoon.

In essence, the Chihuahua is a canine that warrants consideration and respect. This is not a consequence of its size, but rather an outcome of its unique functionality within that size. This canine displays a high level of energy and intelligence, which is manifested through its physical characteristics, namely its fur. The dog's behavior indicates an eagerness to explore the world, establish connections with its human owners, and engage in activities that challenge its abilities. Upon observing a Chihuahua, one does not merely perceive a toy dog; rather, one encounters a diminutive, relentless mind that seeks to comprehend the intricacies of the world and its position within one's own. Once this process is initiated, the result will not be limited to the immediate environment of the pet. The entity in question will serve as a constant presence, a protective guardian, a steadfast companion, and, above all, a reliable friend.

References

- American Kennel Club. (n.d.). *Chihuahua Dog Breed Information*. https://www.akc.org/dog-breeds/chihuahua/
- Coren, S. (2006). *The Intelligence of Dogs*. Free Press.
- Cesar's Way. (n.d.). *Understanding Small Dog Syndrome*. https://www.cesarsway.com
- DogTime. (n.d.). *Chihuahua Temperament and Personality*. https://dogtime.com/dog-breeds/chihuahua
- Smith, R. (2021). *Training Small Dogs: Big Results for Little Breeds*. Canine Press.
- PetMD. (n.d.). *Mental Stimulation for Dogs: Why It's Important*. https://www.petmd.com

Chapter 3: Choosing the Right Chihuahua

Breeder vs. Rescue

Bringing a Chihuahua into your life is a big decision, despite the breed's small size. It means committing to years of care, companionship, and responsibility. One of the first and most important choices you'll face is where to get your dog: through a breeder or by adopting from a rescue or shelter. Each path has its pros and cons, and the right choice depends on your lifestyle, values, and what you're looking for in a canine companion.

Getting a Chihuahua from a Breeder

Getting a Chihuahua from a reputable breeder is a wise decision for anyone looking for a healthy and well-adjusted pet. Reputable breeders are dedicated to preserving and improving the breed, which means they invest considerable time, resources, and knowledge into raising puppies. When you choose a breeder, you are more likely to find Chihuahuas with specific traits that you may be looking for. This could range from having the classic apple-shaped head to particular coat colors. If you have intentions of entering dog shows, a breeder is usually the best option, as they often have lineage that meets the standards for competition.

One of the key practices of good breeders is performing genetic testing on their dogs. This testing helps to minimize the risk of inherited health problems, which is essential for anyone who wants a healthy pet. When puppies are raised in a home environment, they are more likely to become well-socialized. This early socialization is critical, as it allows puppies to become comfortable with various people and situations. Furthermore, reputable breeders take the time to carefully match puppies with their new owners based on the temperament of both the dog and the prospective owner. This means that when you go to adopt, there is a higher likelihood that the puppy's personality will fit well with your lifestyle.

When you start the process of finding a Chihuahua, it's common to find yourself on a waiting list. Breeders who are selective about who they sell to are usually a good sign. A waiting list indicates that the breeder values each puppy and is committed to ensuring that they go to suitable homes. Quality breeders are also usually very transparent about the puppy's medical history, including vaccinations and care. This transparency helps you understand what to expect as the puppy grows.

However, not all breeders operate ethically. The popularity of Chihuahuas has led to an increase in puppy mills and backyard breeders, which are unethical operations focused more on profit than on the welfare of the animals. These places often keep dogs in poor conditions and might produce puppies that are undersocialized. Such dogs can end up being fearful or prone to health issues, making life challenging for the new owners. To avoid these problems, always visit the breeder in person, if possible. Ask questions about the breeding practices and request to meet the puppy's parents. This gives you a clearer picture of the environment the puppies were raised in.

Expectations around cost are important to consider when working with a reputable breeder. Prices for Chihuahuas can vary significantly, typically ranging from $800 to over $3,000. Factors like pedigree, appearance, and demand play essential roles in determining the price. Higher costs can be discouraging, but it's vital to understand that with this expense comes a certain level of predictability. When you invest in a puppy from a reputable breeder, you gain insights into the dog's background, potential size, and possible health risks. This knowledge can lead to fewer surprises down the road.

When selecting a breeder, it's beneficial to examine their reputation. Take time to read reviews and get feedback from previous clients. Many reputable breeders have websites or social media pages showcasing their puppies and their commitment to responsible breeding practices. You can also reach out to local breed clubs for recommendations. This helps ensure that you find a breeder who aligns with ethical practices, giving you confidence in your choice.

In addition to checking the breeder's reputation, assessing the conditions in which the puppies are raised is crucial. This includes looking for cleanliness, space for the dogs to play, and signs of good nutrition. A well-maintained facility often indicates that the breeder cares for their animals. Pay attention to how the puppies interact with each other and with their human caretakers. Puppies that are playful and curious are likely to have been raised in a loving environment, making them easier to train and socialize as they grow.

Another step in the process is understanding the importance of puppy evaluations. Good breeders should conduct evaluations to gauge each puppy's temperament. This assessment helps to match the right puppy with the right owner. If you have children or other pets, it may be useful to discuss these with the breeder so they can identify a puppy that is more likely to mesh well with your family dynamic.

Once you find a reputable breeder and select a puppy, be prepared for the immediate responsibilities of puppy ownership. This includes setting up your home for the new arrival. You will need to purchase supplies such as a crate, food and water bowls, quality puppy food, a leash, and toys. Preparing your space will help your new Chihuahua feel comfortable in its new home from day one.

Training is also an essential aspect of puppy ownership. Chihuahuas respond well to positive reinforcement training. Start with basic commands like sit, stay, and come. A good training session can help to develop a strong bond between you and your puppy. Considering enrolling in a puppy training class can provide both guidance and socialization opportunities for your new pet.

Remember, patience is important during this phase. Puppies, including Chihuahuas, can be energetic and playful, but they require consistent training and care. If issues arise, do not hesitate to consult your breeder or a veterinarian for advice. Taking these necessary steps allows you to enjoy a fulfilling relationship with your new Chihuahua while giving them a stable and loving home.

Adopting a Chihuahua from a Rescue or Shelter

On the other side of the decision is adoption. Every year, thousands of Chihuahuas end up in shelters and breed-specific rescues. Many of these dogs were surrendered due to no fault of their own—owners may have underestimated the breed's needs, experienced life changes, or simply failed to provide long-term care.

Adoption offers a second chance. It's a compassionate choice, often more affordable, and deeply rewarding. Rescues typically charge a modest fee that covers vaccinations, spaying or neutering, and sometimes microchipping. The cost ranges from $100 to $500. Many Chihuahuas in rescue are adults, which means they're often house-trained and past the high-energy demands of puppyhood. Their personalities are more developed, making it easier to find a dog that fits your lifestyle.

Breed-specific rescue groups can be especially helpful. They understand the Chihuahua temperament, work to rehabilitate dogs from all kinds of backgrounds, and take time to match the right dog with the right person. Shelter workers and foster parents can give honest insights into a dog's behavior, quirks, and needs.

One consideration with rescue dogs is the unknown. You might not get full medical or behavioral history. Some Chihuahuas may come from neglectful or abusive situations and need extra patience and training. But with time, many adopted Chihuahuas blossom into loyal, loving companions. Their capacity for bonding—especially with someone who gave them a second chance—is profound.

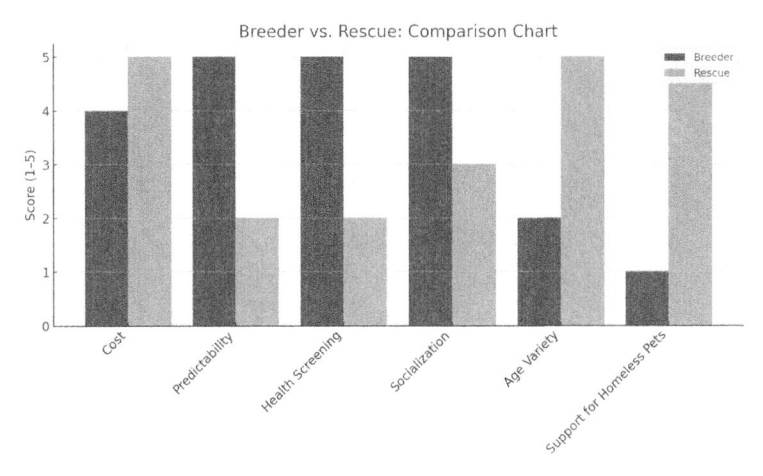

Breeder vs. Rescue: Comparison Chart

Which Path is Right for You?

Choosing the right path when it comes to adopting a dog is an important decision. It can set the tone for your relationship with your new furry friend. You will need to carefully consider whether you want to go through a breeder or a rescue organization. Each option comes with its own set of rewards and challenges. The choice you make should align with your personal preferences and lifestyle.

Understanding Breeders

If you're leaning towards a breeder, it's vital to understand what that entails. Breeders typically focus on producing dogs with specific traits. This means that if you want to raise a dog from puppyhood, a breeder could be the perfect fit. When you choose a breeder, you often know the dog's lineage and can learn about its parents and grandparents. This insight can help you better understand what to expect in terms of health, temperament, and behavior.

For example, if you're interested in dog sports or conformation shows, a breeder can guide you in choosing a dog that possesses the qualities necessary for these competitive fields. It also allows you to familiarize yourself with puppy training schedules and developmental milestones, which can be crucial for raising a well-adjusted dog. Be ready to ask questions about the breeding process, the dog's health screenings, and any potential concerns that might arise down the road.

The Advantages of Rescuing

On the other hand, choosing to adopt from a rescue organization has its own unique set of benefits. If you are open to giving an older dog a second chance at life, rescue might be the most fulfilling route for you. Many dogs in rescue shelters are often already trained and have a good understanding of basic commands. This means you might not need to start from scratch, which can save you both time and effort.

Rescue can also fill you with a sense of purpose. By adopting a dog from a rescue organization, you are actively helping to reduce pet homelessness. In many cases, these dogs have faced hardships, and giving them a safe and loving home can be a profoundly rewarding experience. For example, when you adopt a senior dog, you are giving it a fresh start, maybe even during its twilight years. This act of kindness not only enriches the dog's life but also brings immense joy to your own.

The Importance of Patience

Regardless of which path you choose, patience is crucial. It is essential that you take your time to find the right match for your home and lifestyle. Do not feel pressured to make a snap decision. Instead, consider what kind of dog best suits your energy levels and family dynamics.

Ask yourself important questions about your daily routine and expectations. If you have a busy lifestyle, a high-energy puppy might not be the best choice. It could make training and socializing more challenging. Alternatively, if you're looking for a calmer companion, an older dog might align better with your situation. Take the time to visit different breeders or shelters, interact with the dogs, and understand their individual personalities.

Matching Your Home and Dog

As you explore options, keep in mind that the right dog will match your home and intentions. You might find joy in knowing you are providing a home for a small dog like a Chihuahua. This breed is known for its unique charm and small stature, but more importantly, it has a big heart. Each dog, regardless of its background, deserves a family that appreciates and understands its character.

The connection between you and your future dog should feel right. Spend time reflecting on your needs and the traits you would appreciate in a dog. Consider lifestyle factors, such as how much time you can commit to exercise, play, and daily care. Each dog brings its own personality and quirks, and it is essential to find a match with which you can build a nurturing relationship.

Seeking Guidance

Whether you decide to go with a breeder or a rescue, do not hesitate to seek guidance. Speak with individuals who have experience in dog ownership, such as friends, family, or professionals. They can provide valuable insights that will help you feel more prepared for the journey ahead.

In a breeder's case, ask about their breeding practices, health screenings, and even visit their facility if possible. This can give you peace of mind regarding the genetic health of your future puppy. If you are choosing to go through a rescue, learn about the organization's mission and processes. Understanding their approach will help you feel confident in your choice and ensure a successful match between you and your new pet.

Final Thoughts

In making your decision, remember that every dog is unique, and the bond you build will be shaped by your mutual understanding and communication. Whether it's a carefully bred puppy or a senior dog looking for a fresh start, the love and companionship that await you are worth every moment of research and consideration. Enjoy the journey of finding the right furry friend who will bring joy and love into your life.

References:

- American Kennel Club. *How to Find a Responsible Dog Breeder.* https://www.akc.org
- Chihuahua Club of America. *Buying or Adopting a Chihuahua.* https://www.chihuahuaclubofamerica.org
- ASPCA. *Adopting a Pet.* https://www.aspca.org/adopt-pet/adoption-tips
- Petfinder. *Chihuahua Adoption Guide.* https://www.petfinder.com/dog-breeds/chihuahua
- Best Friends Animal Society. *Why Rescue?* https://bestfriends.org

Health and Pedigree Considerations

Chihuahuas are known for their long lifespans and lively personalities, but like all purebred dogs, they come with specific health concerns that owners and breeders must take seriously. Understanding these issues is key to ensuring a healthy, happy life for the dog and maintaining the integrity of the breed through responsible breeding practices.

On average, Chihuahuas live between 12 to 20 years. Their extended lifespan is largely due to their small size and relatively low risk of many large-breed diseases. However, they are not immune to health issues—many of which are common in toy breeds or are inherited through generations of selective breeding.

One of the most common health problems is patellar luxation, a condition where the kneecap slips out of place. This can range from mild discomfort to serious lameness requiring surgery. Regular vet checkups and breeding dogs with sound joint health help reduce its occurrence. Another widespread issue is dental disease. Due to their small mouths and crowded teeth, Chihuahuas are highly susceptible to tartar buildup, gingivitis, and early tooth loss. Daily brushing and professional cleanings are strongly recommended.

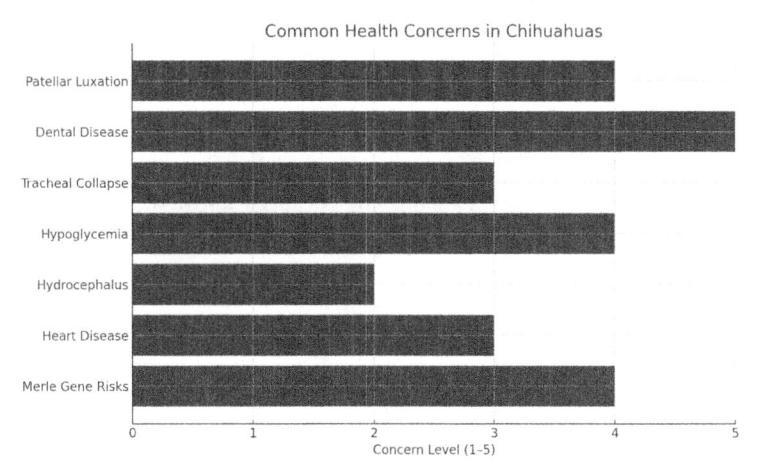

Common Health Concerns in Chihuahuas

Condition	Concern Level (1-5)
Patellar Luxation	4
Dental Disease	5
Tracheal Collapse	3
Hypoglycemia	4
Hydrocephalus	2
Heart Disease	3
Merle Gene Risks	4

Tracheal collapse is another concern. This condition causes the windpipe to weaken and collapse, leading to chronic coughing and breathing difficulties. Using a harness instead of a collar can reduce pressure on the neck and help prevent this problem. Chihuahuas may also suffer from hypoglycemia, especially as puppies. A sudden drop in blood sugar levels can lead to weakness, confusion, or even seizures. Feeding them small, frequent meals and having a sugar source like honey available in emergencies can be lifesaving.

Hydrocephalus, or water on the brain, is a more serious but less common condition. Affected puppies may have an enlarged skull, seizures, and poor coordination. Unfortunately, there is no cure, though some cases can be managed with medication. Heart disease, particularly mitral valve disease, can develop in older Chihuahuas, so routine veterinary visits are essential, especially for seniors.

Pedigree plays a major role in health. Ethical breeders work hard to eliminate harmful genetic traits from their lines. This includes health screenings for hereditary conditions, maintaining genetic diversity, and avoiding inbreeding. Prospective buyers should always ask for health clearances and detailed family histories. Reputable breeders will provide documentation and be transparent about any risks.

The merle coat pattern, while visually appealing, is another area of concern. Dogs that inherit two copies of the merle gene (one from each parent) are at a significantly higher risk for deafness, blindness, and neurological problems. Many kennel clubs discourage or even ban merle-to-merle breeding due to these risks.

Owning a Chihuahua also means being proactive with routine care. This includes vaccinations, parasite prevention, dental hygiene, grooming, weight management, and proper nutrition. Spaying or neutering can also help prevent reproductive system diseases and reduce behavioral issues.

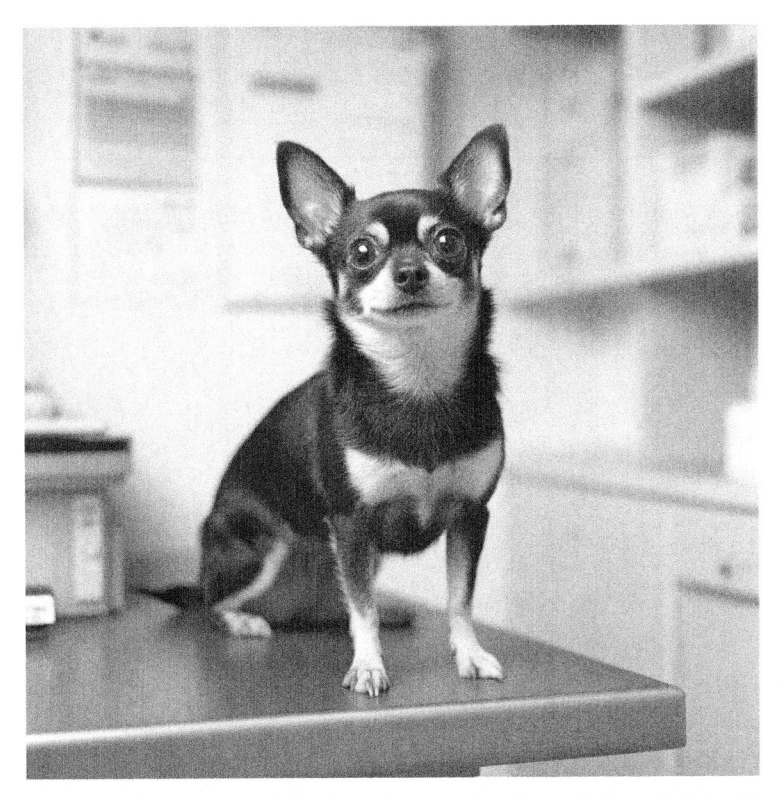

For those adopting a Chihuahua from a rescue or shelter, full health histories may not be available. However, a veterinary checkup can establish a health baseline and help catch any emerging issues early. Many rescue Chihuahuas are adults or seniors, which can make health assessment more straightforward.

Ultimately, Chihuahuas can live long, vibrant lives when their health is prioritized. Proper breeding, early intervention, and consistent care form the foundation for their well-being. Their small size may make them physically delicate, but with the right attention and commitment, they can be robust, energetic, and loving companions for many years.

References:

- American Kennel Club. (n.d.). *Chihuahua Dog Breed Information*. Retrieved from https://www.akc.org/dog-breeds/chihuahua/
- Orthopedic Foundation for Animals. (n.d.). *Patellar Luxation Statistics*. Retrieved from https://www.ofa.org

- Banfield Pet Hospital. (2020). *State of Pet Health Report*. Retrieved from https://www.banfield.com
- ASPCA. (n.d.). *Common Health Issues in Small Dogs*. Retrieved from https://www.aspca.org
- Taylor, D. (2021). *The Complete Guide to Chihuahuas*. LP Media Inc.
- UC Davis Veterinary Genetics Laboratory. (n.d.). *Merle Gene in Dogs*. Retrieved from https://vgl.ucdavis.edu
- Veterinary Centers of America. (n.d.). *Tracheal Collapse in Dogs*. Retrieved from https://vcahospitals.com

Puppy or Adult?

Choosing between a Chihuahua puppy or an adult dog is a decision that goes beyond simple preference. It involves lifestyle, experience, patience, and the kind of bond you want to build. Both options come with unique benefits and challenges, and understanding the differences can help future owners make the choice that fits their needs.

A Chihuahua puppy is undeniably adorable—tiny, wide-eyed, and full of energy. Raising a puppy allows you to shape its behavior from the beginning. You're in control of its training, socialization, and daily habits. With the right guidance, a well-raised puppy grows into a balanced, confident adult. Puppies also tend to adapt easily to new environments, people, and other animals. Their personalities are still forming, which means they're more likely to adjust to your household routine and bond tightly with the people around them.

However, raising a Chihuahua puppy requires serious commitment. They are fragile and need to be handled with care. Their small size puts them at risk of injury from falls, rough play, or being accidentally stepped on. Puppies also need frequent feeding, bathroom breaks, and constant supervision. House training a Chihuahua can be a slow process, as small breeds sometimes struggle with bladder control and require extra patience. Chewing, barking, and boundary testing are all normal stages, and owners need the time, consistency, and willingness to work through them.

Puppies are also more susceptible to stress and illness, especially in the first few months. They need a stable environment, regular vet visits, vaccinations, and social exposure to avoid developing anxiety or reactivity later in life. The critical early weeks determine how well they'll adjust to life as an adult dog. If you're someone with a flexible schedule and the energy to raise a puppy properly, it can be incredibly rewarding. The bond formed from early puppyhood is often very strong, especially with a breed as loyal as the Chihuahua.

On the other hand, adopting an adult Chihuahua offers its own set of advantages. Adult dogs generally come with a clearer sense of personality, behavior, and temperament. You know what you're getting —whether the dog is quiet or vocal, independent or cuddly, easygoing or high-strung. This predictability can be helpful for first-time dog owners or people who want a specific type of companion.

Adult Chihuahuas are usually past the destructive puppy phase. They're less likely to chew on furniture, have accidents in the house, or need constant supervision. Many adult dogs already know basic commands, walk well on a leash, and have established routines. This can make the transition into a new home much smoother. In rescue or shelter situations, adult Chihuahuas are often spayed or neutered, vaccinated, and health-checked—removing many of the initial costs and responsibilities of puppy ownership.

However, adopting an adult dog isn't without challenges. Some Chihuahuas may come from homes where they experienced neglect, abuse, or poor socialization. These dogs might be fearful, aggressive, or slow to trust. They may have bad habits that take time to unlearn, and they might need training just like a puppy. But with patience and consistency, many adult Chihuahuas learn to trust again and thrive in loving homes. In fact, giving a second chance to an older dog can be one of the most meaningful experiences for an owner.

There's also the option of adopting a **senior Chihuahua**, which some people overlook. These dogs often require less exercise, are calmer, and make excellent companions for people with slower-paced lifestyles. They tend to be grateful, low-maintenance, and already house-trained. While they may come with some health concerns, senior Chihuahuas have a lot of love to give, and they can be the perfect fit for someone looking for a quiet, affectionate pet.

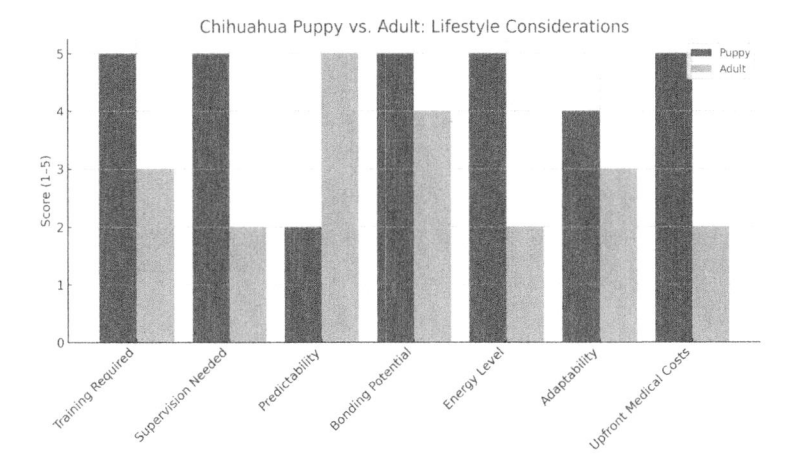

Chihuahua Puppy vs. Adult: Lifestyle Considerations

[Bar chart comparing Puppy vs. Adult scores (1-5) across: Training Required, Supervision Needed, Predictability, Bonding Potential, Energy Level, Adaptability, Upfront Medical Costs]

Ultimately, the choice between a puppy and an adult Chihuahua depends on your lifestyle, experience, and what kind of relationship you're looking to build. Puppies offer a blank slate and a long-term journey. Adults offer personality you can see upfront and often settle into homes more easily. Neither is better than the other—just different paths to the same destination: sharing life with a small dog full of love, loyalty, and personality.

References:

- American Kennel Club. (n.d.). *Chihuahua Dog Breed Information*. Retrieved from https://www.akc.org/dog-breeds/chihuahua/
- Palika, L. (2007). *Chihuahuas for Dummies*. Wiley Publishing.
- ASPCA. (n.d.). *Adopting a Dog: Puppy or Adult?* Retrieved from https://www.aspca.org/pet-care/dog-care/general-dog-care
- McKinney, C. (2013). *The Everything Chihuahua Book*. Adams Media.
- RSPCA. (n.d.). *Should I Get a Puppy or an Older Dog?* Retrieved from https://www.rspca.org.uk/adviceandwelfare/pets/general/puppyvsadult

Lifestyle Match

The Chihuahua's small size and oversized personality make it a breed that can fit into many different types of homes, but they're not for everyone. Choosing a Chihuahua isn't just about liking cute dogs—it's about making sure your lifestyle aligns with their physical and emotional needs. While their adaptability is one of their strong suits, they require a certain kind of attention and understanding to truly thrive.

Perfect for Small Spaces, But Not Low Energy

Chihuahuas are often thought of as perfect apartment dogs—and in many ways, they are. Their small stature means they don't need a big backyard, and they're easy to carry or travel with. But being small doesn't mean they don't need stimulation. They may not need long, intense exercise sessions, but they do need movement, interaction, and regular mental challenges. A couple of short walks each day, combined with some indoor playtime or training, can keep them healthy and happy. Just because they can live in small spaces doesn't mean they'll be content being left alone or ignored.

Social, Loyal, and Deeply Attached

Chihuahuas form strong bonds, usually with one or two people in particular. They tend to be "velcro dogs," meaning they want to be with you all the time—on your lap, in your bed, under your desk. This makes them ideal companions for people who are home often, like remote workers, retirees, or stay-at-home individuals. If you're looking for a dog to keep you company throughout the day, a Chihuahua fits that role perfectly. They thrive on closeness and can become anxious or depressed if they're left alone too often or for too long.

On the flip side, they're not well-suited for people with extremely busy schedules who are away from home most of the day. Chihuahuas are prone to separation anxiety and can act out by barking excessively, chewing, or becoming withdrawn. If you're frequently traveling or working long hours without access to dog care, this may not be the best match. A lonely Chihuahua is not just sad—it's likely to become behaviorally difficult.

Families and Children: Handle with Care

In a family setting, Chihuahuas can truly thrive if they receive the right socialization. This means introducing them to various experiences, people, and sounds in a gradual and positive way. Early socialization helps these little dogs become more confident and adaptable. For families with young children, it's crucial to think carefully about the dynamics involved. Chihuahuas, due to their small size, are better suited for homes where the children are older and can understand how to behave around pets.

The delicate nature of a Chihuahua's tiny frame means they are easily injured. When young kids play, they may not always realize that their actions can be too rough. For instance, if a child pulls a Chihuahua's tail or picks it up without support, the dog could get hurt. This is why it is essential to supervise interactions between young children and Chihuahuas. Teaching kids about respecting a dog's space and understanding their body language is important. You can explain to them that a dog may not want to be held the same way they hold their toys, promoting a safer environment for the pet.

While young children may have a harder time relating to a Chihuahua's needs, many of these dogs form strong bonds with older kids and adults who can show them kindness. When an older child or an adult engages gently with a Chihuahua, the little dog often responds with playfulness and affection. For example, they may enjoy playing fetch with a soft toy or simply sitting close for cuddles on the couch. It's crucial for families to spend quality time together, building a connection. Over time, as trust develops, Chihuahuas can show their silly and entertaining sides, making them delightful companions.

Chihuahuas love to learn tricks and engage in fun games. Teaching them simple commands like "sit" or "stay" can be a rewarding experience for both the Chihuahua and the family member involved. When teaching these commands, it is beneficial to use positive reinforcement like treats or praise. This encourages the dog to learn while also strengthening the bond between pet and owner. Games can involve chasing a ball or tugging on a toy, which can keep the Chihuahua happy and physically active.

In a family, it's common for a Chihuahua to develop a special connection with one person, often referred to as their "favorite." However, this doesn't mean that they cannot bond with other family members as well. Creating positive experiences for each family member is key to fostering these relationships. Taking turns walking the dog, feeding them, or engaging in play can help strengthen these bonds. Encouraging each person in the household to take part in caring for the Chihuahua builds a deeper connection, ensuring that the dog feels loved and included by all.

Maintaining an environment that allows Chihuahuas to feel safe is equally important. High places, like the top of a couch or bed, can be favorite spots for these little dogs, but it's vital that they have safe access and a way to get down without falling. Additionally, providing a cozy space like a soft bed or blanket can help them establish a sense of security in their home. This security makes it easier for them to interact calmly, whether with children or other pets.

Additionally, regular vet check-ups are necessary for Chihuahuas to monitor their health. Since they are small breed dogs, they may be predisposed to certain health issues. By visiting the vet, families can get advice on proper diet, exercise, and dental care. Maintaining their health contributes significantly to the overall happiness of the Chihuahua and helps prevent accidents related to their delicate physical structure.

Recognizing the signs of stress in a Chihuahua is another important aspect of family life with this breed. Dogs often display their discomfort through body language. For instance, if a Chihuahua tucks its tail or tries to hide, it may be feeling scared or overwhelmed. Understanding these signs allows family members to step in and provide comfort. Training children to recognize when a dog is feeling anxious can also help maintain peaceful interactions and a harmonious household.

In a family with a Chihuahua, patience and understanding are essential. When introducing the dog to new family members or situations, the process may take time. Allowing the dog to acclimate at its own pace is important for building trust. Creating a structured routine for feeding, training, and playtime can help the Chihuahua understand what to expect. This routine can also give family members a helpful guideline to follow, ensuring that everyone is on the same page regarding the care of their furry friend.

Socialization can extend beyond the family to other pets and people. If feasible, exposing a Chihuahua to other friendly dogs and individuals can help them grow into well-rounded animals. Enrolling them in socialization classes or play groups can be a fun way for families to help their dog meet others. These experiences can also ease the Chihuahua into different environments while reinforcing their bond with family members.

Ultimately, the journey of raising a Chihuahua in a family environment can be rewarding and fulfilling. By providing proper care, supervision, and understanding, families can create a loving home where their Chihuahua feels safe and cherished. Through continuous engagement and positive experiences, Chihuahuas can flourish and bring joy and laughter to their families.

Seniors and Solo Dwellers

Chihuahuas are often a favorite among older adults—and for good reason. Their small size makes them manageable for people who may have physical limitations, and their loyal nature provides emotional support and companionship. They don't require excessive physical activity, but they do enjoy short walks and regular routines. A calm, predictable household is ideal for a Chihuahua, and many seniors find joy in the close relationship these dogs form.

For solo dwellers, especially those who live in small spaces or don't have the time or interest for high-maintenance breeds, a Chihuahua can be a wonderful partner. They offer constant companionship, stay close, and often become a kind of shadow to their owner. But it's important to understand that their emotional needs are big. A Chihuahua wants attention, affection, and involvement in your life. They don't just want to sit on the sidelines—they want to be at the center of your day.

Climate Sensitivity

Due to their size and thin coat, Chihuahuas are highly sensitive to temperature extremes. They get cold easily, even indoors if there's a draft or chill. In colder climates, they'll need sweaters or coats, especially during outdoor walks. Heated dog beds, blankets, and cozy spots around the home help them stay comfortable. In hot weather, their small bodies can overheat quickly. Walks should be scheduled for cooler times of the day, and water should always be available. Never leave a Chihuahua in a hot car or direct sun for long periods—they're just too small to regulate their body temperature effectively.

Traveling and Social Lifestyles

For people who love to travel or live a more social lifestyle, Chihuahuas can be ideal. They're one of the most portable breeds—easy to bring on planes, stay in pet-friendly hotels, or join you at outdoor cafes. With proper training and socialization, they're adaptable and confident in new environments. A well-socialized Chihuahua can enjoy being around people, meeting other dogs, and participating in activities like road trips or camping (as long as their safety is considered). But without that early exposure, they can become nervous or aggressive in unfamiliar situations. Investing in training and positive social experiences early in life will help your Chihuahua become more adaptable and less fearful.

Not for Everyone

Chihuahuas aren't the right match for people looking for a low-maintenance or independent pet. They need involvement, routine, and affection. Their loyalty is deep, but they can also be demanding. If you're seeking a quiet companion who doesn't need much interaction, you're better off with a more reserved breed. Chihuahuas want to be where the action is, even if the "action" is just you folding laundry or watching TV.

But for the right person—someone who wants a close, expressive, intelligent, and loyal dog—the Chihuahua offers a truly unique bond. They're entertaining, emotionally in tune, and often surprising in their strength and bravery. A good lifestyle match doesn't come down to house size or income—it comes down to time, attention, and willingness to meet this little dog on its big terms.

References

- American Kennel Club. (n.d.). *Chihuahua Dog Breed Information*. https://www.akc.org/dog-breeds/chihuahua/
- ASPCA. (n.d.). *General Dog Care*. https://www.aspca.org/pet-care/dog-care/general-dog-care
- DogTime. (n.d.). *Chihuahua Temperament and Personality*. https://dogtime.com/dog-breeds/chihuahua
- PetMD. (n.d.). *Separation Anxiety in Dogs: What It Looks Like and How to Help*. https://www.petmd.com
- Stanley, B. (2019). *How to Raise the Perfect Dog: Through Puppyhood and Beyond*. Penguin Random House
- Small Dog Place. (n.d.). *Best Dogs for Seniors*. https://www.smalldogplace.com
- Coren, S. (2006). *The Intelligence of Dogs*. Free Press

Chapter 4: Bringing a Chihuahua Home

First 24 Hours

The first 24 hours after bringing a Chihuahua home are crucial. This small, sensitive breed thrives on routine, trust, and environment. Whether your new companion is a young puppy from a breeder or a rescue adjusting to a new chapter, how you handle their first day can shape their long-term comfort, security, and behavior. It's not just about making your dog feel welcome—it's about laying the groundwork for a healthy bond and structured life together.

Preparing Your Space

Before your Chihuahua arrives, it is important to prepare your home adequately. Since Chihuahuas are small, they can be more vulnerable to dangers that other, larger dogs might navigate easily. Start by securing any loose wires around your home. These can be potential hazards, as curious puppies might chew on them. Next, remove any small objects that could be swallowed or choked on; think about things like coins, buttons, or small toys that you might overlook but that could pose a safety risk.

Additionally, ensure that staircases are blocked off. Chihuahuas can have difficulty navigating stairs due to their size, which can lead to falls and injuries. Creating a safe area for them is essential. This space can be a cozy crate, a small playpen, or even a room that is gated off from the rest of your home. The idea is to provide them with a secure place where they can relax and feel safe, especially when they first arrive and are adjusting to new surroundings.

Having the necessary supplies ready before your Chihuahua comes home is also crucial. Start with a soft bed where they can rest comfortably. Access to clean water is vital as well, so ensure you have a bowl that's easy for them to drink from. Since their nutritional needs will vary based on their age, invest in high-quality dog food that is appropriate for their life stage. Don't forget the essentials like a harness and leash for walks, along with training pads if housebreaking is still a work-in-progress. A few chew-safe toys will also keep them entertained and help with teething if they are young. Finally, place all these items in the designated safe area so your Chihuahua begins to recognize it as their own space.

The Arrival

When you are ready to bring your Chihuahua home, it's important to remain calm and composed. As excited as you might feel, avoid giving them an overwhelming welcome with lots of noise or attention. Instead, you can gently guide them into your house using a leash or securely carrying them if they seem nervous. Let them explore their new environment at their own pace while you supervise their movements. They may want to sniff around, pause in certain spots, or even take a few steps back. This behavior is normal for Chihuahuas, as they tend to be cautious and observant, especially when they are in unfamiliar territory.

If there are other pets in your home, do not introduce them right away. It's best to let your new Chihuahua settle in on their own first. Allow a few hours for them to get used to the sights, sounds, and smells of their new environment. Once they have had some time to adjust, you can manage a slow and controlled introduction to the other pets. Doing this outdoors on neutral ground is often a good choice. This can help alleviate any territorial behaviors. After your Chihuahua has a chance to meet the other pets outside, you can all return indoors together.

During these early introductions, it is vital to closely observe the body language of both your Chihuahua and the existing pets. Signs of stress or aggression should be monitored carefully. Ensure that all interactions are supervised, as this will help create a safe and positive experience for everyone involved. Taking it slow can help establish trust and comfort in these new relationships.

Feeding and Bathroom Breaks

When you bring a Chihuahua into your home, you may notice they can be picky when it comes to food. It's important to remember that these little dogs can be easily stressed by changes in their environment, including new food. For this reason, if your Chihuahua does not eat much on their first day, do not be alarmed. Stick to the same food they were eating before you brought them home. If you want to switch to a different brand later, do it gradually over several days. This can help prevent an upset stomach, which can make them uncomfortable and more anxious.

Create a designated area for feeding. This space should be quiet and away from distractions, so your Chihuahua can eat in peace. It's best to offer food and water without hovering nearby. Allow them the space they need. You can place the food and water bowls on a sturdy mat to help keep the area tidy and make it easy to clean up. If you notice them taking their time to eat, just let them proceed at their own pace.

In addition to feeding, addressing bathroom needs is equally crucial, especially for puppies or dogs that are not yet house-trained. Once you arrive home with your new Chihuahua, take them to their potty area right away. This is the perfect opportunity to establish a routine. It's important to encourage frequent bathroom breaks. Aim to take them out every one to two hours, especially in the beginning. This will help them understand when and where to go.

When your Chihuahua successfully uses the potty in the right place, offer calm praise. A simple "good job" or a gentle pat can go a long way in reinforcing the behavior. Positive reinforcement helps them connect going to the bathroom outside with a reward, making it more likely they will remember to go outside in the future.

Consistency is key for any new pet. Try to keep their bathroom breaks at the same times each day, which helps create a routine they can rely on. Also, recognize and learn their signs for needing to go out. Many dogs will sniff around or circle when they need to relieve themselves. By paying attention to these behaviors, you can respond quickly to their needs and prevent accidents in the house.

As your Chihuahua settles in, you should gradually increase the time between bathroom breaks. Watch for signs that they are becoming more comfortable and house-trained. However, remember that each dog is different. Some may take longer to adjust than others. Patience is essential during this time.

Overall, the goal is to create a safe and comfortable environment for your Chihuahua, where they feel secure enough to eat properly and know where to go to the bathroom. Establishing clear routines for feeding and bathroom breaks will help you and your Chihuahua create a strong bond. Building trust with them will also encourage better behavior in both eating and house training.

If at any point you find that your Chihuahua continues to be a picky eater or has ongoing issues with going to the bathroom, do not hesitate to reach out to your veterinarian. They can provide additional guidance and check for any underlying health issues that could be affecting your dog's eating habits or potty training. Working closely with your vet ensures that your Chihuahua stays healthy and happy as they adjust to their new home.

Rest and Observation

Chihuahuas are highly alert but also need plenty of rest—especially puppies or rescues adjusting to a new environment. Don't overstimulate them with play or attention. Let them nap undisturbed in their bed or crate, and avoid loud noises, rough handling, or overwhelming them with toys or new people.

This is also your time to observe. Watch for signs of anxiety, discomfort, or medical issues. Are they sneezing, coughing, limping, or excessively scratching? Are they eating or drinking at all? Mild stress is expected, but anything that seems unusual should be monitored or discussed with a vet, especially within the first 24 hours.

Establishing Trust

Building trust between you and your pet starts with simple, consistent actions. The way you communicate with your Chihuahuas matters a lot. Using a soft, friendly voice can help them feel more at ease. Imagine speaking to a nervous child; your tone can either calm them down or make them more anxious. It's important to keep your voice gentle and reassuring.

When interacting with your Chihuahuas, avoid sudden movements. Reaching over their heads abruptly can make them feel threatened or scared. Instead, try to lower yourself to their level. This not only makes you appear less intimidating but also encourages them to approach you. When they do come close, it's essential to acknowledge their bravery. A small reward like treats can reinforce this behavior. For example, if your pet approaches you, offer them a small treat. If they wearily enter their crate or successfully use the potty area, reward them again. These small wins build towards a larger sense of trust.

Routine is another important aspect in building trust. A consistent schedule creates comfort and predictability for your Chihuahuas. Start by establishing regular feeding times. Pets thrive on routine, so feeding them at the same time every day will help them understand when to expect their meals. This can reduce anxiety around food, making it easier for them to trust you.

In addition to feeding, establish regular potty breaks. By taking your Chihuahuas out at the same times each day, you help them learn when it's time to go outside. They will appreciate the structure this brings to their day. Short, quiet walks around your neighborhood can also be scheduled at similar times. This repetition not only helps them understand the flow of the day but also fosters a stronger bond between you and your pet.

Chihuahuas are quick learners, especially when they feel safe. Creating a predictable environment allows them to learn more effectively. When they can anticipate what will happen next, they will feel more secure and trust you even more. For instance, if they know that after breakfast, they will go for a short walk, they will begin to look forward to that routine. Each element of the schedule reinforces their trust in you as a reliable caregiver.

It's important to be patient. Trust does not build overnight. Sometimes, your Chihuahua may not approach you right away or may react cautiously to new experiences. This is normal. Allow them the time they need to adapt. You can sit quietly on the floor, reading a book or playing with a toy. This non-threatening presence can encourage your Chihuahua to come to you when they feel comfortable.

Moreover, engage in activities that promote positive experiences. Play with them using toys they like. Use praise and kind words whenever they interact with you in a positive way. This strengthens the bond and helps them associate you with good feelings. The more enjoyable experiences they have with you, the more trust they will build.

Remember that every dog is different. Some may take longer to trust than others. If you have a particularly shy Chihuahua, it might be helpful to create a safe space where they can retreat if they feel overwhelmed. This could be a cozy bed or a specific area in your home where they feel secure. Allow them to explore at their own pace. Never force them into situations they aren't comfortable with, as this can damage trust.

Alongside these strategies, observe your Chihuahua. Pay attention to their body language. Signs of relaxation, such as wagging tails or playful postures, indicate that they are becoming more comfortable with you. Conversely, if they exhibit signs of stress, like cowering or hiding, step back. Give them some space until they are ready to engage again.

In summary, building trust with your Chihuahua requires consistency, patience, and understanding. Use a soft voice and gentle interactions to make them feel safe. Establish routines for feeding, potty breaks, and walks to instill a sense of predictability. Reward their brave actions with treats and positive reinforcement. Always be aware of their comfort level and allow them to approach you on their own terms.

These steps will lead to a deeper connection and a trusting relationship that benefits both you and your furry friend.

Introducing the Crate or Sleep Area

Night one is often the toughest. Chihuahuas don't like feeling alone and may cry or bark when first crated or left in their designated sleep area. Don't panic. Place the crate near your bed so they don't feel isolated. Give them a warm blanket, a comfort toy, or an item that smells like you. Resist the urge to remove them at every whimper—they'll learn that noise gets attention.

Gentle reassurance, not indulgence, helps them settle. Keep lights low, noise minimal, and stay calm. Some owners find soft music or a white noise machine helps calm anxiety during the first night.

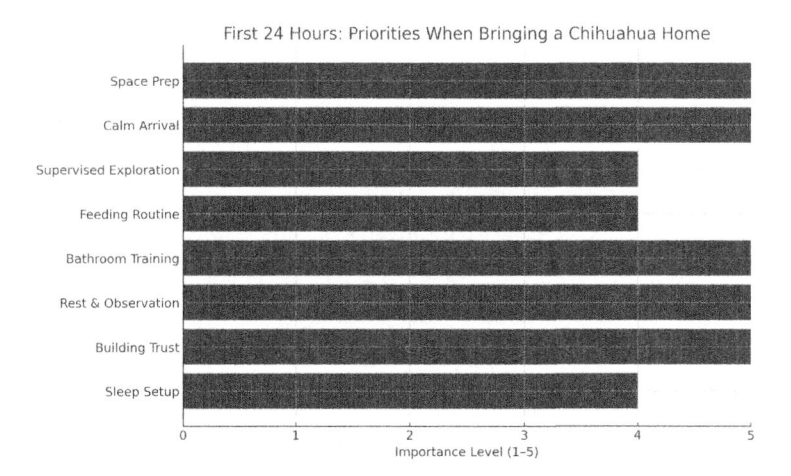

First 24 Hours: Priorities When Bringing a Chihuahua Home

Priority	Importance Level (1-5)
Space Prep	5
Calm Arrival	5
Supervised Exploration	4
Feeding Routine	4
Bathroom Training	5
Rest & Observation	5
Building Trust	5
Sleep Setup	4

Final Thoughts for Day One

The first 24 hours are not about perfect training or instant bonding—they're about respect, calm, and observation. This is a transitional period for your Chihuahua. Even if they're quiet or withdrawn, they're absorbing everything: your tone, your movements, your environment. How you handle this first day will influence how safe they feel moving forward.

Give them patience, space, and quiet structure. You're not just welcoming a dog into your home—you're becoming their entire world.

References:

- American Kennel Club. *Bringing Home a New Puppy.* https://www.akc.org/expert-advice/training/puppys-first-day-home
- Chihuahua Club of America. *New Owner Resources.* https://www.chihuahuaclubofamerica.org
- ASPCA. *Pet Care: Dog Basics.* https://www.aspca.org/pet-care/dog-care
- Cesar's Way. *First 24 Hours With Your New Dog.* https://www.cesarsway.com
- Rizzuto, D. *Your Chihuahua's First Day: What to Expect.* Dog Care Manual, 2020.

House Rules

Bringing a Chihuahua into your home means more than just feeding and walking it—it involves creating a structured, safe, and consistent environment that matches the breed's specific needs. Despite their small size, Chihuahuas have big personalities, and without clear boundaries, they can become stubborn, territorial, and even aggressive. Establishing house rules early on helps build a respectful, balanced relationship between the dog and everyone in the household.

One of the most important things to remember is that Chihuahuas are highly intelligent and observant. They quickly pick up on routines and patterns and can just as quickly learn how to bend the rules if they sense inconsistency. This is why rules should be clearly defined and consistently enforced by all members of the household. If one person allows the dog on the couch while another doesn't, the Chihuahua will likely ignore both and do whatever it wants.

Training should start the moment the Chihuahua arrives home. Basic rules—such as where the dog is allowed to go, when it eats, where it sleeps, and how it interacts with humans—should be established and kept consistent. Chihuahuas respond well to positive reinforcement methods, including praise, treats, and play. Harsh discipline, however, can backfire and lead to fear-based behaviors or defiance.

Housebreaking is another key rule area. Due to their small bladders, Chihuahuas can be harder to potty train than larger breeds. Frequent bathroom breaks, crate training, and reward-based methods are highly effective. Accidents should be cleaned thoroughly to eliminate lingering odors that might encourage repeat mistakes. Patience is essential, especially in the early months.

Essential House Rules for Chihuahuas

Rule	Importance Level (1-5)
Consistency Among Family	5
Housebreaking	5
Barking Control	4
Socialization Rules	4
Safety for Small Size	5
Feeding Discipline	4
Guest Guidelines	3
Alone Time Training	4

Chihuahuas are territorial by nature and may bark at strangers, visitors, or even household noises. Setting rules about barking—when it's acceptable and when it's not—helps avoid nuisance behavior. Teaching a command like "quiet" or "enough" and rewarding silence can be an effective way to manage this. Leaving excessive barking unaddressed can turn into a long-term problem, especially in apartment settings.

Social behavior is another area where rules matter. Chihuahuas often bond deeply with one person and may become possessive or even snappy toward others. To avoid this, it's important to socialize them early and frequently with a variety of people, pets, and environments. House rules should encourage inclusivity—such as feeding and playing being done by different family members—to prevent attachment to just one person.

Safety rules are especially important for such a small and fragile dog. Chihuahuas can be injured easily by accidental drops, rough handling, or interactions with larger pets. Children should be taught how to hold and interact with the dog gently, and furniture access should be monitored—small ramps or stairs can help prevent injuries from jumping off couches or beds.

Feeding rules should also be established to prevent overfeeding and obesity, which is a serious issue in small breeds. Human food should be limited or eliminated from the dog's diet, and begging at the table should not be tolerated. Scheduled feeding times and portion control keep the dog healthy and reinforce discipline.

Visitors and guests should be informed of any house rules related to the dog. This might include asking them not to feed the dog, to approach calmly, or to avoid picking it up without permission. Consistency from everyone interacting with the Chihuahua reinforces the dog's understanding of acceptable behavior.

Lastly, it's helpful to establish quiet or alone time. Chihuahuas can become overly dependent and suffer from separation anxiety if they are never left alone. Creating a comfortable space—like a crate or a specific bed—where the dog learns to rest on its own builds independence and helps reduce anxiety when you leave the house.

House rules aren't about control—they're about setting your Chihuahua up for success. Clear expectations, structure, and gentle but firm boundaries create a safe and respectful environment where the dog can thrive. A Chihuahua that understands the rules will be more confident, well-behaved, and easier to live with in the long run.

References:

- American Kennel Club. (n.d.). *Chihuahua Training Tips*. Retrieved from https://www.akc.org
- Cesar's Way. (n.d.). *Small Dog Syndrome: Breaking Bad Habits Early*. Retrieved from https://www.cesarsway.com
- ASPCA. (n.d.). *Dog Behavior and Training Basics*. Retrieved from https://www.aspca.org
- Taylor, D. (2021). *The Complete Guide to Chihuahuas*. LP Media Inc.
- The Humane Society of the United States. (n.d.). *Housetraining Your Puppy or Dog*. Retrieved from https://www.humanesociety.org

Introducing to Kids and Pets

Chihuahuas may be small, but their personalities are strong—and so are their instincts. When introducing a Chihuahua to children or other animals, understanding the breed's temperament is key. These dogs can be loving and loyal companions in multi-pet or family households, but the success of that relationship depends on how introductions are handled and whether everyone—human and animal—is respectful and properly prepared.

Chihuahuas are naturally wary of strangers, loud noises, and unpredictable movements. This cautious nature comes from their history as alert watchdogs and companion dogs bred for close human contact, not roughhousing or group play. When it comes to children, this sensitivity can be both a benefit and a challenge. On one hand, Chihuahuas form strong bonds with their human families, including older, gentle kids. On the other, their small size and delicate frame make them vulnerable to injury from toddlers or younger children who may not understand how to handle a dog with care.

For families with young kids, it's essential to set clear expectations from the beginning. Children should be taught never to grab, squeeze, or pick up the Chihuahua without supervision. Sudden movements or loud voices can startle the dog, which might react by snapping or retreating. Because of their instinct to protect themselves, Chihuahuas might not tolerate teasing or rough handling. This is not aggression in the traditional sense—it's self-defense in a fragile animal. Supervised interactions, calm energy, and age-appropriate handling lessons are all part of ensuring safety and building trust.

Older children, particularly those raised around animals, usually have better success with Chihuahuas. These kids can learn the dog's body language, understand when it needs space, and enjoy a close, affectionate bond. Chihuahuas often thrive in these settings, curling up next to their chosen person, following them from room to room, and becoming a reliable best friend. They may still display some protectiveness or pick a "favorite," but with regular socialization, they can form attachments to multiple people in the home.

Introducing a Chihuahua to other pets is also highly individual, depending on the other animal's temperament and the Chihuahua's past experiences. When raised with other dogs, especially those of similar size and energy, Chihuahuas can coexist peacefully and even form strong social bonds. However, when meeting new dogs—particularly larger breeds—Chihuahuas may show signs of fear or aggression. It's not uncommon for them to bark, lunge, or stand their ground, seemingly unaware of the size difference. This is where careful, structured introductions are vital.

The key is gradual exposure. Start by keeping both dogs on leashes, allowing them to observe each other from a safe distance. Let them sniff under supervision, and watch for signs of stress—stiff body language, growling, or snapping. Never force interaction. If the larger dog is well-trained and calm, it may help reassure the Chihuahua and ease its anxiety. Short, positive experiences build trust. Over time, they can learn to live and even play together, but constant supervision is necessary, especially early on.

Cats are another common companion animal in Chihuahua households. In many cases, the dog's size puts it closer to a cat than another dog, which can work in their favor. With slow introductions, most Chihuahuas can learn to coexist with cats, especially if the cat is confident and not easily spooked. Some Chihuahuas may try to chase or assert dominance at first, but consistent boundaries and calm correction usually smooth things out. As with dogs, successful integration relies on temperament and training on both sides.

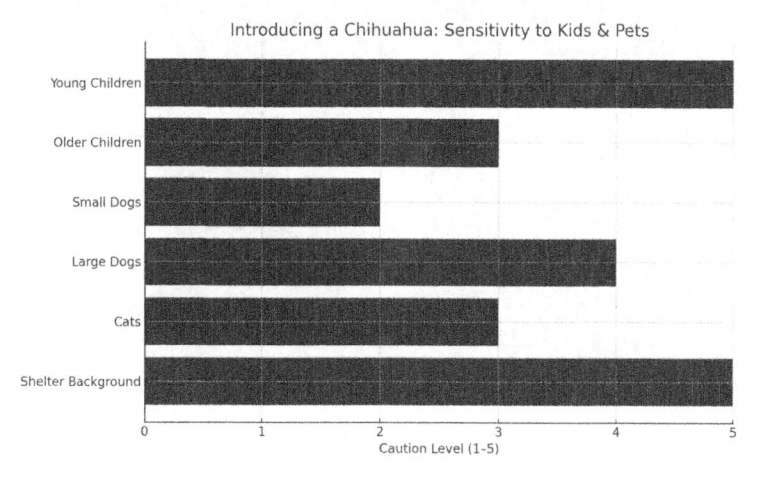

Introducing a Chihuahua: Sensitivity to Kids & Pets

Category	Caution Level (1-5)
Young Children	5
Older Children	3
Small Dogs	2
Large Dogs	4
Cats	3
Shelter Background	5

It's also important to consider the Chihuahua's past. Dogs adopted from shelters or uncertain backgrounds may have a history of trauma, poor socialization, or negative experiences with kids or other animals. These dogs need extra patience and space. Professional guidance from a trainer or behaviorist can be helpful in building a calm, structured environment for introductions.

In all cases, the foundation is the same: patience, supervision, and respect for boundaries. Chihuahuas are loyal and adaptable, but they need to feel safe. With proper handling and gradual exposure, they can become loving members of homes with children, other dogs, cats, and even small animals. Each successful introduction builds their confidence—and strengthens the bond they share with the people and animals around them.

References:

- American Kennel Club. (n.d.). *Chihuahua Dog Breed Information.* Retrieved from https://www.akc.org/dog-breeds/chihuahua/
- Palika, L. (2007). *Chihuahuas for Dummies.* Wiley Publishing.
- ASPCA. (n.d.). *Introducing Your Dog to New Pets and Children.* Retrieved from https://www.aspca.org/pet-care/dog-care/dog-behavior-tips
- McKinney, C. (2013). *The Everything Chihuahua Book.* Adams Media.
- HSUS. (n.d.). *Introducing Pets to New Family Members.* Retrieved from https://www.humanesociety.org/resources/introducing-pets-new-family-members

Bonding Techniques

Building a strong bond with a Chihuahua takes time, consistency, and genuine attention. These dogs are known for choosing a "favorite person" and forming intense attachments—but that kind of loyalty doesn't happen by accident. Bonding with a Chihuahua requires more than basic care; it's about creating trust, understanding their emotional cues, and being present in a way that makes them feel secure.

Chihuahuas are deeply sensitive animals. They pick up on tone of voice, body language, and even mood. If you're stressed or angry, they'll likely sense it and may become anxious or withdrawn. That's why calm, positive energy is one of the most important foundations for bonding. Speaking gently, avoiding loud or sudden movements, and using encouraging words help a Chihuahua feel safe around you.

Physical Touch and Presence

One of the easiest ways to bond is through physical closeness. Chihuahuas are lap dogs by nature. They love to curl up next to their person, burrow under blankets, or sit quietly in your arms. Letting them be near you—whether you're working, watching TV, or resting—gives them comfort. Gently petting or scratching their favorite spots (often behind the ears or under the chin) reinforces that bond. Over time, your scent and presence become sources of safety.

However, respect their space too. If they move away, don't force interaction. For Chihuahuas, trust means knowing they can approach you on their terms. Trying too hard can backfire—let the bond build naturally.

Routine and Predictability

Chihuahuas thrive on routine. Feeding times, walk times, bedtime—it all helps them feel secure. The more predictable their environment, the more they relax and open up. Establishing daily rituals, like morning cuddles or evening walks, gives them something to look forward to and helps strengthen the connection.

Consistency in your behavior is equally important. If you're affectionate one day and distracted the next, they may get confused or clingy. Show up for them the same way every day, and their trust in you will deepen.

Communication and Training

Training sessions are not just about obedience—they're bonding opportunities. When you teach your Chihuahua a command or trick and reward them with praise or treats, you're reinforcing that good things happen when they're engaged with you. Keep sessions short, fun, and upbeat. Avoid frustration or punishment. Even five minutes a day builds connection.

Chihuahuas are smart and expressive. Pay attention to their body language—how their ears, tail, or posture changes. Learning their signals helps you respond appropriately, which in turn makes them feel understood. That sense of being "heard" is powerful in building a bond.

Playtime and Enrichment

Interactive play is another great bonding tool. Tug toys, fetch (yes, even indoors), and puzzle feeders all engage their body and brain. Playing together creates shared experiences and memories. It's also a chance for them to see you as a fun, positive part of their world—not just the person who feeds them.

Mental stimulation is as important as physical activity. Teaching new tricks, scent games, or rotating toys keeps their mind sharp and builds trust in your leadership. A mentally stimulated Chihuahua is more balanced, less anxious, and more connected to you.

Building Confidence Through Exposure

Part of bonding is helping your Chihuahua feel confident. Expose them gradually to new environments, people, and other animals—always with reassurance and positive reinforcement. When they see that you're a safe anchor in unfamiliar situations, their trust in you grows.

For shy or fearful Chihuahuas, this step is especially important. Never force them into overwhelming situations. Let them explore at their own pace while staying nearby. Confidence grows slowly, and your calm support during that process becomes a bonding force.

Respect Their Unique Personality

Every Chihuahua has its own distinct personality. Some Chihuahuas are bold and social, enjoying the company of people and other animals. They may wag their tails enthusiastically when they meet new friends and march confidently into new situations. On the other hand, some

Chihuahuas are more timid and reserved. They might hide behind their owners or approach new experiences with caution. Understanding this individuality is key to forming a strong bond with your Chihuahua.

Bonding with your Chihuahua means adapting to their personality rather than trying to change it. For a bold Chihuahua, you might want to encourage their social behavior by introducing them to new experiences gradually. This could be as simple as taking them to a dog park or inviting friends over to meet them. It's important to do this slowly, allowing your dog to become comfortable at their own pace. On the other hand, if your Chihuahua tends to be more reserved, it's essential to give them the space they need. For example, when introducing them to new people, make sure that they have a safe spot to retreat to if they feel overwhelmed. Understanding their reactions and respecting their need for space can help solidify the bond you share.

Celebrating your Chihuahua's quirks can also strengthen your connection. Each dog has unique behaviors and traits that make them special. Perhaps your Chihuahua tilts its head when it hears a specific sound, or maybe it has a favorite toy it carries around everywhere. Acknowledging and appreciating these cute and funny habits can create positive interactions. If your Chihuahua has a tendency to bark at the mailman, instead of getting frustrated, you could focus on giving praise when they are calm. This way, you reward them for good behavior rather than punishing them for what seems like misbehavior.

As you spend time with your Chihuahua, make sure to use positive reinforcement to encourage their progress. Whether your dog is learning a new command or adjusting to a new environment, offering treats, praise, or petting can go a long way. For example, if your Chihuahua is learning to sit on command, reward them right after they sit down. This reinforces the behavior and helps them understand what you want from them. With every small success, your Chihuahua learns to trust you more.

For a deeper bond, being reliable and attentive is crucial. Chihuahuas, like all dogs, thrive on routine and knowing what to expect. Feeding them at the same time every day, providing regular exercise, and maintaining a consistent training schedule can alleviate their anxiety. When they know they can count on you, they feel safe. This sense of security is vital for trust-building. If you establish that you are a reliable source of care and companionship, your Chihuahua will likely become more affectionate in return.

Emotional presence is another essential aspect of bonding. Being emotionally present means being in tune with your dog's feelings and needs. It involves paying attention to their body language and vocalizations to understand when they are happy, anxious, or in need of attention. For instance, if your Chihuahua is shaking, it might be feeling scared or cold. A calm, reassuring response can help them relax. Even spending quiet time together, like sitting beside them while they chew on a toy, can provide comfort and build a strong emotional connection.

As you nurture this bond, you may find that your Chihuahua returns your efforts with loyalty and affection. Once trust is established, you're likely to witness a transformation in your pet's behavior. They may become more eager to follow you around the house, show excitement when you come home, or cuddle up beside you while you relax. These moments are markers of a deepening relationship and highlight the importance of mutual respect.

Having a relationship based on mutual respect is vital. Rather than striving for control, which can lead to frustration, focus on creating a partnership with your Chihuahua. This means recognizing their needs, allowing their personalities to shine, and valuing the bond you share. When your Chihuahua feels respected for who they are, they respond with behavior that reflects their love and loyalty.

Ultimately, the more time and energy you invest in understanding your Chihuahua, the stronger your connection will become. As you engage with them daily, you'll not only learn about their distinctive traits but also discover the depth of the bond that forms over time. Each interaction helps shape the relationship, building a foundation of love and trust that can last a lifetime.

The journey to bond with your Chihuahua requires patience and understanding, but it's incredibly rewarding. By respecting their unique personality, being attentive, and celebrating their quirks, you can build a lasting relationship. When you approach your Chihuahua with love and respect, the bond that develops is not just about ownership; it's about partnership. This partnership leads to memories and experiences that both you and your Chihuahua will cherish.

References

- American Kennel Club. (n.d.). *How to Bond with Your Dog.* https://www.akc.org

- DogTime. (n.d.). *Chihuahua Personality and Temperament.* https://dogtime.com

- Cesar's Way. (n.d.). *Bonding With Your Dog: The Foundation of Training.* https://www.cesarsway.com

- Coren, S. (2006). *The Intelligence of Dogs.* Free Press

- PetMD. (n.d.). *Understanding Dog Body Language.* https://www.petmd.com

- Animal Humane Society. (n.d.). *Positive Reinforcement Training.* https://www.animalhumanesociety.org

Chapter 5: Training Your Chihuahua

Potty Training Tips

Potty training is one of the first and most essential lessons for your Chihuahua. While these dogs are intelligent and eager to please, they also have a reputation for being one of the more challenging breeds to house-train. Their small size, independent streak, and occasional stubbornness can lead to accidents if the right approach isn't used. But with consistency, patience, and the right setup, your Chihuahua can learn quickly and reliably.

Why Potty Training Can Be Tricky for Chihuahuas

One of the main challenges is their size. Chihuahuas have tiny bladders and fast metabolisms, which means they need to go more often than larger dogs. What seems like frequent accidents may actually be your dog simply unable to hold it. Weather sensitivity is another factor—many Chihuahuas dislike going outside in the rain or cold, which can lead to indoor accidents. Lastly, their alert, sometimes anxious nature can distract them from doing their business outdoors if they don't feel completely comfortable.

Start With a Schedule

The first step to effective potty training is a consistent schedule. Take your Chihuahua out—or to their indoor potty spot—first thing in the morning, after meals, after naps, after playtime, and right before bed. For puppies under six months old, this may mean going out every 1–2 hours.

Keep feeding times consistent too. Predictable meals make it easier to anticipate when they'll need to go. Free-feeding (leaving food out all day) often leads to unpredictable bathroom habits, which can delay progress.

Pick a Designated Spot

Choose a specific potty area and always lead your Chihuahua there using a leash, even indoors if needed. Use a cue word like "go potty" or "do your business." Keep the cue short and say it in a calm, upbeat tone.

Don't rush them. Let them sniff and walk around the spot for a few minutes. The familiar scent helps reinforce the idea that this is the right place. When they go, offer enthusiastic praise and a treat immediately —within two seconds—so they connect the reward to the action.

Crate Training as a Tool

Crate training can greatly speed up potty training. Dogs naturally avoid soiling their sleeping space. Use a crate just large enough for your Chihuahua to stand, turn, and lie down comfortably. If it's too big, they may potty in one corner and sleep in the other.

Take them straight to the potty area each time you let them out. If they go, reward them and allow some supervised play. If not, return them to the crate for 10–15 minutes and try again. Crate time should never feel like punishment—it's a place of rest and security.

Supervise and Limit Access

When not in the crate, supervise your Chihuahua closely. If you can't keep both eyes on them, use a leash indoors or confine them to a small, puppy-proofed room. This helps you spot signs that they need to go: circling, sniffing the floor, whining, or pacing.

Interrupt accidents in progress with a firm but gentle "No" and immediately take them to the potty spot. Never punish after the fact. Chihuahuas don't associate past messes with discipline, and scolding only creates fear or confusion.

Indoor Potty Options

Because of their size and weather aversion, many Chihuahua owners use indoor potty systems. Pee pads, artificial grass pads, or litter boxes with paper pellets can work well. The key is to be just as consistent as with outdoor training. Pick a spot, use a cue, and reward successes. Don't change the location once you've started, or it may confuse them.

If you plan to eventually transition your Chihuahua from pads to going outside, do it gradually. Move the pad closer to the door over several days, then outside the door, and finally to the desired outdoor location.

Positive Reinforcement Works Best

Chihuahuas respond best to positive reinforcement. Use high-value treats—small, soft, and irresistible—and don't hold back on praise. Keep your tone upbeat, and celebrate each success with genuine enthusiasm. This builds trust and motivation, and your dog begins to associate pottying in the right place with positive experiences.

Watch the Water Intake

Regulate water, especially before bedtime. Don't withhold it entirely, but avoid letting your Chihuahua drink a large amount right before sleep. Always give access to fresh water during the day, and offer a final potty trip just before turning in for the night.

Stay Patient and Realistic

Potty training a Chihuahua isn't an overnight task. Puppies may take several weeks to months to be fully reliable. Even adult rescues may need time to adjust to a new environment. Be patient, and don't expect perfection too soon. Setbacks are normal, especially during schedule changes, illness, or stress.

Track your dog's progress and celebrate improvements, even small ones. The key is consistency—when rules and routines are steady, Chihuahuas learn faster and with less confusion.

Common Mistakes to Avoid

- Free-roaming too early. Give freedom gradually after consistent success.
- Inconsistent training times. Stick to a schedule.
- Using punishment. It leads to fear-based behavior, not learning.
- Expecting them to hold it too long. Young puppies especially need frequent breaks.

Final Thoughts

Potty training is a process, and every dog learns at their own pace. With Chihuahuas, a little extra patience and structure go a long way. Set clear boundaries, reward good behavior, and handle mistakes calmly. You're not just teaching them where to go—you're building trust, confidence, and lifelong habits that make your home cleaner, happier, and more peaceful.

References:

- American Kennel Club. *Housebreaking Your Puppy: Do's and Don'ts.* https://www.akc.org
- Chihuahua Club of America. *Puppy Training Basics.* https://www.chihuahuaclubofamerica.org
- ASPCA. *House Training Your Dog or Puppy.* https://www.aspca.org/pet-care/dog-care/house-training
- Dunbar, I. *Before and After Getting Your Puppy.* New World Library, 2004.

- Pryor, K. *Don't Shoot the Dog: The New Art of Teaching and Training.* Bantam Books, 1999.

Basic Commands

Training a Chihuahua is an essential part of ensuring they become well-behaved and well-adjusted pets. Though small in size, Chihuahuas are known for their big personalities and intelligence, which can sometimes lead to stubbornness or a tendency to challenge authority. By teaching basic commands, you establish a foundation of communication and mutual respect that helps keep the dog safe, confident, and in control of their environment.

Starting with basic commands early in a Chihuahua's life is the best way to avoid behavioral problems later on. While Chihuahuas are generally eager to please, consistency, patience, and positive reinforcement are key to making training successful. Here are the most important basic commands every Chihuahua should learn:

1. Sit

The "sit" command is one of the simplest yet most useful commands you can teach your Chihuahua. It helps control your dog's behavior in various situations, such as when you need them to settle down before feeding, walking, or meeting visitors. To teach this command, hold a treat close to your dog's nose, then move it upwards and backward toward their head. As their rear end touches the ground, say "sit" in a clear, calm voice, and reward them immediately with praise and the treat. With repetition, your Chihuahua will quickly learn to sit on command.

2. Stay

The "stay" command is an important tool for maintaining control over your Chihuahua in various environments, especially when you need them to remain in place for safety. To teach "stay," ask your Chihuahua to sit first. Hold your palm out toward them, say "stay," and take a step back. If they stay in place, return to them, praise them, and reward them with a treat. Start by practicing for short periods and gradually increase the duration and distance as they become more confident with the command. Keep in mind that Chihuahuas, like most small breeds, can be energetic and may need some time to master this skill.

3. Come

The "come" command is one of the most crucial commands for any dog, regardless of breed, as it ensures that your Chihuahua will return to you when called. To teach this command, begin by calling your dog in a playful, enthusiastic tone when they are a few feet away. Use their name followed by "come," and reward them immediately with praise and a treat when they approach you. Practice this command in different locations and situations, and always reward them for coming to you. Be sure not to scold your Chihuahua if they take too long to respond, as this can create negative associations with the command.

4. Down

Teaching the "down" command helps instill good behavior, especially if your Chihuahua tends to jump up on people or furniture. Begin by asking your dog to sit, then gently guide them into a lying position by moving a treat from their nose to the floor. When they lie down, immediately say "down" and reward them with praise and a treat. Over time, your Chihuahua will learn to associate the action of lying down with the verbal command. This command also serves as a great way to calm an excited or anxious dog.

5. Leave It

The "leave it" command is vital for Chihuahuas, especially since they can be very curious and may attempt to pick up something harmful or unsafe. To teach this command, hold a treat in your hand and show it to your Chihuahua, but don't let them grab it. Close your fist around the treat and say "leave it" in a firm, calm voice. When your dog stops trying to get the treat and looks away, open your hand, and reward them with a different treat. With time and practice, they will learn to stop and leave objects alone when you say "leave it."

6. No

The "no" command is essential for correcting unwanted behaviors. It's important to say "no" firmly and clearly, but never with anger or frustration. When your Chihuahua engages in undesirable behavior—such as chewing on something they shouldn't or barking excessively—use the "no" command. Immediately redirect their attention to a more appropriate behavior and reward them for complying. Repeating this consistently will help your Chihuahua understand that certain actions are not acceptable.

7. Watch Me

"Watch me" is an excellent command for gaining your Chihuahua's focus, especially in distracting environments. To teach this, hold a treat close to your face, and when your dog looks at you, say "watch me." Immediately reward them with the treat and praise. This command is helpful when you want to get their attention before giving further instructions, and it's especially useful during training sessions or when they're distracted by something else.

8. Crate Training

While not a traditional "command," crate training is an essential part of creating a safe and structured environment for your Chihuahua. Introduce the crate as a positive, comforting space by placing treats, toys, and their bedding inside. Use commands such as "go to your crate" or "bed" to encourage your dog to enter it willingly. Over time, they will learn that the crate is their designated space, providing both security and a place for rest.

Tips for Effective Training:

- **Consistency is key**: Always use the same command words and gestures to avoid confusing your Chihuahua.
- **Positive reinforcement**: Reward good behavior with praise, treats, or toys, and always be sure to make training a fun experience.
- **Short sessions**: Keep training sessions short (about 5-10 minutes) to prevent your Chihuahua from becoming bored or frustrated.
- **Patience**: Chihuahuas are quick learners, but they can also be stubborn. Stay patient and positive, especially when teaching more complex commands.

With the right approach, you'll build a strong foundation of trust and communication with your Chihuahua, and they will become a well-behaved companion in your home.

References:

- American Kennel Club. (n.d.). *Chihuahua Training Tips*. Retrieved from https://www.akc.org/dog-breeds/chihuahua/
- Cesar's Way. (n.d.). *Dog Training Techniques and Tips*. Retrieved from https://www.cesarsway.com
- ASPCA. (n.d.). *Basic Dog Training and Behavior*. Retrieved from https://www.aspca.org/pet-care/dog-care

Behavior Problems

Chihuahuas, like any breed, can exhibit a range of behavioral issues. While many of these issues stem from their natural temperament, size, or early experiences, they can often be managed with the right training, consistency, and understanding. Because of their small size and strong personalities, Chihuahuas are sometimes labeled as "yappy" or "stubborn," but it's important to remember that behavior problems can arise in any dog. With the right approach, most of these issues can be addressed effectively.

1. Excessive Barking

One of the most common behavior problems with Chihuahuas is excessive barking. While barking is a natural way for dogs to communicate, Chihuahuas are particularly vocal. Their alert nature makes them excellent watchdogs, but it can also result in continuous barking, especially when they hear noises outside, see other animals, or sense unfamiliar people.

Excessive barking can quickly become a nuisance, but with proper training, it's manageable. One effective technique is teaching the dog a "quiet" command. This can be achieved by rewarding your Chihuahua for remaining quiet after it has barked, gradually increasing the duration of silence before offering a reward. Avoid rewarding barking behavior, as this can reinforce it. Regular exercise and mental stimulation can also reduce the likelihood of barking due to boredom or anxiety.

2. Separation Anxiety

Chihuahuas tend to form strong bonds with their owners, and when left alone for extended periods, they can develop separation anxiety. This is particularly common in Chihuahuas that have been overly pampered or overattached to one person. Dogs with separation anxiety may engage in destructive behavior, like chewing furniture, digging, or having accidents in the house. They might also bark excessively or whine when left alone.

The best way to manage separation anxiety is to gradually increase the amount of time spent apart. Starting with short separations and gradually extending the time can help the dog become more comfortable being alone. Providing distractions like puzzle toys or chew items can keep the dog occupied while you're away. In more severe cases, working with a professional dog trainer or behaviorist can be beneficial to address the root cause and help your dog build confidence.

3. Small Dog Syndrome

Small Dog Syndrome, sometimes referred to as "small dog complex," is a common behavioral issue in many toy breeds, including Chihuahuas. These dogs often act out in an attempt to compensate for their small size. A Chihuahua suffering from Small Dog Syndrome may act aggressively, try to dominate other animals, or become possessive of its owner or territory. They may bark aggressively at larger dogs or strangers, attempting to assert authority even when they are outmatched in size.

This behavior is usually the result of inconsistent training, lack of boundaries, or overindulgence. It's essential for Chihuahua owners to establish rules early on and enforce them consistently. Teaching your dog basic commands like "sit," "stay," and "leave it" helps promote respect and reduces unwanted behaviors. A well-behaved Chihuahua knows its place in the household hierarchy, which can help curb dominance issues.

4. Aggression Towards Other Pets

Chihuahuas are known for their protective and territorial nature. While many get along well with other pets, some may exhibit aggression, especially towards dogs of different sizes or unfamiliar animals. Their small size can make them nervous around larger dogs, and they may feel the need to protect themselves or their owners. This can lead to growling, snapping, or even biting.

Introducing a Chihuahua to other pets, especially new ones, should always be done gradually and under supervision. Positive reinforcement training can help the dog feel more secure and reduce fearful or aggressive behaviors. It's also important to provide each pet with its own space, so the Chihuahua doesn't feel threatened or crowded by other animals in the house.

5. Potty Training Issues

While most Chihuahuas are quick to learn potty training, their small bladders can make it a bit more challenging. Some Chihuahuas may have accidents in the house more frequently than larger dogs simply because they need to relieve themselves more often. Additionally, Chihuahuas can be stubborn, and if potty training isn't established early and consistently, they may continue to have accidents indoors, even in adulthood.

The key to successful potty training is consistency. Chihuahuas should be taken outside frequently, especially after meals, naps, or playtime. Using a crate or playpen can also help them learn to control their bladder. Accidents should never be punished, as this can increase anxiety and worsen the behavior. Instead, praise and reward the dog when it goes potty outside, reinforcing good behavior.

6. Destructive Chewing

Chewing is a natural behavior for dogs, especially puppies. However, some Chihuahuas, particularly those with high energy levels or anxiety, may chew destructively on furniture, shoes, or even electrical cords. This can be a sign of boredom, stress, or lack of sufficient mental and physical stimulation.

To prevent destructive chewing, provide your Chihuahua with plenty of toys and activities to keep its mind occupied. Puzzle toys, chew toys, and interactive games can help reduce the desire to chew on inappropriate objects. If your Chihuahua is particularly destructive, crate training may be helpful when you're not home to supervise. Training your dog to use a designated area for chewing will help redirect its energy.

7. Fearfulness or Shyness

While Chihuahuas are often bold and confident, some may be more reserved or fearful, especially if they have not been adequately socialized. A fearful Chihuahua may exhibit behaviors like hiding, shaking, or retreating from unfamiliar people, animals, or situations. This fear can lead to anxious behaviors such as excessive barking or aggression when the dog feels threatened.

Early and consistent socialization is key to preventing fearfulness in Chihuahuas. Exposing them to various people, pets, and environments from a young age helps build their confidence and ensures they are more adaptable as adults. Positive reinforcement can help fearful dogs associate new experiences with rewards, easing their anxiety.

Conclusion

While Chihuahuas can experience a range of behavioral issues, most of these problems can be addressed with the right approach. Understanding the breed's temperament and providing appropriate training, socialization, and consistent care are crucial to fostering a well-behaved and happy Chihuahua. With patience, positive reinforcement, and a clear structure, Chihuahuas can be wonderful, well-adjusted pets that thrive in a loving home.

References:

- American Kennel Club. (n.d.). *Chihuahua Dog Breed Information*. Retrieved from https://www.akc.org/dog-breeds/chihuahua/
- Palika, L. (2007). *Chihuahuas for Dummies*. Wiley Publishing.

- McKinney, C. (2013). *The Everything Chihuahua Book*. Adams Media.
- Fogle, B. (2000). *The Encyclopedia of the Dog*. DK Publishing.
- ASPCA. (n.d.). *Behavioral Issues in Dogs*. Retrieved from https://www.aspca.org/pet-care/dog-care/dog-behavior-tips

Socialization Essentials

For a Chihuahua, socialization is not just a luxury—it's an absolute necessity. Despite their small size, Chihuahuas can be naturally wary of new people, environments, and other animals. Proper socialization ensures that your Chihuahua grows up to be a well-rounded, confident, and happy dog who can handle new experiences without becoming fearful or aggressive.

Early Socialization: The Foundation

The best time to begin socializing your Chihuahua is during puppyhood, ideally between 3 and 14 weeks of age. This critical window helps them form positive associations with people, other pets, and different situations. During this period, they are most receptive to new experiences, so exposing them to a variety of sights, sounds, and people can set the stage for a calm, confident adult dog.

However, socialization doesn't stop in puppyhood. While early exposure is crucial, socialization must continue throughout a Chihuahua's life. The more experiences they have, the more adaptable and confident they become. You must remain patient and committed to introducing your Chihuahua to new environments, people, and animals throughout their adulthood to ensure they stay well-socialized.

Meeting New People

Chihuahuas can be especially cautious or even fearful of strangers, often barking excessively when they sense something unfamiliar. While this is partly due to their protective nature, it's essential to help them learn how to appropriately respond to new faces without becoming overly anxious or aggressive.

Start by introducing your Chihuahua to new people in a calm, controlled manner. Allow your dog to observe newcomers from a distance before deciding whether to approach. Never force interaction —let your Chihuahua come to new people on their own terms. Positive reinforcement goes a long way. Reward them with treats and praise when they behave calmly during introductions. Over time, they will learn that meeting new people is a pleasant experience and not something to fear.

Socializing with Other Dogs

Chihuahuas can sometimes show territorial behavior. This behavior stems from their small size, which can make them feel threatened in the presence of larger dogs. To help your Chihuahua thrive, it is crucial to expose them to other dogs of different sizes, breeds, and temperaments. Doing so helps them develop appropriate interaction skills and prevents them from becoming overly aggressive or overly fearful. It is best to start with calm and friendly dogs. As you introduce them, supervision is key. Make sure to watch their interactions closely. Keeping the experience positive is essential for their social development.

You should pay close attention to your dog's body language during these interactions. Signs of stress or fear can include behaviors like growling, snapping, or hiding. If you notice any of these signs, it's important to take a step back. Allow your dog to process the encounter at their own pace. By doing this, you give them the chance to feel secure and comfortable in these situations. Socializing should never feel like a chore or a punishment for your pet.

One effective way to help your Chihuahua socialize with other dogs is by enrolling them in puppy classes or doggy playgroups. These structured environments provide safety and control while allowing your dog to meet others. Puppy classes often feature professionals trained to guide both you and your dog through the process of socialization. These instructors know how to create a positive atmosphere and help dogs learn better interaction habits.

In these types of settings, your Chihuahua can learn proper dog-to-dog manners. For example, they can discover how to communicate effectively with other dogs using body language. This is crucial because dogs rely heavily on body language to understand each other. A wagging tail often indicates friendliness, while a stiff posture may suggest a dog is feeling threatened. By learning these cues, your Chihuahua can become more adept at navigating social situations with confidence.

Additionally, puppy classes encourage learning how to share space. Sharing space is a vital skill for any dog, as it allows them to coexist peacefully with others. Available space can often lead to conflicts, so teaching your dog to be aware of their surroundings and respect boundaries is important. With guided play, dogs can learn to find their place and feel comfortable around other animals.

Being in a structured class also helps dogs avoid feeling overwhelmed. In an environment designed for their benefit, Chihuahuas can meet new friends without the pressure of uncontrolled settings. This allows them time to acclimate. For example, they might first interact from a distance where they can observe other dogs before engaging in closer play. It's important to let them approach at their own speed.

Furthermore, early socialization through classes or playgroups can prevent behavioral issues later on. When Chihuahuas do not receive proper social exposure, they may develop issues such as fearfulness or aggression. Open socialization can help curb these tendencies, making your dog more adaptable and less likely to react negatively in new situations.

Remember, consistency is crucial when socializing your Chihuahua. Attend classes or playgroups regularly to help reinforce positive experiences with other dogs. The more opportunities they have to meet new friends, the better they will become at handling various situations. Familiarity and practice can make a significant difference.

Aside from classes, you can also look for local dog parks or community events where dogs are welcome. These spaces can offer additional chances for socialization. As you bring your Chihuahua to these communal areas, start with quiet times when there are not too many dogs present. This gradual introduction helps them avoid feeling overwhelmed.

Before heading to a dog park, it's advisable to observe how dogs interact from a distance. Watch for any aggressive behaviors or signs of discomfort in both your dog and others. This observation helps you judge when it may be a good time to let your dog off-leash for play.

Once you feel comfortable, allow your Chihuahua to explore. Even if they take their time, let them investigate the environment at a pace that feels secure for them. Encouraging gentle interactions with other dogs will help them grow more confident. You can reward positive behaviors with treats or praise, reinforcing their good social conduct.

Also, involve yourself in the interaction. Engage with your dog during play so they feel supported. Your presence can reassure them, helping reduce anxiety while meeting new friends. Encourage friendly play and be ready to intervene if necessary, especially in larger crowds where things might get too boisterous.

By providing an abundance of social opportunities and closely monitoring their interactions, you set your Chihuahua up for future successes. The emphasis on positive experiences helps foster their development into well-adjusted and sociable pets. Keep in mind that patience is key. Every dog has their own timeline for adjustment and socialization. Celebrate the small victories along the way, no matter how trivial they may seem.

In essence, socializing your Chihuahua opens doors to friendships and enhances their quality of life. As they learn to navigate the dog world, they will become more fulfilled and happier. Engaging in social activities regularly enriches their experiences and strengthens the bond between you and your furry companion. The goal is to create a friendly environment where they can grow, learn, and enjoy the companionship of others.

Exposure to New Environments

Socializing your Chihuahua isn't just about people and other dogs. It's also about getting them accustomed to different environments and situations. A Chihuahua that is not exposed to various experiences may develop anxiety when faced with unfamiliar places. Gradual exposure to different environments helps them stay calm and relaxed no matter where they are.

Start with simple outings. Take your Chihuahua for short walks in different areas, such as the park, a busy street, or even a pet-friendly café. The goal is to expose them to new smells, sounds, and sights without overwhelming them. Keep these outings positive by bringing treats and offering praise for calm behavior. Over time, your Chihuahua will learn to enjoy being out and about, building confidence with each new adventure.

Don't forget about sounds. Chihuahuas are sensitive to noise, and sudden loud sounds can be a source of fear. If possible, gently expose your dog to different noises, such as vacuum cleaners, traffic, doorbells, or even thunderstorms. Gradual, positive exposure helps them learn to cope with the everyday sounds they may encounter in the real world.

Handling Fear and Anxiety

Many Chihuahuas can develop fear-based behaviors, especially if they have not been properly socialized. This lack of exposure to different environments, sounds, and other animals can cause them to react in ways that are concerning for their owners. They may bark excessively, growl at perceived threats, or even avoid situations that are unfamiliar to them. It is crucial to address these signs of fear and anxiety in a thoughtful and patient manner. Forcing a Chihuahua into situations that trigger their fear will often make the problem worse, leading to more anxiety and stress. Therefore, understanding how to help them is vital for their well-being.

To start, employing positive reinforcement techniques can be very effective in building a Chihuahua's confidence. Positive reinforcement involves rewarding your pet with treats, praise, or playtime when they display calm behavior in situations that previously caused them fear. This technique helps them learn that they can trust their environment. When your dog realizes that they will receive rewards for staying calm, they begin to perceive the world as a safer place.

A key aspect of addressing fear is gradual exposure. Begin with slowly and carefully introducing your Chihuahua to the source of their fear. For instance, if your dog is afraid of other dogs, start by allowing them to observe another dog from a distance where they feel safe. You can give them treats and praise when they remain calm during this observation. This step can help instill a sense of security, as they begin to associate the presence of other dogs with positive experiences, rather than fear.

Once your Chihuahua responds well to seeing other dogs from afar, you can slowly decrease the distance between them. However, it is essential to do this at a pace that your dog is comfortable with. If you notice signs of anxiety, such as backing away, barking, or showing a tense body posture, it's important to give them space. In this case, return to the previous distance where they felt safe and continue working at that level for a while longer before attempting to close the gap again.

In addition to systematic desensitization, it may be helpful to create a secure space for your Chihuahua at home where they can retreat if they feel overwhelmed. This space can be a cozy bed or a crate in a quiet room away from loud noises or bustling activity. Encourage them to use this area by placing some of their favorite toys or treats inside. The goal is to establish a refuge where they can relax and feel safe.

It is also important to age and temperament when working with a fearful Chihuahua. Older dogs may take longer to adjust than younger puppies, as they may have had more ingrained fears. A calm and patient approach is needed to help them overcome these challenges. Consider consulting with a professional dog trainer or a veterinary behaviorist if the anxiety persists. These professionals can provide tailored strategies to assist in overcoming fear-based issues.

Building a strong bond with your Chihuahua will also play a crucial role in alleviating their fears. Spend quality time together through play and gentle interactions. Engage them in activities they enjoy, like basic training or simple games that stimulate their mind. By creating positive experiences together, you'll reinforce your relationship, making your dog feel more secure in your presence. They should be able to trust that you will keep them safe.

Moreover, consistent routines can help reduce anxiety in Chihuahuas. Dogs thrive on predictability, and establishing a daily routine for meals, walks, and playtime can help create a sense of stability. This structure can alleviate uncertainty and help them feel more secure in their environment.

Sometimes, addressing basic needs like exercise can also contribute to a reduction in fear-based behavior. Regular physical activity helps to burn off excess energy and can lead to a calmer disposition. Even a few short walks daily, in a controlled and familiar environment, can significantly impact their overall anxiety levels.

It is important to remember that change takes time. You should not expect immediate results. Celebrate small victories along the way, such as your Chihuahua being able to sit calmly during a stroll in the park or showing curiosity towards a new person. These progressions are steps forward in your dog's emotional health. By staying patient and committed to helping your Chihuahua face their fears, you'll pave the way for a happier and more confident pet. Ultimately, your care and understanding will foster a trusting relationship that enhances both your lives.

The Role of Obedience Training

Obedience training is a key component of socialization. It helps your Chihuahua understand boundaries, respect, and calm behavior in various situations. Basic commands like "sit," "stay," "come," and "leave it" are essential in everyday life and can help control your dog during moments of socialization.

Training your Chihuahua also helps establish you as a confident leader, making it easier to guide them through new situations. The more confident you are, the more your dog will trust you, and the more willing they will be to follow your cues.

Group Classes and Socialization Events

Group training classes or organized socialization events, such as playdates or dog meetups, are a great way to expose your Chihuahua to a variety of new experiences and people in a structured, supportive environment. These events are typically led by professional trainers who can guide your Chihuahua through safe and positive interactions with other dogs and people.

Group classes not only provide socialization opportunities, but they also allow you to work on obedience training in a distracting environment, helping your dog focus and respond to commands despite the distractions. This level of engagement is valuable for their development and confidence.

Lifelong Socialization

Socialization doesn't end when your Chihuahua reaches adulthood. In fact, continued exposure to new experiences and environments is crucial for maintaining their well-being and preventing anxiety-related behaviors. As your dog ages, try to incorporate new experiences into their routine. Expose them to different people, places, and activities to keep their social skills sharp. A well-socialized Chihuahua is more likely to remain calm and well-adjusted throughout their life.

In conclusion, socializing your Chihuahua is a lifelong commitment that requires patience, consistency, and dedication. By exposing them to new people, environments, and experiences, you help them grow into confident, well-adjusted adults. Through positive reinforcement, controlled exposure, and ongoing training, you can ensure that your Chihuahua enjoys a rich and fulfilling life, full of healthy relationships with both humans and other animals.

References

- American Kennel Club. (n.d.). *How to Socialize Your Dog.* https://www.akc.org

- PetMD. (n.d.). *Socialization for Puppies: Why it's Important.* https://www.petmd.com

- Cesar's Way. (n.d.). *How to Socialize a Dog: The Right Way to Introduce New People and Pets.* https://www.cesarsway.com

- DogTime. (n.d.). *How to Socialize a Dog and Why It's Important.* https://dogtime.com

- Stanley, B. (2019). *How to Raise the Perfect Dog: Through Puppyhood and Beyond.* Penguin Random House

Chapter 6: Nutrition and Feeding

Feeding by Age

Proper nutrition is critical to the health and well-being of your Chihuahua, and feeding them according to their age is one of the most important factors in ensuring they live a long, happy, and healthy life. Like all dogs, Chihuahuas have different dietary needs at different stages of life, from puppyhood through adulthood and into their senior years. Understanding these needs and adjusting their diet accordingly will help prevent obesity, maintain a healthy coat, promote healthy digestion, and provide the energy they need to thrive.

Feeding a Chihuahua Puppy (8 Weeks to 1 Year)

The first year of a Chihuahua's life is crucial for their development. During this time, they experience rapid growth, with puppies gaining weight, muscle mass, and bone density. Feeding your Chihuahua the right nutrients during this period is vital for supporting healthy development. A balanced diet that includes high-quality protein, essential fatty acids, vitamins, and minerals is key to setting them up for a healthy life.

Choosing Puppy Food:

Look for a puppy-formulated food that is specifically designed for small-breed dogs. Puppy foods are generally richer in calories, protein, and fat than adult formulas, which is important for supporting the energetic and growing needs of your Chihuahua. Small-breed puppy foods often come in smaller kibble sizes that are easier for tiny mouths to chew. Additionally, puppy food often contains more calcium and phosphorus to support bone growth and development.

Puppies need more frequent meals throughout the day due to their small stomachs. Typically, you should feed your Chihuahua puppy three to four meals per day. As they grow older, you can gradually reduce the frequency of meals. At around 6 months, you can transition to feeding them twice a day—morning and evening.

Portion Control:

Although Chihuahuas are small, they have big personalities and can be quite energetic. However, like all puppies, they can easily overeat if left to their own devices. It's important to follow the feeding guidelines provided by the food manufacturer, but always adjust portions based on your individual dog's needs. Keep track of your Chihuahua's growth and body condition and talk to your vet if you're unsure about portion sizes. Keep in mind that too much food can lead to obesity, which is especially concerning in such a small breed.

Feeding a Chihuahua Adult (1 to 7 Years)

As your Chihuahua transitions into adulthood, their nutritional needs shift. At this stage, they're no longer growing, but they still require a diet that supports energy levels, maintains healthy organs, and ensures proper weight management. The goal is to maintain a balanced diet that keeps your Chihuahua lean and healthy while still providing them with all the nutrients they need.

Choosing Adult Food:

Adult Chihuahuas need a diet that is lower in calories compared to puppy food, as their growth has plateaued, and their energy requirements are now stabilized. However, because of their small size and fast metabolism, it's still important to provide them with a nutrient-dense food that will meet their daily needs in smaller portions.

Look for an adult small-breed formula that's high in animal-based protein, moderate in healthy fats, and contains a balance of carbohydrates like rice or sweet potatoes for energy. Omega fatty acids —such as those from fish oil—are important for a shiny, healthy coat, while antioxidants like vitamins E and C help maintain a strong immune system. Avoid foods with unnecessary fillers like corn or soy, which can cause digestive issues in some dogs.

Meal Frequency:

Adult Chihuahuas typically do well with two meals a day—one in the morning and one in the evening. This helps keep their energy levels stable and prevents them from becoming too hungry between meals. For Chihuahuas with a high energy level, you can also split their meals into three smaller portions per day, especially if they're active or have a fast metabolism.

It's important to adjust your Chihuahua's food based on their activity level, weight, and age. If your dog is more sedentary, they may need fewer calories, while active dogs may require a bit more. Regularly monitor their weight and body condition score to ensure they're at a healthy weight.

Feeding a Senior Chihuahua (7 Years and Older)

As your Chihuahua enters their senior years, their nutritional needs continue to change. They may become less active, develop health problems like arthritis, or face dental issues that can make chewing more difficult. Adjusting their diet to reflect these changes can help keep them comfortable, healthy, and mobile for as long as possible.

Choosing Senior Food:

Senior dog foods are typically lower in calories and fat than adult formulas, as older dogs tend to be less active and may gain weight more easily. Senior diets often include joint-supporting supplements like glucosamine and chondroitin, which are essential for maintaining cartilage health and managing the pain of arthritis or other joint issues that many older Chihuahuas experience.

Look for a senior formula that's rich in easily digestible proteins, such as chicken or turkey, along with moderate fat content. This provides sufficient energy without the risk of excessive weight gain. Additionally, some senior foods contain higher fiber levels to support digestion and maintain healthy bowel movements.

Meal Frequency:

Senior Chihuahuas, especially those with slower metabolisms, may benefit from three smaller meals per day. This helps maintain stable blood sugar levels and reduces the risk of obesity, which is more common in older dogs. If your senior Chihuahua has dental issues or trouble chewing, consider switching to a softer food or wet food options that are easier to eat.

If your Chihuahua is prone to health problems like kidney disease, heart issues, or diabetes, talk to your vet about a specialized diet. Many senior dogs benefit from food that is tailored to their specific health needs, and your vet can help guide you toward the best options.

Weight Management Across Life Stages

Maintaining a healthy weight is crucial for your Chihuahua's health at any age. Their small size means that even a small amount of extra weight can put stress on their joints, heart, and overall health. Ensure that you're feeding them the appropriate portions based on their age, activity level, and metabolism. If your Chihuahua is overweight, you may need to reduce food intake, increase exercise, or consider a weight management food formulated for small breeds.

Treats and Snacks:

While treats are a fun way to bond with your Chihuahua, they should be used sparingly. Choose healthy, low-calorie treats and avoid giving them human food, as it can lead to digestive issues and excessive weight gain. Chihuahuas are often motivated by food, so use treats to reinforce good behavior or during training sessions.

Water Intake:

Chihuahuas, like all dogs, need access to fresh water at all times. Because of their small size, they may not drink as much as larger dogs, but it's important to monitor their water intake, especially if they are eating dry food. Make sure their water bowl is always clean and full, and encourage them to drink regularly, particularly after meals and playtime.

Final Thoughts on Feeding Your Chihuahua

From the first days of puppyhood to the golden years of senior life, feeding your Chihuahua is about more than just choosing the right food—it's about tailoring their diet to meet their ever-evolving needs. By providing the right nutrition, portion sizes, and feeding schedule, you are helping them live a longer, healthier life. Always keep in mind that the best diet for your Chihuahua is one that supports their individual health needs, and consult your vet regularly to ensure they are on the path to a happy, balanced life.

References:

- American Kennel Club. *Feeding Your Dog: A Guide to Proper Nutrition.* https://www.akc.org
- Chihuahua Club of America. *Feeding Your Chihuahua: What You Need to Know.* https://www.chihuahuaclubofamerica.org
- The Pet Health Network. *The Best Diet for Small Dogs.* https://www.pethealthnetwork.com
- Waltham Petcare Science Institute. *Small-Breed Dog Nutrition.* https://www.waltham.com

- Dunbar, I. *Before and After Getting Your Puppy*. New World Library, 2004.

Common Allergies and Sensitivities

Chihuahuas, like many small dog breeds, can be prone to certain allergies and sensitivities, both environmental and dietary. Due to their small size, delicate skin, and unique metabolic systems, Chihuahuas can sometimes experience discomfort from common allergens that might not affect other breeds. Understanding the most common triggers and how to manage them can help you provide your Chihuahua with a healthier, more comfortable life.

1. Food Allergies

Food allergies are relatively common in Chihuahuas, and they can manifest in a variety of ways, from digestive issues to skin irritations. The most common food allergens for Chihuahuas are proteins such as **beef**, **chicken**, **lamb**, and **dairy**, but grains like **corn**, **wheat**, and **soy** can also cause allergic reactions.

Symptoms of food allergies may include:

- Vomiting or diarrhea
- Excessive gas or bloating
- Skin rashes, hives, or itching
- Ear infections or paw licking

If you suspect that your Chihuahua is experiencing a food allergy, it's best to consult with your veterinarian. They may recommend an **elimination diet**, where you feed your dog a single protein and carbohydrate source to see if symptoms improve. If the symptoms resolve, you can slowly introduce other ingredients to identify the specific allergen.

Some Chihuahuas may also have a sensitivity to grains or by-products commonly found in commercial dog foods. Switching to a high-quality food with minimal additives and preservatives can help reduce the risk of allergic reactions.

2. Environmental Allergies

Like many small breeds, Chihuahuas are prone to **environmental allergies**, which are triggered by substances like **pollen**, **dust mites**, **mold**, and **pet dander**. These allergies are particularly common during the spring and fall when pollen counts are higher.

Signs of environmental allergies may include:

- Itchy skin, especially around the ears, paws, and face
- Sneezing, coughing, or wheezing

- Red, watery eyes
- Excessive licking or rubbing of the face or paws

One way to manage environmental allergies is by minimizing exposure to known allergens. This might involve:

- Keeping your Chihuahua indoors on high pollen days
- Bathing them more frequently to remove pollen and dust from their fur
- Using air purifiers or keeping windows closed during peak allergy seasons
- Regularly washing their bedding and toys

For more severe cases, your vet may recommend **antihistamines** or **steroidal treatments** to manage symptoms. In some cases, allergy testing may be performed to identify the specific environmental allergens affecting your dog.

3. Flea Allergies

Chihuahuas can also suffer from **flea allergy dermatitis (FAD)**, a condition where a dog has an allergic reaction to flea saliva. Even a single flea bite can cause extreme itching, hair loss, and inflamed skin, especially around the back, neck, and tail.

Symptoms of flea allergies include:

- Intense itching and scratching, often to the point of creating sores or bald spots
- Red, inflamed skin, particularly in areas where fleas are most likely to bite
- Hair loss or thinning fur

Preventing flea infestations is crucial in managing flea allergies. Regular use of flea prevention treatments, such as oral medications, topical treatments, or flea collars, can help. Additionally, keeping your home and yard free of fleas through regular cleaning and vacuuming will reduce the risk of an outbreak.

4. Seasonal Allergies

Chihuahuas can also develop **seasonal allergies** that occur at specific times of the year. This can be due to the presence of pollen from trees, grasses, or flowers, or from mold in the fall when leaves decompose. These allergies tend to be more prevalent during the change of seasons, particularly in spring and autumn.

Symptoms are similar to environmental allergies, with itching, watery eyes, and respiratory issues being common. Seasonal allergies can often be managed by limiting your dog's exposure to allergens, but in more severe cases, your vet may recommend medications such as corticosteroids or antihistamines to alleviate symptoms.

5. Skin Sensitivities

Chihuahuas have delicate skin, and some can develop **skin sensitivities** or conditions like **atopic dermatitis**, which can result from environmental factors or food allergies. The skin may become red, inflamed, or flaky, and scratching or licking is common. Dry air, harsh chemicals in cleaning products, or frequent bathing can also contribute to skin sensitivities.

To help manage skin sensitivities:

- Use hypoallergenic shampoos that are gentle on your dog's skin
- Avoid over-bathing your Chihuahua, as this can dry out their skin
- Consider adding omega-3 fatty acids or supplements to their diet to help maintain a healthy coat and skin
- Make sure your Chihuahua's environment is clean and free of irritants like dust, strong fragrances, or harsh chemicals

6. Medications and Allergic Reactions

While not common, Chihuahuas may sometimes experience allergic reactions to medications. These reactions can range from mild skin rashes to more serious symptoms like swelling or difficulty breathing. Always consult your veterinarian before giving your dog any new medication, and inform them of any known allergies.

Managing Allergies in Chihuahuas

Managing allergies in Chihuahuas requires a combination of prevention, diagnosis, and treatment. Regular vet visits are essential to ensure your dog's allergies are properly managed. If you suspect your dog is suffering from allergies, a vet will be able to provide guidance on how to identify the trigger, reduce exposure, and alleviate symptoms.

In some cases, your veterinarian may recommend allergy testing, either through blood tests or intradermal skin tests, to pinpoint the specific allergens that are causing problems. This information can help tailor a treatment plan to your dog's unique needs, which may include dietary changes, medications, or even immunotherapy (allergy shots) in extreme cases.

Overall, while allergies and sensitivities can be a challenge for Chihuahuas, with proper care, attention, and veterinary support, your dog can live a happy, healthy life free from discomfort.

References:

- American Kennel Club. (n.d.). *Chihuahua Health and Care*. Retrieved from https://www.akc.org/dog-breeds/chihuahua/
- ASPCA. (n.d.). *Common Dog Allergies and Sensitivities*. Retrieved from https://www.aspca.org
- PetMD. (n.d.). *Flea Allergy Dermatitis in Dogs*. Retrieved from https://www.petmd.com

- Merck Veterinary Manual. (n.d.). *Allergies in Dogs: Environmental and Food Sensitivities*. Retrieved from https://www.merckvetmanual.com

Portion Control

When it comes to feeding a Chihuahua, portion control is critical to ensuring their health and well-being. Due to their small size and high energy levels, Chihuahuas require a balanced diet that provides the right amount of nutrients without leading to overfeeding or underfeeding. Maintaining a proper weight is essential for the breed, as Chihuahuas are prone to certain health issues, such as obesity and joint problems, which can be exacerbated by improper feeding habits.

Understanding Nutritional Needs

Before diving into portion control, it's important to understand what Chihuahuas need from their diet. Like all dogs, Chihuahuas require a diet rich in high-quality proteins, fats, and carbohydrates, along with essential vitamins and minerals. Their small size means they have a higher metabolism compared to larger breeds, so they require a nutrient-dense diet to meet their energy needs. However, because they are so small, their portion sizes will naturally be much smaller than those of larger dogs.

Generally, adult Chihuahuas require around 200 to 300 calories per day, depending on their age, activity level, and overall health. Puppies and active dogs may need more, while less active or senior Chihuahuas may require fewer calories to maintain a healthy weight. Always check with your veterinarian to get a personalized recommendation for your Chihuahua's specific needs, as factors like metabolism, activity level, and health conditions can influence their daily calorie intake.

Measuring Portions

Since Chihuahuas are prone to gaining weight, portion control begins with accurate measurements. It's easy to overestimate how much food a small dog needs, but using a measuring cup ensures your Chihuahua is getting the right amount. Most commercial dog foods provide serving size recommendations on the packaging, based on your dog's weight and age. These are a good starting point, but always remember that each dog's needs can vary.

Using a food scale can also be helpful, especially if you're feeding homemade food or raw diets. Weighing your dog's food ensures that you're not giving too much or too little. For dry food, it's recommended to divide their daily food intake into two or three meals to help regulate their metabolism and prevent hunger-related behaviors. For wet food or a raw diet, similar portion control principles apply, but be mindful that wet food tends to have fewer calories than dry food.

Preventing Overfeeding

One of the biggest challenges with small dogs like Chihuahuas is the temptation to overfeed. Their adorable appearance can lead to owners wanting to give them extra treats or larger portions. However, overfeeding can quickly lead to obesity, which can cause serious health problems like joint issues, diabetes, and heart disease. Additionally, Chihuahuas have small stomachs, and feeding them too much at once can lead to digestive issues, such as upset stomach or vomiting.

To avoid overfeeding, follow the feeding guidelines provided on the food packaging or your veterinarian's recommendations. Always measure their food and stick to the recommended portions. Avoid giving in to the urge to offer table scraps, as many human foods can be harmful to dogs and contribute to unhealthy weight gain. If you feel the need to give treats, opt for low-calorie, healthy options, and consider using part of your Chihuahua's daily food allotment for training rewards, ensuring the total calories remain within their target range.

Preventing Undereating

On the flip side, some Chihuahuas may not eat enough due to picky eating habits, stress, or health issues. Since they are so small, even a slight reduction in food intake can have a significant impact on their health. If your Chihuahua refuses to eat or loses interest in food, it could be a sign of an underlying issue, such as dental problems, digestive upset, or an emotional issue like stress or anxiety.

If your Chihuahua is underweight or refusing to eat, it's important to consult your veterinarian to rule out health concerns. A lack of appetite can also occur when there's a change in their environment or routine, so maintaining a consistent feeding schedule is crucial. Some Chihuahuas are simply more finicky eaters and may need a variety of food to keep their interest. Offering different types of food or warming up their meals slightly can make a difference. For very picky eaters, a food topper, such as a small amount of low-fat canned food or boiled chicken, can encourage eating.

Managing Treats

While treats are an essential part of training and bonding, they should never replace regular meals or make up a large portion of your Chihuahua's daily intake. Treats should be given in moderation and should be accounted for in the total daily calorie count. A good rule of thumb is to limit treats to no more than 10% of your Chihuahua's daily calories. If you're using treats as a reward during training sessions, consider using small, low-calorie options like freeze-dried chicken, carrot pieces, or commercial dog treats made specifically for small breeds.

Adjusting Portions Based on Life Stage

Portion control is different for puppies, adult dogs, and senior Chihuahuas. Puppies are still growing and developing, so they need more calories and nutrients for proper growth. While the exact amount will depend on your puppy's age and activity level, they typically need more food per pound of body weight than an adult Chihuahua. As your puppy matures, you can gradually reduce their food intake to the standard adult portion.

Senior Chihuahuas, on the other hand, may have slower metabolisms and less energy, which means their portion sizes should be adjusted downward to prevent weight gain. Some senior Chihuahuas may also develop health issues like arthritis or dental problems, which can affect their ability to exercise or chew. In these cases, your veterinarian may recommend a special diet that's easier to digest or supports joint health.

Conclusion

Proper portion control is essential for keeping your Chihuahua healthy, happy, and at a healthy weight. By measuring their food accurately, avoiding overfeeding, and monitoring their weight regularly, you can help prevent common health problems like obesity, digestive issues, and nutritional imbalances. Additionally, tailoring their diet to their age, activity level, and health needs will ensure they get the best nutrition possible. Remember, a balanced diet and appropriate portion sizes are key to a long, healthy life for your beloved Chihuahua.

References:

- American Kennel Club. (n.d.). *Chihuahua Dog Breed Information*. Retrieved from https://www.akc.org/dog-breeds/chihuahua/
- Palika, L. (2007). *Chihuahuas for Dummies*. Wiley Publishing.
- McKinney, C. (2013). *The Everything Chihuahua Book*. Adams Media.
- ASPCA. (n.d.). *Feeding Your Dog: A Guide to Healthy Portion Sizes*. Retrieved from https://www.aspca.org/pet-care/dog-care/nutrition-tips
- Fogle, B. (2000). *The Encyclopedia of the Dog*. DK Publishing.

Raw, Kibble, or Cooked?

When it comes to feeding your Chihuahua, the choice of diet can be a complicated one. There are multiple options available, including raw food, kibble, and home-cooked meals, each with its own benefits and potential drawbacks. Deciding which diet is right for your Chihuahua depends on various factors, including your dog's health, your lifestyle, and your willingness to invest time in meal preparation. Let's take a closer look at each of these options to help you make an informed choice for your small companion.

Raw Food Diet: A Natural Approach

The raw food diet, often called "BARF" (Biologically Appropriate Raw Food), is based on the idea that dogs should eat the same types of foods that their ancestors, like wolves, consumed. This typically includes raw meat, bones, fruits, vegetables, and sometimes organ meat. Proponents of the raw food diet claim that it can provide numerous benefits, such as healthier skin and coat, improved digestion, and increased energy levels.

For Chihuahuas, a raw food diet can offer high-quality protein, which is essential for their muscle health and energy. Because Chihuahuas are small dogs, they often have higher metabolic rates, making protein-rich diets especially important for maintaining their energy levels and muscle mass. The raw food diet also provides essential nutrients that can be lost during the processing of kibble.

However, there are significant considerations when feeding a Chihuahua raw food. First, raw diets require careful planning to ensure nutritional balance. Dogs require a specific ratio of nutrients, and improperly prepared raw food can lead to deficiencies or imbalances, affecting their overall health. Additionally, there's the risk of bacterial contamination—raw meat can carry bacteria such as Salmonella or E. coli, which can be harmful to both dogs and humans, especially in small breeds like Chihuahuas, whose immune systems might be more vulnerable.

Raw food diets also require more time and effort to prepare. You'll need to ensure that your dog's meals are properly stored and that they receive a variety of proteins and other nutrients. Not every pet owner is equipped for the level of commitment this diet demands. For those interested in the raw food diet, it's crucial to consult a veterinarian or a pet nutritionist to ensure that you're meeting your Chihuahua's nutritional needs safely.

Kibble: Convenient and Balanced

Kibble is one of the most common and convenient feeding options for Chihuahuas. It offers a complete and balanced meal in each bite, with carefully calculated amounts of protein, fat, fiber, vitamins, and minerals. Commercial dog foods are typically formulated to meet AAFCO (Association of American Feed Control Officials) standards, ensuring that your dog gets a nutritionally complete diet.

The advantages of kibble are clear—it's easy to store, doesn't require refrigeration, and is simple to serve. For busy pet owners, kibble can be a time-saving option that still meets a Chihuahua's dietary needs. Additionally, kibble is available in a wide variety of formulations, including options for puppies, seniors, and dogs with special dietary requirements (e.g., weight management, joint health, etc.).

However, not all kibble is created equal. Low-quality kibble may contain fillers, preservatives, or artificial additives that may not be ideal for your dog's health. It's important to select high-quality kibble made with real meat as the primary ingredient and free of unnecessary additives. Some Chihuahuas may also develop dental problems from eating kibble if they don't chew it properly, although kibble can help reduce plaque buildup when your dog chews it correctly.

Another issue to consider is the carbohydrate content in many kibbles. While dogs do require some carbohydrates, too many can lead to obesity, especially in small breeds like Chihuahuas. It's important to monitor portion sizes and avoid overfeeding, as small dogs can be prone to weight gain.

Cooked Food: Fresh and Customizable

Home-cooked meals for dogs, especially Chihuahuas, offer a fresh and customizable option compared to both raw food and kibble. Many pet owners decide to prepare meals at home to ensure they know exactly what ingredients are being fed to their pets. This approach allows them to meet the specific dietary needs of their dogs. When cooking for your Chihuahua, there are various ingredients you can use, such as meats like chicken, beef, or turkey, alongside vegetables and grains like rice or quinoa. By taking charge of your dog's diet, you can tailor meals to help with issues like allergies or food sensitivities.

One benefit of choosing cooked food over raw meat is the reduced risk of harmful bacteria. Raw diets can sometimes lead to health problems due to contamination, while cooked meals can still provide the advantages of a whole-food diet without the same health risks. Cooking enables you to create a balanced meal that meets the specific requirements of your Chihuahua. For example, if your dog has digestive issues, you can choose ingredients that are gentler on their stomach and avoid those that may trigger discomfort. This customization allows you to focus on what makes your dog feel its best.

However, preparing meals for your dog is not without challenges. It takes time, effort, and a solid understanding of canine nutrition. Just like with any diet, it is important to maintain a balanced recipe for your dog. Dogs need a precise combination of proteins, fats, carbohydrates, vitamins, and minerals to thrive. Ensuring your home-cooked meals meet these nutritional guidelines can be tricky without proper knowledge. If the meals lack essential nutrients or include incorrect proportions, it could lead to health problems for your dog.

Planning and preparation are significant parts of cooking for your Chihuahua. You will need to allocate time for cooking, which sometimes can be more than just a quick meal prep. It's important to either prepare meals in bulk or create a meal plan for your dog's diet. After cooking, you should portion the food according to your Chihuahua's dietary needs. Proper storage of the meals is also essential. For example, you can use airtight containers to keep the food fresh and ensure that it is safe for your dog.

If you decide to shift to a cooked diet for your furry friend, it is a good idea to seek guidance from a veterinarian or a pet nutrition expert. They can offer valuable insights into what a balanced diet for your Chihuahua looks like. Their expertise can help you better understand the nutritional needs required at different life stages or individual health conditions. Consulting professionals can save you from common mistakes and help you feel more confident in the meals you prepare.

One practical step you can take is to start with simple recipes that contain a mix of meat, vegetables, and grains. For example, you might create a chicken and rice dish. Begin by boiling some chicken breast until it is fully cooked, then shred it into small pieces. In a separate pot, cook rice according to the package instructions. Finally, mix both together with some well-cooked, diced vegetables like carrots or peas. Be sure to introduce new ingredients slowly to watch for any adverse reactions.

Furthermore, the preparation process can also include portions for storing. Once you've cooked a batch of food, you can divide it into daily portions. This means that no matter how busy your schedule gets, your Chihuahua will still have nutritious meals ready to go. Storing portions in the freezer can also keep them fresh for longer periods. When you need to serve, simply thaw the portion in the refrigerator overnight or warm it up as needed. This planning approach helps you maintain a regular cooking routine without it becoming overwhelming.

Another aspect to consider is the importance of variety in your Chihuahua's diet. Dogs, just like humans, can get bored with the same meals every day. By changing the ingredients occasionally, you can keep your dog interested in their food. This might mean rotating between different types of meat, such as beef one week and turkey the next, or introducing various vegetables to the mix. It is crucial, however, to ensure that any new ingredients are safe for dogs. Researching which foods are dog-friendly can help you make these dietary changes confidently.

Monitoring your dog's response to the home-cooked meals is also essential. Keep an eye out for any changes in their behavior, coat condition, or energy levels. If you notice any negative effects, it may be necessary to adjust the recipe or consult with a vet again. Being proactive about your dog's health is an important part of cooking for them. Taking notes may be helpful in tracking what works and what doesn't. Over time, this will guide you in creating the best meals for your Chihuahua.

Through this cooking journey, you build a closer bond with your Chihuahua. Preparing their food personally can be a rewarding experience. It allows you to express your love and care while also ensuring they receive the health benefits they need. By investing time into cooking, you are taking a significant step toward being a responsible pet owner. This thoughtful approach to feeding your dog will not only enhance their wellness but also contribute to their happiness at home.

What's Best for Your Chihuahua?

When it comes to choosing the best diet for your Chihuahua, there are several factors to consider. Each dog is unique, with different needs based on their health, activity level, and even personal preferences. Your own lifestyle also plays a big role in this decision. Understanding these elements will help you make the right food choices for your furry friend.

Raw Food

One option to consider is a raw food diet. This kind of diet can be very beneficial for Chihuahuas, especially for those who are active and need a lot of energy. Raw food typically includes raw meat, bones, fruits, and vegetables. The diet is rich in high-quality proteins, which can help your dog maintain strong muscles and overall wellness. However, raw food preparation requires a commitment of time and effort.

If you decide to go this route, it's important to learn about canine nutrition. You will need to balance the meals to ensure your Chihuahua gets all the vitamins and minerals they need. One way to do this is to research what types of meat and vegetables are best suited for Chihuahuas. Consulting with a veterinarian who understands raw diets can also provide you with guidance. This way, you can make sure your Chihuahua stays healthy and happy while enjoying a varied and nutritious diet.

Kibble

Another popular option is kibble, which is often the most convenient choice for busy dog owners. Kibble is dry dog food that comes in a bag and is easy to serve. It provides a complete and balanced diet, which is essential for any Chihuahua. When selecting kibble, it's crucial to look at the ingredients list. High-quality brands are recommended because they use quality ingredients and avoid fillers that can be harmful to your dog.

Fillers like corn, wheat, and soy may fill up your Chihuahua but offer little in terms of nutrition. To choose the right kibble, look for food that lists a high-quality source of protein, such as chicken or beef, as the first ingredient. Also, consider your dog's specific needs. Some Chihuahuas might be overweight or have certain health conditions, and a high-protein, low-carb kibble could be a better option for them.

Lastly, kibble has the added benefit of being shelf-stable, which makes it an easy feeding solution for those with limited time.

Cooked Food

If you enjoy cooking and have time to prepare meals, you might consider a cooked food diet. This option allows you to use fresh, high-quality ingredients to make meals for your Chihuahua. When cooking for your dog, it's important to provide a balanced diet that includes proteins, carbohydrates, and essential fats. This can help you cater to any specific dietary needs your Chihuahua may have.

For instance, if your dog has food sensitivities or allergies, you can control what goes into their meals. You might choose to include chicken, rice, and vegetables like carrots and peas, which are all nutritious options. There are plenty of resources available to help you create balanced recipes. You can consult a veterinarian or look for books that specialize in homemade dog food. This ensures that your meals are not only tasty but also meet all the nutritional requirements for your Chihuahua.

Final Thoughts

Choosing the right diet for your Chihuahua is ultimately about finding what works best for your dog and your lifestyle. Whether you go for raw food, kibble, or cooked meals, the focus should always be on providing balanced nutrition. Regular consultation with your veterinarian is a great way to ensure you're making the best choices for your pet's long-term health. As you make diet decisions, take into account any changes in your Chihuahua's health or activity level, and be ready to adjust their food as necessary. By keeping a close eye on their nutritional needs, you can help them lead a happy and healthy life.

References

- American Kennel Club. (n.d.). *Feeding Your Dog: Raw, Kibble, or Cooked?*. https://www.akc.org

- PetMD. (n.d.). *Raw Diets for Dogs: Pros and Cons.* https://www.petmd.com
- Coren, S. (2006). *The Intelligence of Dogs.* Free Press
- DogTime. (n.d.). *Choosing the Right Dog Food for Your Pet.* https://dogtime.com
- Stanley, B. (2019). *How to Raise the Perfect Dog: Through Puppyhood and Beyond.* Penguin Random House

Chapter 7: Health and Vet Care

Genetic Health Risks

Owning a pet is a lifelong commitment that includes ensuring their health and well-being. While regular veterinary visits, a balanced diet, and exercise routines are fundamental, it's also essential to consider the role of genetic health risks. Many animals, especially purebred pets, are predisposed to certain genetic conditions. Being aware of these risks allows you to take the necessary steps to help prevent or manage these health issues.

Understanding Genetic Health Risks

Genetic health risks are conditions passed down from one generation to the next through genes. They are often breed-specific, meaning certain breeds are more susceptible to particular health problems. Purebred animals, due to selective breeding, are often at higher risk for genetic disorders compared to mixed-breed pets. While some conditions may not manifest until later in life, others may require immediate attention and management from an early age.

Some of the most common genetic health risks include hip dysplasia, heart disease, eye problems, and certain cancers. Many of these conditions can be managed with early diagnosis and proper veterinary care, which is why it's important to be proactive about your pet's health.

Common Genetic Health Conditions

Hip Dysplasia

Hip dysplasia is a common genetic condition that affects larger dog breeds. This disorder occurs when the hip joint doesn't develop properly, leading to joint instability. Over time, this can cause pain, arthritis, and mobility issues. Common breeds affected by hip dysplasia include German Shepherds, Golden Retrievers, and Labrador Retrievers. Early detection through X-rays and regular check-ups can help manage the condition, and in severe cases, surgery may be necessary.

Progressive Retinal Atrophy (PRA)

PRA is a degenerative disease that affects the retina of the eye, leading to progressive vision loss. It is an inherited condition and affects many dog breeds, including Miniature Schnauzers, Cocker Spaniels, and Collies. Although PRA leads to blindness, early diagnosis through eye exams can help pet owners manage the condition and make adjustments to their pet's lifestyle, such as providing a familiar environment to reduce the impact of vision loss.

Brachycephalic Syndrome

Brachycephalic syndrome affects dogs with short snouts, such as Bulldogs, Pugs, and Shih Tzus. These dogs often have narrow airways, which can lead to breathing difficulties, especially in hot weather or during physical exertion. Brachycephalic dogs may experience snoring, labored breathing, or even heatstroke in extreme conditions. Ensuring that your pet has a cool, comfortable environment and managing their weight can help reduce symptoms.

Cataracts

Cataracts are a genetic condition where the lenses of the eyes become clouded, impairing vision. Certain dog breeds, like Cocker Spaniels and Boston Terriers, are more prone to cataracts. While cataracts can be treated through surgery, early diagnosis is crucial for success. Regular eye exams at the vet can help catch the condition early, preventing further vision loss.

Heart Disease

Some breeds are more prone to heart disease, particularly conditions like dilated cardiomyopathy and mitral valve disease. Breeds like Doberman Pinschers, Cavalier King Charles Spaniels, and Boxers are particularly at risk. Regular heart screenings, which may include echocardiograms or electrocardiograms (ECGs), can help detect heart disease early. Management often involves medication, a controlled diet, and maintaining a healthy weight.

Cancer

Certain types of cancer are hereditary and more common in specific breeds. For example, Golden Retrievers, Boxers, and Rottweilers are known to be at higher risk for lymphoma and osteosarcoma (bone cancer). Regular veterinary exams and blood tests can help detect early signs of cancer, which may lead to more successful treatments, such as surgery, chemotherapy, or radiation.

Managing Genetic Health Risks

While genetic health conditions can seem daunting, there are many ways to manage them. One of the first steps in prevention is choosing a reputable breeder who screens for genetic conditions. Responsible breeders conduct genetic tests to reduce the risk of inherited diseases and focus on breeding healthy animals.

For current pet owners, being proactive is key. Regular veterinary visits allow for early detection of genetic disorders, which means timely intervention can reduce pain and improve quality of life. DNA testing is also an excellent tool for identifying specific genetic risks in pets. Many pet owners choose to get their animals tested, which can provide insight into potential health concerns before they manifest.

Additionally, lifestyle management is crucial for pets with known genetic predispositions. For example, maintaining a healthy weight is particularly important for dogs at risk of hip dysplasia and heart disease. Joint supplements, such as glucosamine and chondroitin, can help manage joint pain, while a low-sodium diet may benefit pets with heart conditions.

Breed-Specific Genetic Screening

Breed-specific screening is an essential practice in preventing genetic conditions in purebred pets. Many veterinarians recommend routine screenings for certain breeds known to carry genetic disorders. These screenings can include blood tests, eye exams, and X-rays. If a potential health risk is detected, the veterinarian may suggest lifestyle adjustments, medications, or even surgical procedures to manage the condition.

For example, breeds prone to hip dysplasia should undergo hip scoring, which assesses the joints for abnormalities. Dogs with heart conditions may benefit from echocardiograms, which provide an in-depth look at heart function. Regular screening can help detect genetic issues early, making treatment more effective and extending the pet's quality of life.

Conclusion

Genetic health risks are an important consideration for pet owners, especially those with purebred animals. Understanding the conditions that may affect certain breeds, along with proactive management and regular veterinary care, can make a significant difference in your pet's well-being. Early detection, lifestyle management, and genetic screening are key to managing these health risks and ensuring your pet lives a long, healthy life.

References:

- American Kennel Club. "Breed Health Information." AKC.org.
- The American College of Veterinary Surgeons. "Hip Dysplasia in Dogs." ACVS.org.
- Veterinary Partner. "Progressive Retinal Atrophy (PRA)." VeterinaryPartner.com.
- PetMD. "Brachycephalic Syndrome in Dogs." PetMD.com.
- Veterinary Specialty Center. "Heart Disease in Dogs." Vetspecialty.com.
- Canine Cancer Research Foundation. "Genetics and Cancer in Dogs." CanineCancer.org.
- American Veterinary Medical Association. "Genetic Testing in Pets." AVMA.org.

Vaccines and Preventatives

When you bring a Chihuahua into your life, it's important to understand that their small size doesn't make them exempt from the need for regular healthcare. These tiny dogs may have big personalities, but their small frames often mean they are more vulnerable to certain health issues, which is why vaccines and preventatives are so crucial. Ensuring your Chihuahua receives proper vaccinations and preventative care helps keep them safe from potentially life-threatening diseases and parasites.

Vaccinations for Chihuahuas

Vaccinations play a very important role in keeping your Chihuahua healthy. Just like all other dogs, Chihuahuas need vaccines to shield them from serious and contagious diseases. Vaccinating your puppy is crucial, as it helps protect them from illnesses that can lead to severe health issues or even death. Core vaccinations mostly involve the distemper, parvovirus, and rabies vaccines. These vaccinations typically start when your Chihuahua is just a puppy and are given in a series to ensure maximum protection.

Distemper

Distemper is a viral disease that can cause problems in multiple systems of the body, including the respiratory, gastrointestinal, and nervous systems. It can sometimes be fatal, making it essential to vaccinate against it. Puppies are often given their first distemper vaccine as early as 6 weeks old. After that, they will need booster shots throughout their first year to maintain protection. For example, if you schedule your first visit with the vet at 6 weeks, the vet might recommend the first vaccination for distemper along with other puppy vaccines. This early vaccination is crucial because distemper can spread easily between animals.

Parvovirus

Parvovirus is another serious illness that can be particularly harmful to puppies. It is highly contagious and primarily targets the gastrointestinal system, leading to severe dehydration, illness, and potential death. For this reason, it is vital to start vaccinations against parvovirus early. Most puppies receive their first dose between 6 to 8 weeks of age, with follow-up shots given every 3 to 4 weeks until they reach around 16 to 20 weeks. Proper vaccination can keep your Chihuahua safe from this disease. If you've ever heard of a puppy having parvo, this involves a very sick dog with severe diarrhea and vomit, which can rapidly lead to dehydration if not treated immediately.

Rabies

Rabies is a serious and often fatal viral infection that affects the brain and spinal cord of dogs and other mammals. Vaccination against rabies is not just a recommendation; in many places, it's required by law. Rabies is particularly dangerous because it can also be transmitted to humans. Most veterinarians will give the rabies vaccine when your Chihuahua is around 12 to 16 weeks old. For example, if you adopt a Chihuahua puppy that is 12 weeks old, you should book a vet appointment to get this important vaccine administered. Ensuring your Chihuahua is rabies vaccinated can help prevent the spread of this lethal virus in your community.

Non-Core Vaccinations

While core vaccinations are crucial, there are also non-core vaccines that might be recommended based on your dog's lifestyle, environment, and specific exposure risks. These vaccines might include Bordetella for kennel cough, Lyme disease, and leptospirosis. If your Chihuahua frequently encounters other dogs in parks or during daycare, the Bordetella vaccine may be particularly important. Kennel cough is a contagious respiratory condition that can spread easily in crowded places.

Likewise, if you live in an area with a high prevalence of Lyme disease-carrying ticks, your vet might recommend the Lyme vaccine. Ticks can be a significant concern, especially if your Chihuahua enjoys outdoor activities, like hiking or visiting wooded areas. Leptospirosis is another disease that can affect dogs, and it can be contracted through contaminated water or soil. If your Chihuahua is active in areas where these risks are present, being informed about these vaccines can be beneficial.

Importance of Regular Vet Visits

Making regular veterinary visits is essential for your Chihuahua's overall health. At these appointments, the vet can assess your dog's health and determine if any additional vaccinations are necessary. It's a good idea to ask your vet about the vaccination schedule and any new updates or recommendations about non-core vaccinations that may be important for your Chihuahua's health. Regular checkups also provide an opportunity to discuss any behavioral or health concerns, ensuring that your pet receives comprehensive care.

Conclusion

Being proactive about vaccinations will help ensure your Chihuahua's long-term health and well-being. Following the recommended vaccination schedule and keeping up with routine veterinary visits makes it easier to protect your furry friend from serious diseases. Consult with your veterinarian about the best approach to vaccination so that your dog stays vibrant and healthy throughout its life. Remember that vaccinations are not just about protecting your dog; they are also vital for public health and the well-being of other animals in your community.

Preventative Care: Parasites and More

Preventative care is essential for keeping your Chihuahua healthy. Besides vaccines, it is important to focus on protecting your dog from parasites, which can cause a range of health issues. Small dogs, including Chihuahuas, are vulnerable to various parasites such as fleas, ticks, and heartworms. To ensure your Chihuahua remains in good health, it is crucial to implement year-round preventative measures.

Fleas

Fleas present a common problem for dogs of all sizes. While they might appear harmless, fleas can lead to significant issues such as skin irritation and allergies. In some cases, these can escalate to secondary infections, requiring further veterinary intervention. Furthermore, fleas can transmit tapeworms to dogs, posing additional threats to their well-being. To combat fleas effectively, using flea preventatives is key. Options include monthly topical treatments, which can be applied directly to your Chihuahua's skin, or oral medications that are given as a chewable treat. These preventive measures can keep your furry friend free from fleas and the problems they bring.

Ticks

Ticks are more than just annoying—they can carry diseases that affect your Chihuahua's health. One of the most concerning diseases linked to ticks is Lyme disease. This illness can lead to serious complications, including joint pain and, in severe cases, organ damage. To protect your

Chihuahua from ticks, it is beneficial to use tick preventatives. Similar to flea treatments, tick preventatives come in various forms, including topical treatments and oral medications. Regularly checking your Chihuahua for ticks, especially after walks in grassy or wooded areas, is also important. If you find a tick, it is crucial to remove it promptly to reduce the risk of disease transmission.

Heartworms

Heartworms are another serious concern for Chihuahuas, as they are transmitted through mosquito bites. Once inside your dog's body, heartworms can cause severe damage to the heart, lungs, and other organs. The effects of heartworm disease can be irreversible, making prevention critical. Most veterinarians recommend a monthly heartworm preventative medication. These medications come in different formats, such as chewables or topical treatments. It is important to adhere to a consistent schedule for administering these preventatives to ensure your Chihuahua remains protected throughout the mosquito season.

Other Parasites

In addition to fleas, ticks, and heartworms, Chihuahuas face risks from various intestinal parasites. Roundworms, hookworms, and whipworms can cause gastrointestinal issues that lead to symptoms such as lethargy and weight loss. These parasites can often go unnoticed until they prompt significant health concerns. To prevent intestinal parasites, it is important to establish regular deworming schedules for your Chihuahua. Scheduling routine fecal exams with your veterinarian can also help catch these parasites early before they become a serious problem. If your vet finds any issues, they can suggest appropriate deworming medications to eliminate the parasites effectively.

Taking a proactive approach to parasite prevention is vital for the health and happiness of your Chihuahua. By using appropriate flea and tick preventatives, adhering to heartworm prevention protocols, and maintaining regular deworming schedules, you will be supporting your small dog in leading a healthy and active life. Remember to discuss any concerns with your veterinarian, as they can offer tailored advice and recommendations based on your Chihuahua's specific needs.

Routine Veterinary Care

Routine veterinary care is essential for keeping your Chihuahua healthy. It goes beyond just vaccinations and preventative treatments; regular visits to the vet are vital. During these check-ups, veterinarians can keep an eye on your dog's health and catch any potential problems early. These early detections can make a big difference in the treatment options available. For example, if a vet notices weight gain during a routine visit, they might recommend dietary changes or increased exercise before it becomes a more serious issue.

During each visit, your veterinarian will perform a thorough physical examination. This may include checking your dog's weight, listening to their heart, and examining their eyes and ears. Regular monitoring of these aspects will help ensure that your Chihuahua remains healthy. If any irregularities are found, your vet can advise on further tests or immediate care. Additionally, updating vaccinations is important. Vaccinations protect your dog from serious illnesses that could develop if they were not vaccinated.

Dental Health

Chihuahuas are known for being prone to dental issues. Their small mouths and crowded teeth can lead to problems such as gum disease and tooth decay. Because of this, regular dental check-ups and cleanings should be part of your Chihuahua's routine healthcare. A vet will examine your dog's teeth and gums during a visit, looking for signs of plaque buildup or other issues.

To keep your Chihuahua's teeth healthy, you can also take some steps at home. Brushing your dog's teeth regularly, using toothpaste designed for dogs, is a great start. Additionally, there are special dental chews and toys available that can help reduce tartar buildup. For some owners, it might be helpful to ask their vet for recommendations on the best products to use. Keeping your Chihuahua's mouth healthy is crucial for their overall health since dental problems can lead to infections and other serious issues.

Nutrition and Diet

Having a balanced diet is essential for your Chihuahua's health. It's important to choose high-quality dog food that is appropriate for their size and age. Chihuahuas have unique nutritional needs, and feeding them the right food can help prevent weight problems and other health issues. When selecting dog food, look for options that list real meat as the first ingredient. You can also check for added vitamins and minerals that support your dog's health.

In some cases, your vet may recommend a specific feeding schedule. For example, they might suggest dividing your dog's daily food intake into two or three smaller meals instead of one large meal. This can help prevent overeating and reduce the risk of obesity. Always be mindful of how many treats you give your Chihuahua, as these can add up quickly in calories and contribute to weight gain.

Exercise and Activity

Regular exercise is vital for your Chihuahua's physical and mental health. Despite their small size, Chihuahuas are active and playful dogs that need daily exercise. A consistent exercise routine helps keep your dog fit and can improve their mood. Simple walks around the neighborhood or playtime in the backyard can be enough to meet your Chihuahua's needs.

Moreover, engaging your Chihuahua in interactive play can help stimulate their minds. Toys that encourage your dog to think, such as puzzle toys or treat-dispensing toys, can be great for keeping them engaged. Setting aside time each day for play and exercise can lead to a happier, healthier dog.

Behavior Monitoring

Monitoring your Chihuahua's behavior is another important aspect of their overall health. Changes in behavior can sometimes be an indication that something may be wrong. For example, if your Chihuahua suddenly becomes less active or stops eating, these could be signs of health issues. Observing your dog's behavior can help you catch possible problems early so that you can seek veterinary advice.

It's beneficial to establish a routine that allows you to check in on your Chihuahua at home. Spend time interacting with them, and get to know their personality. If you notice changes, such as increased aggression or withdrawal from social interactions, these changes should be discussed with a veterinarian. Your vet can help determine whether these behavioral changes might be linked to health problems or stress.

The Importance of a Proactive Approach

Taking a proactive approach to your Chihuahua's healthcare will greatly improve their quality of life. By staying ahead of potential issues through regular veterinary visits, dental care, proper nutrition, exercise, and behavior monitoring, you create a strong foundation for a happy, healthy life. Your little companion relies on you to meet their needs and ensure they can thrive.

Creating a routine that incorporates all these care aspects may take time and planning, but the rewards are well worth the effort. Your Chihuahua will benefit from a structured lifestyle that contributes to their overall health and well-being. The bond you share will grow as you take the necessary steps to maintain their vitality and happiness.

References:

- American Kennel Club (AKC). (n.d.). *Chihuahua Health: Vaccination and Preventative Care.* Retrieved from https://www.akc.org
- Veterinary Partner. (2021). *Heartworm Prevention and Treatment for Dogs.* Retrieved from https://www.veterinarypartner.com
- PetMD. (2020). *The Importance of Vaccinations for Dogs.* Retrieved from https://www.petmd.com

Dental Health: A Crucial Part of Your Chihuahua's Well-being

Dental health is an often overlooked yet incredibly important aspect of maintaining the overall well-being of your Chihuahua. While their small stature might lead some to underestimate their dental needs, Chihuahuas are actually at a high risk for dental issues due to their tiny mouths and tightly packed teeth. These small dogs are prone to tartar buildup, gum disease, and even tooth loss. If left untreated, poor oral hygiene can lead to more serious complications, including infections that can affect other organs, such as the heart, liver, and kidneys.

Due to their compact jaws, Chihuahuas are more likely to develop dental issues earlier than larger breeds. This is particularly evident in conditions like periodontal disease, which occurs when bacteria infect the gums, leading to swelling, pain, and ultimately the loss of teeth. As a result, it's essential to start a routine of dental care early in your Chihuahua's life to prevent the onset of these problems.

Understanding the Risks

The tight spaces in a Chihuahua's mouth can make it difficult for food particles to be properly cleared away, leading to an increased risk of plaque and tartar buildup. If left unchecked, plaque can harden into tartar, which can irritate the gums and cause inflammation—a precursor to gum disease. In severe cases, untreated gum disease can lead to tooth loss and contribute to systemic infections that can affect the heart and kidneys.

Additionally, Chihuahuas are prone to developing bad breath, which is often a sign of underlying dental issues. While occasional bad breath in dogs can be normal, persistent foul odor is usually indicative of dental problems, such as gingivitis or periodontitis, both of which are common in small breeds like Chihuahuas.

Prevention and Care

The best way to combat dental disease in Chihuahuas is prevention. Regular brushing of their teeth is the most effective method to prevent plaque buildup. Ideally, you should brush your Chihuahua's teeth every day, but at least three to four times a week can make a significant difference. Be sure to use a toothbrush and toothpaste specifically designed for dogs—human toothpaste can be toxic to them.

In addition to brushing, you should schedule regular vet checkups. During these visits, the vet will examine your Chihuahua's teeth and gums for signs of disease, such as swelling or sensitivity. Some veterinarians may recommend a professional dental cleaning, which helps remove tartar that can't be addressed through brushing alone. Professional cleanings may also involve X-rays to check for hidden issues below the gum line.

Dental Chews and Toys

Incorporating dental chews and toys into your Chihuahua's routine can also be beneficial. There are many dental chews available that help reduce plaque and tartar buildup while satisfying your Chihuahua's natural chewing instinct. Be sure to choose chews that are appropriately sized and designed for dental health. Some toys are designed to massage the gums and clean between the teeth, helping maintain healthy oral hygiene in between brushings.

When choosing dental chews or toys, look for products that have been approved by veterinary dental organizations, as these are formulated to help fight plaque and tartar without being too hard, which could potentially damage your dog's teeth. A few minutes of chewing on a dental toy every day can make a world of difference in maintaining your Chihuahua's oral health.

Signs of Dental Problems to Watch For

Even with regular care, dental issues can still arise. It's important to recognize the signs of dental problems early. If your Chihuahua is experiencing difficulty eating, has a noticeable decrease in appetite, or starts drooling excessively, these could be signs of pain or infection in the mouth. Other signs to watch for include pawing at the mouth, sensitivity when eating certain foods, or unusually smelly breath that doesn't improve with regular brushing.

If you notice any of these symptoms, it's crucial to seek veterinary attention right away. Early intervention can help prevent more severe issues from developing, such as tooth loss or systemic infections. The longer dental problems go untreated, the more challenging and costly they can become to address.

The Benefits of Proper Dental Care

Maintaining good dental health for your Chihuahua is essential. It prevents tooth decay and gum disease, which can lead to more serious health issues. A healthy mouth is not just about keeping teeth clean; it's about fostering an environment that promotes overall well-being. When dental problems arise, they can affect not only your dog's mouth but also their body. For example, untreated dental infections can lead to serious conditions like heart disease. This is because bacteria from the infected gums can enter the bloodstream and affect the heart. Therefore, taking care of your Chihuahua's teeth and gums is a step towards ensuring they live a longer and healthier life.

Regular dental care is a habit that should start early. A good practice is to introduce dental care routines when your Chihuahua is still a puppy. You can begin by brushing their teeth with dog-specific toothpaste. This toothpaste is formulated for pets and is safe for them to swallow. The act of brushing helps to remove plaque before it hardens into tartar. Aim to brush your Chihuahua's teeth at least two to three times a week. If daily brushing is possible, it's even better. Make the experience enjoyable by rewarding them with a treat after each session. Over time, your dog will start to associate tooth brushing with positive experiences.

In addition to brushing, dental chews can be helpful. They come in different shapes and sizes, made specifically for cleaning teeth while your Chihuahua chews. Look for products that carry a seal of approval from veterinary dental associations, as these have been tested for their effectiveness. Offering dental chews can help to scrub the teeth and reduce bad breath. It also provides an outlet for your Chihuahua's natural instinct to chew, keeping them engaged and happy.

Another helpful addition to your dental routine is regular veterinary check-ups. During these visits, the vet can perform a thorough cleaning and check for any signs of dental disease. Professional cleanings usually involve scaling and polishing, removing built-up tartar and plaque that brushing at home might miss. It is generally recommended to have your dog's teeth cleaned by a veterinarian at least once a year, depending on their dental health. Your veterinarian can give personalized recommendations based on your Chihuahua's specific needs.

Monitoring your Chihuahua's mouth for signs of dental problems is also crucial. Look for signs such as bad breath, swollen gums, or difficulty chewing. If you notice any of these symptoms, it's important to consult with your veterinarian right away. Ignoring these issues can lead to significant pain for your dog and potential health complications. Early intervention can make a big difference in treatment outcomes.

Aside from the health benefits, proper dental care can significantly improve your dog's quality of life. Just like humans, dogs experience pain from toothaches or gum infections. By taking preventive measures, you ensure that your Chihuahua avoids unnecessary discomfort. A toothache can lead to changes in behavior; a dog in pain may become less active or more irritable. Keeping their teeth and gums healthy will enable them to enjoy their daily activities without pain.

Fresh breath is also a notable benefit of regular dental care. Many dog owners can relate to the unpleasant experience of bad dog breath. It can create awkward moments during snuggles or kisses. With proper dental hygiene, you can reduce or eliminate bad breath. This means you can enjoy your dog's company even closer without worrying about the smell.

Hydration plays a role in dental health too. Ensuring that your Chihuahua has access to fresh, clean water is important. Keeping them hydrated can help wash away food particles and bacteria in their mouth. Additionally, consider using water additives designed for dental health. These products can help control plaque and freshen breath when added to their water bowl. Speak with your veterinarian about suitable options that are safe for your dog.

In summary, proper dental care for your Chihuahua goes beyond just having clean teeth. It is an important aspect of their overall health and happiness. By incorporating regular brushing, using dental chews, scheduling professional cleanings, and monitoring for any dental issues, you are investing in your dog's well-being. This commitment to dental health will not only lengthen their life but also enhance the quality of their daily experiences. A healthy smile on your Chihuahua will certainly bring joy to both you and your furry friend.

Conclusion

Dental health is a key component of caring for your Chihuahua. It requires consistent attention and proactive steps, such as brushing, professional cleanings, and providing dental chews and toys. By prioritizing your Chihuahua's dental care, you're not only helping them maintain a bright, healthy smile but also ensuring they live a long, happy life free from the pain and complications of dental disease.

References

- American Veterinary Dental College (AVDC). "Periodontal Disease." Retrieved from https://www.avdc.org.
- American Kennel Club (AKC). "Dental Health for Dogs." Retrieved from https://www.akc.org.
- PetMD. "How to Keep Your Dog's Teeth Clean." Retrieved from https://www.petmd.com.

- Veterinary Oral Health Council (VOHC). "Dental Care for Your Dog." Retrieved from https://www.vohc.org.

Emergency Signs

Living with a Chihuahua is a rollercoaster of emotions—big love packed into a small, lively body. These tiny creatures may be small in stature, but their hearts are colossal, and their loyalty knows no bounds. However, despite their courageous personalities, Chihuahuas have some unique traits that can make them prone to certain health issues. As a Chihuahua owner, it's essential to be vigilant and aware of the emergency signs that could indicate your dog is in distress.

One of the first signs you might notice when something is wrong with your Chihuahua is a change in behavior. Chihuahuas are known for their boundless energy and spunky attitude. If your Chihuahua, usually playful and full of life, suddenly becomes lethargic or disinterested in activities they typically enjoy, it could be a warning sign. This shift may signal underlying health problems, such as heart disease, infection, or even stress. If your Chihuahua appears unusually tired, weak, or reluctant to move, it's important to seek veterinary attention promptly.

Another critical sign to watch for is changes in your Chihuahua's breathing. Chihuahuas, with their small tracheas and compact chests, are prone to respiratory issues. If your dog begins to breathe rapidly, wheeze, or struggle to catch their breath, it could indicate a serious problem like a respiratory infection, heart disease, or even heatstroke. Overheating is a particular concern for these small dogs, especially during hot weather. A Chihuahua in distress due to heat will show signs such as excessive panting, drooling, or restlessness. Always be prepared to cool your dog down with water and provide shade, but seek emergency care immediately if their breathing continues to be labored.

Chihuahuas are also prone to dental issues due to their small mouths. If your Chihuahua is suddenly reluctant to eat, is drooling excessively, or seems to be in pain while chewing, it could be a sign of dental disease. Gum infections, broken teeth, or even abscesses can cause significant discomfort, and without treatment, they can lead to more serious health complications. Regular dental checkups and cleaning are essential to avoid these issues. However, if you notice any of these signs, a visit to the vet is necessary to prevent further damage and to provide your Chihuahua with the relief they need.

Vomiting or diarrhea is another major emergency sign in Chihuahuas. While an occasional upset stomach may not be cause for alarm, frequent vomiting or diarrhea—especially if it persists for more than 24 hours—could indicate a more severe problem. Infections, poisoning, or even a blockage in the intestines can all cause gastrointestinal distress in Chihuahuas. These conditions can quickly lead to dehydration, a serious concern for small dogs. If your Chihuahua refuses food, continues to vomit or have diarrhea, or exhibits additional signs of distress like lethargy or fever, it's crucial to get them checked by a vet right away.

Lastly, changes in body temperature can signal an emergency. Due to their small size and thin coat, Chihuahuas are highly susceptible to temperature extremes. If your Chihuahua feels unusually hot or cold, it could be a sign of hypothermia or heatstroke. Hypothermia, which can occur in cold weather, will cause shivering, weakness, and even confusion. On the other hand, heatstroke can result from exposure to high temperatures, leading to excessive panting, drooling, or even collapse. In either case, you need to act quickly. If your Chihuahua is overheated, move them to a cooler place and offer them water. If they're too cold, wrap them in blankets and try to warm them gradually. In both situations, a visit to the vet is necessary to prevent serious health complications.

As a Chihuahua owner, it's essential to be aware of these emergency signs. Although they may seem small, Chihuahuas have big hearts, and their health is fragile. Recognizing when something is wrong and acting swiftly can make a significant difference in your Chihuahua's well-being and even save their life. Always trust your instincts, and if you're in doubt, don't hesitate to contact your veterinarian.3

References:

- American Kennel Club (AKC). (2023). *Chihuahua Health and Care.* Retrieved from https://www.akc.org/dog-breeds/chihuahua/

- PetMD. (2022). *Signs Your Dog May Be in Pain or Distress.* Retrieved from https://www.petmd.com/dog/care/evr_dg_signs_your_dog_is_in_pain

- Veterinary Partner. (2021). *Chihuahua Health Issues and Concerns.* Retrieved from https://www.veterinarypartner.com

Chapter 8: Grooming and Maintenance

Brushing and Bathing

Proper grooming is an essential part of pet care, ensuring that your animal stays healthy, comfortable, and happy. Regular brushing and bathing are fundamental components of a grooming routine. These practices not only keep your pet's coat looking great but also contribute to their overall well-being. In this chapter, we will explore the importance of brushing and bathing your pet, along with the best practices for maintaining a clean and healthy coat.

The Importance of Brushing

Brushing your pet's coat regularly has several benefits, both for their appearance and health. The primary purpose of brushing is to remove dirt, debris, and loose hair. For pets with long or thick coats, regular brushing helps prevent tangles and mats, which can lead to skin irritation or infections if left untreated. It also helps distribute natural oils throughout the coat, promoting a healthy shine and reducing shedding.

Brushing also serves as an opportunity to inspect your pet's skin for signs of irritation, rashes, or parasites like fleas and ticks. Regular grooming allows you to spot any abnormalities early, enabling you to address potential health issues before they become serious.

Choosing the Right Brush for Your Pet

When it comes to grooming pets, choosing the right brush is crucial. Different pets have unique coat types, and using the appropriate brush for their specific needs can make a big difference. It is important to understand the different types of brushes available and how each one can be beneficial to your pet.

Slicker Brush

Slicker brushes are a popular choice for pets that have long and dense coats. These brushes feature fine, short wires designed to reach deep into the fur. This means they can effectively remove tangles, mats, and loose hair. If you own a breed such as a Poodle or a Shih Tzu, investing in a slicker brush can help keep their coat looking neat. To use a slicker brush, gently work through your pet's coat in small sections, starting from the roots. Try to be patient, as it may take some time to work through tough tangles. The key is to use smooth, even strokes to avoid pulling on your pet's skin.

Pin Brush

For pets with medium-length coats or fine hair, a pin brush is often the best option. Pin brushes have longer pins with rounded tips, which allows them to untangle hair without causing discomfort. Breeds like Spaniels, which often have silky coats, benefit from this type of brush. When using a pin brush, remember to approach it gently. Start brushing from the roots and gradually move toward the tips to avoid breaking the hairs. Incorporating this method can help keep your pet's coat looking healthy and shiny.

Bristle Brush

If you have a short-haired pet, a bristle brush might be the right choice. These brushes are designed to help distribute natural oils throughout the coat while also removing any loose fur. Breeds like Beagles and Bulldogs, which are known for their short, sleek coats, can greatly benefit from regular use of a bristle brush. To use this brush effectively, simply glide it over the coat in the direction of hair growth. This not only helps clean the fur but also stimulates the skin, promoting overall health.

Deshedding Brush

For pets that shed a lot, deshedding brushes are an essential tool. These brushes are designed to target and remove loose undercoat hair, significantly reducing shedding around the house. Breeds known for heavy shedding, such as Huskies and Golden Retrievers, will benefit from regular use of a deshedding brush. To get started, make sure to brush your pet outside or in an easy-to-clean area. Gently run the deshedding brush through your pet's coat in the direction of hair growth, focusing on areas that tend to shed the most. This will help keep your home cleaner and your pet more comfortable.

Brushing Tips

Brushing your pet should always be a gentle experience. It's not just about getting rid of loose fur; it's also about creating a calm and enjoyable grooming routine. Using gentle strokes is key to avoiding discomfort or skin irritation. Make sure to pay close attention to your pet's reaction. If they seem uncomfortable, you may need to adjust your technique or switch to a different brush.

Regular brushing is another important aspect of grooming. Depending on your pet's coat type, you might need to brush them anywhere from two to several times a week. Long-haired pets may require more frequent brushing to keep mats and tangles at bay. For example, if you have a Golden Retriever, brushing three to four times a week can help maintain their beautiful coat.

Always remember to work from the roots of the fur and proceed to the tips. This method is effective in removing tangles while minimizing breakage. By starting from the roots, you ensure that you are addressing any tangles at their source, making the process smoother for both you and your pet.

Lastly, consider incorporating treats and praise during brushing sessions. This not only rewards your pet for their good behavior but can also make grooming an enjoyable experience. Offering treats can encourage your pet to stay calm and relaxed while you groom them. Over time, they will start to associate grooming with positive experiences, making future sessions easier.

Taking the time to choose the right brush and develop a consistent brushing routine is well worth the effort. Your pet will thank you, and you will enjoy a happier grooming process.

The Importance of Bathing

Bathing is an important part of grooming that helps keep your pet clean. It removes dirt, oils, and odors that can build up on your pet's skin and fur. Regular bathing is also beneficial for your pet's health. It can help eliminate allergens such as pollen and dust mites that might irritate your pet's skin. When you bathe your pet, you also have the chance to check their skin for any unusual signs like bumps, redness, or infections. However, it is essential to be careful about how often you bathe your pet. Over-bathing can strip the skin of its natural oils, leading to dryness and irritation. Finding the right balance in bathing frequency is key to keeping your pet comfortable and healthy.

How Often Should You Bathe Your Pet?

The frequency of bathing your pet can vary. It mainly depends on their breed, how active they are, and the type of coat they have. Some pets have oilier coats that may need more regular cleaning, while others might only require a wash every few months. Understanding your pet's specific needs will help you determine the best bathing schedule for them.

Short-Haired Dogs

For short-haired dogs, bathing is generally less frequent. These pets can typically go about six to eight weeks between baths unless they become particularly dirty from playing outside or have a skin condition that requires more regular washing. If your short-haired dog spends time in muddy places or has allergies, you might find that they need a bath sooner. Pay attention to their fur and skin. If they start to smell or their fur feels greasy, it might be time for a wash.

Long-Haired Dogs

Long-haired dogs often need more attention when it comes to bathing and grooming. Their hair can trap dirt and oils more easily, and they may be more prone to tangling and mats. For these pets, a good rule of thumb is to bathe them every four to six weeks. This frequent bathing helps keep their coat healthy and manageable. Regular grooming in between baths is crucial as well. Brushing can help remove loose fur and prevent mats, which makes bathing easier and more effective.

Active Pets

If you have an active pet, such as one that loves to run around outside, splash in puddles, or dig in the dirt, they may need baths more often. Pets that have a lot of outdoor adventures often come back home dirty, which means their coats will need more regular cleaning. It's important to monitor how dirty they get after their outings. You might find that once a month is not enough for these lively animals. Regular cleaning helps remove dirt and debris that can cause skin irritations or lead to infections if left unchecked.

Bathing Techniques

When you decide it's time for a bath, there are some basic techniques to use that can make the process smooth for both you and your pet. Start by gathering all your supplies, including dog shampoo, towels, a brush, and non-slip mats for the tub or bathing area. Using a non-slip mat can help your pet feel more secure while bathing. Wet your pet gently with lukewarm water, avoiding the face area initially to help them feel more comfortable. Apply the appropriate pet shampoo and work it into their coat, making sure to follow the instructions on the bottle for the right amount to use.

Remember to rinse thoroughly. Leaving soap on their skin can lead to irritation. After rinsing, you can apply a conditioner if it is suitable for your pet's coat type, especially for long-haired breeds. Pay attention to rinsing out the conditioner as well. Once the bathing is complete, towel dry your pet gently to remove excess water. If your pet is comfortable with it, you can use a hairdryer on a low setting, keeping it at a distance to avoid overheating.

After Bath Care

After bathing, it's important to keep an eye on your pet's skin and coat. Look for any signs of irritation or discomfort that may have arisen during the bath. It's also a good time to check for any skin issues or unusual bumps. If your pet seems to be scratching more than usual or is uncomfortable, it may be worth discussing with your vet. Additionally, make sure to reward your pet after their bath with a treat or some playtime. This can help create a positive association with the bathing experience.

Finding the Right Products

Choosing the right products for bathing your pet is also crucial. Not all human shampoos are safe for pets, as they may have ingredients that can irritate their skin. Always opt for shampoos specially formulated for pets, as these will have the right pH balance for their skin. Additionally, consider your pet's specific needs. For example, if your pet has allergies, look for hypoallergenic shampoos. If they have a specific skin condition, your veterinarian may recommend medicated shampoos. Always read the labels and ask your vet if you're uncertain about what product is best for your pet.

Careful attention to bathing your pet will ensure they stay healthy and happy. Finding a routine that works for them will help you maintain their cleanliness while ensuring their skin remains moist and irritation-free. Being mindful of their grooming needs helps build a stronger bond between you and your pet, making for a happier companion.

Coat Type	Brushing Frequency	Bathing Frequency
Short-haired	1-2 times/week	Every 6-8 weeks
Medium-length	2-3 times/week	Every 4-6 weeks
Long-haired	Daily or every other day	Every 4-6 weeks
Heavy shedders	3-4 times/week	Every 4-6 weeks
Outdoor-active pets	As needed (may be daily)	Every 2-4 weeks

Choosing the Right Shampoo

Selecting the right shampoo for your pet is essential for keeping their skin and coat healthy. It's important to remember that using human shampoo on your pet is not a good idea. Human shampoos can upset the natural pH balance of your pet's skin. This can lead to problems like dryness, irritation, and even more serious skin issues. Pet shampoos are specifically designed for animals. They work to maintain the health of your pet's skin and coat without causing harm.

There are special pet shampoos available that are medicated. These shampoos are created to tackle specific skin problems such as allergies, dry skin, or even flea infestations. If your pet has sensitive skin or allergies, it's best to choose a hypoallergenic and fragrance-free shampoo. For pets that are dealing with fleas or ticks, you might need to look for a specialized flea shampoo. These types of shampoos contain ingredients that can effectively eliminate or repel these pests, keeping your pet comfortable and healthy.

Bathing Tips

Prepare the Area

Before beginning the bath, make sure to prepare the area where you'll be cleaning your pet. Whether you choose to bathe them indoors or outdoors, the space should feel safe and comfortable. It's best to use lukewarm water for bathing. Hot water can be harsh on your pet's skin, potentially causing irritation, while cold water can make them uncomfortable during the bath.

Wet and Lather Gently

When you start the bathing process, use either a cup or a gentle spray nozzle to wet your pet's coat. Be careful to avoid their face and ears during this step. Once their coat is wet, apply the shampoo gently. It is best to start lathering from the neck and then move down the body slowly. This method ensures that you do not miss any spots while carefully avoiding sensitive areas like the eyes, ears, and genital region.

Thoroughly Rinse

Once you have lathered the shampoo, it is crucial to rinse all of it out of your pet's coat. Leaving any shampoo residue can lead to irritation and dryness of the skin. Take your time during this step and make sure to run your hand through your pet's coat while rinsing to ensure that all shampoo is completely washed away.

Dry Properly

After the bath, drying your pet the right way is just as important. Use a towel to gently dry off your pet and remove excess water. If your pet has long hair, you might find it helpful to use a blow dryer on a low heat setting. This will help speed up the drying process. It's essential that your pet is completely dry after bathing to prevent fungal infections or other skin issues. Make sure to check all areas of their body to confirm that they are dry, especially if they have thick or long fur.

Importance of Regular Grooming

Brushing and bathing are crucial elements of a regular grooming routine for your pet. They contribute significantly to your pet's overall hygiene, comfort, and health. Regular brushing helps to remove dirt, debris, and loose fur from your pet's coat. This not only keeps their coat looking shiny and healthy but also prevents mats from forming. Small mats can quickly turn into larger tangles if not addressed.

Bathing your pet plays a critical role as well. It removes dirt, oils, and allergens that can irritate your pet's skin. Keeping your pet clean is vital for their well-being, as buildup from dirt and oils can lead to itching and discomfort. By sticking to a consistent grooming schedule and using the right techniques and products, you can make sure your pet remains healthy and happy.

Tools for Grooming

To make grooming as effective as possible, it's important to have the right tools on hand. You will need a good quality brush that is suitable for your pet's coat type. For instance, if your pet has a long coat, a slicker brush can be very helpful in getting through tangles. For shorter coats, a rubber grooming brush can be more effective in removing loose fur and dirt.

In addition to brushes, you might also find pet combs valuable for specific tasks, such as untangling knots or working through areas where mats may form. It's also beneficial to have nail clippers made specifically for pets, as well as ear cleaning solutions that are safe for animal use. By investing in the right grooming tools, you can make the grooming process smoother for both you and your pet.

Establishing a Routine

Establishing a consistent grooming routine is beneficial for you and your pet. Regular grooming can help your pet become accustomed to the process. Start slowly, allowing your pet to get used to being brushed or bathed. Over time, they will learn to associate grooming with comfort and affection, making future sessions easier for both of you.

Try to set specific days or times for grooming. This helps your pet learn that grooming is a regular part of their care. Additionally, if your pet is comfortable, you might consider turning grooming into a bonding activity. Spend some time petting and praising them during and after grooming to strengthen your connection.

By following these guidelines for choosing the right shampoo and bathing your pet, you can contribute significantly to their health and happiness. Proper grooming ensures that they feel comfortable and secure in their environment, ultimately enriching their quality of life.

References:

- American Kennel Club. "Grooming Your Dog." AKC.org.
- PetMD. "How Often Should You Bathe Your Dog?" PetMD.com.
- The Spruce Pets. "How to Bathe Your Dog." TheSprucePets.com.
- ASPCA. "Dog Grooming Tips." ASPCA.org.
- VCA Animal Hospitals. "Brushing and Bathing Your Pet." VCAhospitals.com.

Nail Trimming

Nail trimming is an important aspect of caring for a Chihuahua, despite their small size. While it might seem like a minor task, regularly trimming your dog's nails can have a significant impact on their overall health and well-being. Chihuahuas, like all dogs, need their nails kept at a manageable length to prevent discomfort, injuries, and other potential health issues.

Why Nail Trimming is Important

If left unchecked, a Chihuahua's nails can grow too long, which can lead to various problems. Long nails can cause your dog to walk awkwardly, putting unnecessary strain on their joints and paws. This could lead to joint pain, arthritis, or more serious musculoskeletal issues over time. Additionally, excessively long nails can become snagged on surfaces, leading to painful tears or breakage.

Another concern is the risk of nails curling into the paw pads. This condition, known as *onychocryptosis*, can be very painful and may require veterinary intervention if not managed. Regular trimming helps prevent this, ensuring your Chihuahua can walk comfortably without pain or injury.

How Often Should You Trim Your Chihuahua's Nails?

The frequency of nail trimming depends on several factors, including your Chihuahua's activity level and the surfaces they walk on. If your dog spends a lot of time outdoors on concrete or asphalt, the natural wear on their nails might reduce the need for trimming. However, if your Chihuahua is mostly indoors or has minimal exposure to hard surfaces, their nails might grow longer and require more frequent attention.

As a general rule, you should check your Chihuahua's nails every two weeks. If you can hear them clicking on the floor as they walk, it's time for a trim. For some Chihuahuas, nail trimming might be needed once a month, while others might require more frequent care.

Activity Level / Environment	Surface Type	Trim Frequency
Mostly indoors	Carpet/tile	Every 2-3 weeks
Moderate outdoor activity	Mixed (grass/pavement)	Every 3-4 weeks
Daily outdoor walks	Pavement/concrete	Every 4-6 weeks
Elderly or inactive dogs	Mostly indoors	Every 2 weeks

Tools for Nail Trimming

Trimming your Chihuahua's nails requires the right tools to ensure safety and effectiveness. A pair of high-quality, sharp dog nail clippers is essential. There are several types available, including scissor-style clippers, guillotine-style clippers, and grinders. Each tool has its advantages, but scissor-style clippers are often the best choice for small breeds like Chihuahuas because they provide better control and precision.

For more nervous Chihuahuas or owners who prefer a gentler method, a nail grinder can be an excellent alternative. A grinder is a small, rotating tool that smooths the nail instead of cutting it, reducing the risk of trimming too much. This tool is especially helpful for dogs with black nails, where it can be harder to see the quick (the sensitive area inside the nail).

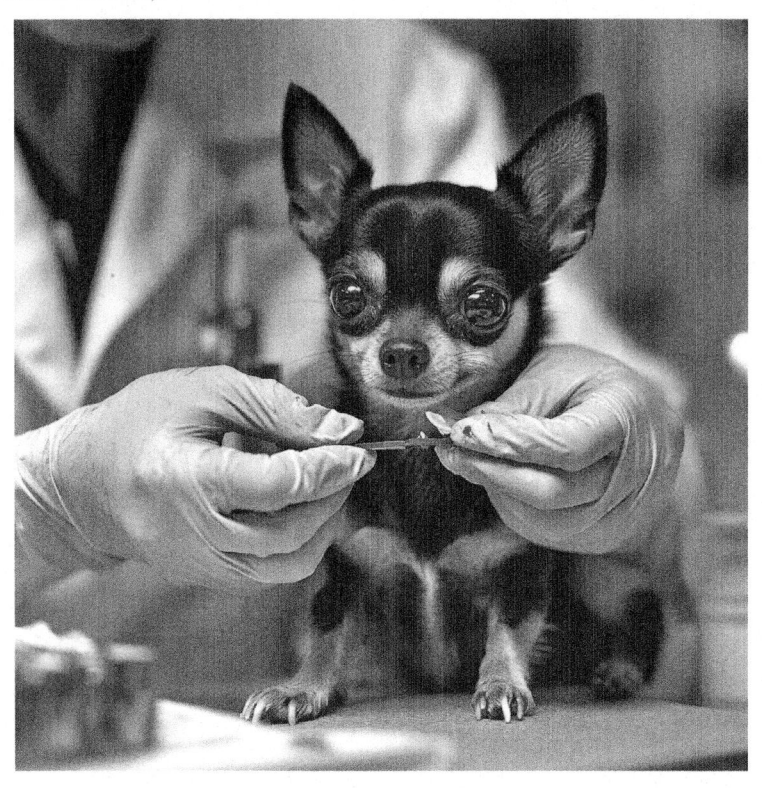

Steps for Trimming Your Chihuahua's Nails

1. **Get Your Chihuahua Comfortable**: Start by making sure your dog is calm and relaxed. You can hold them in your lap or have someone help keep them steady. If your Chihuahua is anxious, consider giving them a treat or using positive reinforcement.
2. **Examine the Nails**: Look closely at your dog's nails. If they are clear or light in color, you can easily see the quick, which should be

avoided. For darker nails, trim small amounts at a time to avoid cutting too far into the quick.

3. **Trim Small Amounts at a Time**: Trim a small part of the nail at a time, avoiding the quick. It's better to trim less and do it more often than to cut too much and cause bleeding. If you accidentally cut the quick, use styptic powder or cornstarch to stop the bleeding.

4. **Smooth the Edges**: After trimming, use a nail file or grinder to smooth out any sharp edges. This will prevent your Chihuahua from accidentally scratching themselves or you.

5. **Reward Your Chihuahua**: After the task is done, give your Chihuahua a treat and plenty of praise. Positive reinforcement helps them associate nail trimming with a rewarding experience, making the process easier the next time.

When to Seek Professional Help

While regular at-home trimming is important, there are times when it's best to seek professional help. If you're unsure how to trim your Chihuahua's nails safely, or if your dog becomes too anxious or aggressive during the process, a professional groomer or veterinarian can handle the task. Additionally, if you notice any signs of injury or infection in your dog's nails or paws, it's important to seek veterinary care promptly.

Conclusion

Nail trimming is a simple yet essential part of your Chihuahua's overall health maintenance. With the right tools and a bit of patience, you can keep your dog's nails at a healthy length and avoid potential discomfort or injury. Regular nail trimming not only promotes your Chihuahua's comfort but also ensures they can continue to walk, run, and play without any unnecessary hindrances. Remember, keeping up with their nail care is a small but crucial step in ensuring your Chihuahua's long-term health and happiness.

References:

- American Kennel Club (AKC). (n.d.). *Nail Trimming Tips for Dogs.* Retrieved from https://www.akc.org
- PetMD. (2020). *How to Trim Your Dog's Nails Safely.* Retrieved from https://www.petmd.com
- Veterinary Partner. (2021). *Dog Nail Care and Trimming.* Retrieved from https://www.veterinarypartner.com

Ear and Eye Care: Ensuring Comfort and Health for Your Chihuahua

As a devoted Chihuahua owner, it's crucial to keep an eye on the health of your dog's ears and eyes. These small dogs are prone to a range of health concerns, and the delicate nature of their ears and eyes makes them especially vulnerable. Maintaining proper care and vigilance in these areas is essential to ensure that your Chihuahua stays comfortable, happy, and healthy.

Ear Care: Keeping Those Tiny Ears Clean and Comfortable

Chihuahuas, with their large, expressive eyes and ears, may seem to be the picture of health, but their ears require attention. Because of their relatively large ear size compared to their tiny heads, they are more prone to developing ear infections. The primary cause of ear infections in Chihuahuas is the accumulation of dirt, wax, and moisture in their ears, which creates an ideal environment for bacteria or yeast to thrive.

Routine ear cleaning is important, especially if your Chihuahua has floppy ears, as these types of ears trap moisture and can promote infection. Start by inspecting the ears regularly for any signs of redness, discharge, or foul odor, which are often signs of an infection. If you notice any of these symptoms, it's essential to consult your vet for treatment.

When cleaning your Chihuahua's ears, use a veterinarian-approved ear cleaner specifically designed for dogs. Never use cotton swabs as they can damage the sensitive inner structures of your dog's ear canal. Instead, gently wipe the outer ear flap and the visible portion of the ear canal with a soft, damp cloth or cotton ball. Be sure to avoid inserting anything deep into the ear canal to prevent injury.

For dogs that are prone to recurrent ear infections, your vet may recommend using ear drops to help keep the ears clean and prevent the buildup of wax and moisture. Regular ear checks should be part of your Chihuahua's overall grooming routine to ensure any issues are caught early, preventing more severe infections from developing.

Eye Care: Protecting Your Chihuahua's Big, Bright Eyes

Chihuahuas have large, round eyes that are often one of their most endearing features. However, these eyes are also particularly vulnerable to injury, infection, and dryness. Given their prominent placement on the face, they can be prone to scratching or irritation, and their size can also make them more susceptible to certain eye conditions, such as dry eye, conjunctivitis, and cataracts.

One of the most common eye issues in Chihuahuas is dry eye, or keratoconjunctivitis sicca (KCS). This occurs when the tear glands do not produce enough tears to keep the eyes moist, leading to redness, irritation, and a higher risk of infection. If you notice your Chihuahua squinting, rubbing their eyes, or experiencing excessive tear production, it's important to consult your veterinarian. Treatment may involve prescription eye drops or medication to help stimulate tear production.

Chihuahuas are also prone to conjunctivitis, commonly known as "pink eye." This condition can cause the eyes to become red, swollen, and discharge pus. It can be triggered by bacteria, viruses, or allergies. Conjunctivitis is contagious to other animals, so if your Chihuahua develops this condition, it's important to keep them isolated from other pets until it's treated.

Another concern for Chihuahuas with large eyes is the potential for trauma. Their eyes are more prone to injury due to their position, and they can easily scratch their corneas or develop other injuries from rough play or environmental factors. If your Chihuahua is squinting, has excessive tearing, or is sensitive to light, it could be a sign of an eye injury, and immediate veterinary care is required.

In addition to regular checks for infections and injuries, you should also keep your Chihuahua's eyes clean. Gently wipe away any discharge with a soft, damp cloth, being careful not to apply pressure on the eye itself. If you notice excessive tearing or crusty buildup around the eyes, consult with your vet to ensure there are no underlying conditions.

Routine Care and Preventative Measures

Preventing ear and eye issues before they arise is key to ensuring your Chihuahua's overall health. Regular grooming should include checking their ears and eyes for any signs of irritation, discharge, or unusual behavior, such as pawing at the face or ears. Keeping the fur around their eyes trimmed and clean will also help prevent debris from causing irritation or injury.

Another important preventative measure is to protect your Chihuahua from environmental factors that could contribute to eye and ear problems. Keep them away from harsh chemicals, such as cleaning products, and protect them from extreme temperatures or wind. If your Chihuahua enjoys outdoor activities, consider limiting their exposure to allergens or irritants like dust or pollen, which could lead to eye or ear issues.

Conclusion

Ear and eye care are integral components of your Chihuahua's health regimen. By taking the time to regularly clean and inspect your dog's ears and eyes, you can prevent many common problems and ensure that they remain comfortable and pain-free. Whether it's avoiding ear infections, managing tear production, or preventing eye injuries, the goal is to provide your Chihuahua with the best possible care. A little attention to these small but vital areas can go a long way in keeping your Chihuahua happy, healthy, and thriving.

References

- American Kennel Club (AKC). "Chihuahua Health." Retrieved from https://www.akc.org.
- Veterinary Partner. "Ear Infections in Dogs." Retrieved from https://www.veterinarypartner.com.
- PetMD. "Eye Problems in Dogs: How to Protect Your Dog's Eyes." Retrieved from https://www.petmd.com.
- American Veterinary Medical Association (AVMA). "Ear Problems in Dogs." Retrieved from https://www.avma.org.

Tools You'll Need

When you welcome a Chihuahua into your home, you are bringing a small but mighty companion into your life. Caring for such a tiny yet spirited dog requires a few essential tools to ensure their health, safety, and comfort. From daily grooming to emergency care, there are a few items you'll need to make sure that both you and your Chihuahua are prepared for whatever comes your way.

1. Collar and Leash

A collar and leash are the basic essentials for any dog owner, but for Chihuahuas, the importance cannot be overstated. Chihuahuas are very small, and their fragile necks make it crucial that their collar fits snugly but comfortably. Opt for a lightweight collar made of soft material to avoid discomfort. Additionally, a leash will allow you to safely walk your Chihuahua while keeping them under control in busy areas. Given their size, Chihuahuas may be more susceptible to pulling, so a harness could also be a better choice for walks, as it can prevent strain on their neck and spine.

2. Crate or Bed for Comfort and Security

Chihuahuas often seek comfort and warmth, so a small, cozy bed or crate is vital. A well-sized crate not only serves as a safe space for your dog when you're away but also provides a sense of security. Chihuahuas tend to feel more relaxed and at ease when they have a designated space of their own. The crate can also be an essential tool for potty training and helping them understand boundaries. When choosing a bed, look for one that is soft, cushioned, and easy to clean.

3. Grooming Tools

Grooming your Chihuahua is a regular necessity, and the right tools will make this task much easier. Their small size and fine coats mean they require frequent brushing to avoid matting, especially if you have a long-haired Chihuahua. A slicker brush is ideal for removing tangles, while a comb can help you deal with finer areas like around their ears and face. Chihuahuas are prone to dental issues, so investing in dog toothbrushes and toothpaste is crucial for maintaining their oral health. Regular dental care will help prevent gum disease and other complications that can arise from poor hygiene.

4. Nail Clippers

Chihuahuas may have tiny paws, but their nails still require regular trimming. Long nails can cause discomfort or even lead to injury if they get caught in fabric or other materials. A good set of dog nail clippers designed specifically for small breeds will help you manage your Chihuahua's nails at home. If you're unsure about trimming your Chihuahua's nails, you can always take them to a groomer or vet for professional care.

5. Food and Water Bowls

Since Chihuahuas are small dogs, they don't require large portions of food, but they do need high-quality meals tailored to their size and health needs. Invest in a sturdy, non-slip food and water bowl set to keep their meals tidy and prevent spills. Stainless steel or ceramic bowls are a great choice, as they are easy to clean and won't harbor bacteria as plastic can.

6. Chew Toys and Treats

Chihuahuas, like most dogs, love to chew. Having a variety of chew toys available will keep your Chihuahua entertained and help them manage any excess energy. Rubber toys, rope toys, and even puzzle feeders can engage them mentally and physically. Dental chews are particularly important for Chihuahuas, as they help maintain oral hygiene and reduce plaque build-up. These can also serve as great rewards during training sessions.

7. First Aid Kit

Accidents can happen, and being prepared with a dog-specific first aid kit is an essential tool for any Chihuahua owner. A well-stocked first aid kit should include items like gauze, bandages, antiseptic wipes, and tweezers for removing foreign objects. For Chihuahuas, you should also have a thermometer, as small breeds can have more sensitive body temperatures and may need quick attention in case of overheating or hypothermia. If your Chihuahua has any known medical conditions, it's wise to keep their prescribed medications in the kit as well.

8. Flea and Tick Prevention

Due to their small size, Chihuahuas are at risk of flea infestations, which can cause severe discomfort or lead to more serious skin infections. You'll need to be proactive with flea and tick prevention to keep your dog protected. Talk to your vet about the best options, whether it be spot-on treatments, flea collars, or oral medications. Regularly checking your Chihuahua's coat for any signs of fleas or ticks will help you catch infestations early.

9. Car Safety Seat or Carrier

Traveling with your Chihuahua requires special attention to ensure their safety. A car safety seat or carrier designed for small dogs will prevent them from moving around freely, keeping them safe during travel. Many of these products come with secure straps or safety harnesses to keep your Chihuahua in place, reducing distractions while driving. A safe and secure carrier can also double as their crate when traveling, providing them with a familiar, comfortable environment.

10. Emergency Contact Information

While not a physical tool, it's essential to have an emergency contact list for your Chihuahua. This includes the number of your veterinarian, an emergency vet clinic, and the contact details of trusted friends or family who can step in if needed. Always have your dog's medical records readily available in case of an emergency, including vaccination history and any ongoing treatments or allergies.

	Essential Tool
☐	Collar or harness + leash
☐	Crate or comfortable bed
☐	Grooming tools (brush, comb)
☐	Dog nail clippers
☐	Food and water bowls
☐	Chew toys and dental treats
☐	Dog-specific first aid kit
☐	Flea and tick prevention
☐	Car safety seat or carrier
☐	Emergency contact list

By having the right tools and being prepared, you'll ensure that your Chihuahua remains happy, healthy, and safe in your care. These essential items will not only help with their everyday needs but also allow you to respond effectively in case of an emergency. Taking proactive steps to understand your Chihuahua's needs and invest in the right tools will make your time together even more enjoyable.

References:

- American Kennel Club (AKC). (2023). *Chihuahua Health and Care.* Retrieved from https://www.akc.org/dog-breeds/chihuahua/
- PetMD. (2022). *Dog Grooming: Tips for Keeping Your Pet Clean and Healthy.* Retrieved from https://www.petmd.com/dog/care
- The Spruce Pets. (2021). *Essential Supplies for New Chihuahua Owners.* Retrieved from https://www.thesprucepets.com

Chapter 9: Chihuahua Lifestyle

Daily Routine Needs

Chihuahuas, one of the smallest dog breeds in the world, have big personalities and a unique set of needs that must be understood in order to provide the best care. While their compact size often makes them ideal for apartment living or smaller spaces, they require careful attention to their daily routine, exercise, nutrition, and mental stimulation. Understanding and meeting these needs ensures that your Chihuahua remains happy, healthy, and well-adjusted.

Feeding and Nutrition

Chihuahuas are small dogs with unique nutritional needs. Even though they have smaller appetites, they still require high-quality food to keep their energy levels up and to support their overall health. Unlike larger dog breeds, which may need bigger meals, Chihuahuas thrive on smaller portions. This is because their metabolism works best with food that is specifically formulated for small dogs. Such specialized food helps to manage their calorie intake effectively. An example of this would be looking for breeds or types of dog food that are labeled as "small breed" or "toy breed," as these often contain the right balance of nutrients.

When it comes to adult Chihuahuas, it is best to divide their meals into two portions each day. Feeding them in the morning and evening can help prevent overeating, which is vital for maintaining a healthy weight. Structured meal times also help create a routine, making it easier for both the dog and the owner. Additionally, Chihuahuas can be prone to dental issues, so choosing a high-quality dry kibble can be especially important. Dry kibble typically has a texture that helps clean the teeth as they chew. For added variety, some owners choose to mix in a small amount of wet food or high-protein treats. However, keeping an eye on their total calorie intake is crucial to avoid obesity, a common problem for this breed due to their tiny size and slower metabolism.

Puppy Chihuahuas, on the other hand, have slightly different nutritional needs than adults. When they are still growing, they require food that has higher protein and fat content to properly support their rapid growth and development. This additional nutrition is essential for building strong muscles and bones. When feeding a puppy Chihuahua, it is important to pay close attention to their portion sizes. This means measuring their food and ensuring they receive enough nutrients to grow without overfeeding them. Chihuahuas tend to grow quickly, and if they eat too much, they can easily gain excess weight.

When selecting food for a puppy Chihuahua, it's beneficial to look for puppy-specific formulas that are rich in the right nutrients. These formulas are often specially designed to meet the demands of a growing dog, helping to ensure they receive everything they need during this critical stage of their life.

In addition to the type of food, monitoring their feeding behavior is important. If a Chihuahua stops eating or shows disinterest in their food, this could indicate a health problem, and it is wise to consult a veterinarian. Some owners may also choose to provide their Chihuahuas with a mix of dry kibble and wet food to keep things interesting and encourage them to eat. However, any changes in their diet should be introduced gradually to avoid digestive upset.

Feeding schedules can also play a role in a Chihuahua's nutrition. Regular feeding times create stability and help dogs understand when to expect food. This reduces anxiety around mealtime and can promote healthy eating habits. It is essential to avoid feeding them table scraps or human food, as many items are not suitable for dogs and can lead to health issues over time.

In summary, caring for the nutritional needs of Chihuahuas requires a good understanding of what they need at different life stages. Owners must pay attention to portion sizes, choose high-quality dog food, and create a consistent feeding routine. By doing this, they can help ensure their small companions live a healthy and happy life.

Exercise and Physical Activity

Despite their small size, Chihuahuas are known for their energy and playful nature. They require daily exercise to maintain a healthy weight and to burn off excess energy. However, due to their size, their exercise needs are generally less demanding than larger breeds. A daily walk of about 20 to 30 minutes is usually sufficient to keep them physically healthy.

It's important to keep their walks at a comfortable pace, as Chihuahuas can overheat or tire easily. During walks, they may also benefit from carrying a small backpack with their belongings or wearing a jacket in cooler weather, as they can be sensitive to temperature extremes.

In addition to walks, Chihuahuas love to play indoors. Providing them with toys that stimulate both their mind and body, such as puzzle toys or small balls, can keep them entertained for hours. Playtime is crucial to a Chihuahua's overall well-being and helps prevent boredom, which can lead to behavioral problems.

Grooming and Coat Care

Chihuahuas come in two coat types: smooth and long-haired. The smooth-coated variety requires minimal grooming, needing only occasional brushing to keep their coat clean and healthy. For the long-haired Chihuahua, regular grooming is essential to prevent tangling and matting. Brushing their coat two to three times a week helps maintain its shine and prevents any unwanted knots.

Bathing should be done as needed, usually once every month or when your Chihuahua gets particularly dirty. Use a dog-specific shampoo to avoid irritating their skin, and make sure to rinse thoroughly. Drying your Chihuahua after a bath is important, as they are susceptible to cold temperatures and could catch a chill.

Chihuahuas are also prone to dental issues due to their small mouths, so dental care is an important part of their grooming routine. Regular teeth brushing is recommended, and dental chews or toys can help reduce tartar buildup.

Rest and Comfort

Chihuahuas love comfort, and creating a cozy space for them to relax is a must. Given their small size, they often enjoy burrowing into blankets or cuddling up next to their owners. Providing a soft, warm bed in a quiet area of the home will help your Chihuahua feel secure. As a breed, Chihuahuas tend to be a bit clingy and will often seek attention and affection from their owners.

In terms of sleep, Chihuahuas don't need as much rest as puppies, but they still require around 12 to 14 hours of sleep per day, especially if they are active or have had a busy day. They are prone to feeling cold, so make sure their resting area is warm and draft-free.

Training and Socialization

While Chihuahuas are intelligent and eager to please, they are also independent and can sometimes be stubborn. Training is essential, but it requires patience, consistency, and positive reinforcement. Early socialization is critical for Chihuahuas, as it helps them grow into well-rounded, confident adults. Introducing your Chihuahua to other animals, people, and new environments can prevent fearful or aggressive behaviors later in life.

Chihuahuas thrive on routine, so it's beneficial to establish a consistent schedule for feeding, bathroom breaks, and playtime. Positive reinforcement, such as treats and praise, will help reinforce good behavior. Since Chihuahuas are naturally alert, they can be excellent watchdogs, but this may also lead to excessive barking. Training your Chihuahua to respond to commands like "quiet" or "enough" will help reduce unnecessary barking.

Health Considerations

Chihuahuas are generally a healthy breed, but they are prone to certain health issues, especially as they age. Regular veterinary checkups are essential to monitor for conditions like heart disease, dental problems, and patellar luxation, which is a dislocation of the kneecap. Regular vaccinations, parasite control, and a balanced diet are also crucial for maintaining their health.

Chihuahuas are sensitive to both heat and cold due to their small size, so it's important to protect them from extreme temperatures. In the summer, be mindful of the risk of overheating, and in the winter, ensure they are kept warm with a pet sweater or jacket if necessary.

Conclusion

Chihuahuas may be small in size, but their needs are as unique and important as any larger breed. By providing a balanced routine that includes proper nutrition, daily exercise, grooming, training, and regular health checks, you can ensure that your Chihuahua lives a happy, healthy, and fulfilling life. Understanding and meeting their daily routine needs will allow you to form a strong, loving bond with your tiny companion and help them thrive in your care.

References:

- American Kennel Club. "Chihuahua Dog Breed Information." AKC.org.
- PetMD. "Chihuahua Health Problems." PetMD.com.
- The Spruce Pets. "Chihuahua Grooming." TheSprucePets.com.
- VCA Animal Hospitals. "Chihuahua Care and Feeding." VCAhospitals.com.
- The Chihuahua Club of America. "Chihuahua Breed Standard." ChihuahuaClubofAmerica.com.

Traveling with a Chihuahua

Traveling with a Chihuahua can be one of the most delightful experiences for both you and your small companion. Chihuahuas, despite their tiny size, have big personalities, and they tend to enjoy being in the middle of the action. Whether you are embarking on a road trip, hopping on a flight across the country, or simply going for a weekend getaway, it is vital to prepare thoroughly. Proper preparation is the key to a smooth and stress-free journey, ensuring that your Chihuahua's safety and comfort are prioritized.

Preparing for the Trip

Before setting off on your adventure, it is important to get your Chihuahua ready for the trip. As creatures of habit, Chihuahuas can experience anxiety when their environment changes. Taking steps to prepare them ahead of time can help to ease any potential stress for both you and your dog.

Visit the Vet

One of the first steps in preparing for travel is to schedule a visit to the veterinarian. It is crucial to ensure that your Chihuahua is up-to-date on vaccinations and has a clean bill of health. This is especially important if you plan to fly, as many airlines require a health certificate from the vet confirming that your dog is fit for travel. During the visit, communicate with your vet about any issues your Chihuahua might have, such as motion sickness or anxiety. They may recommend certain medications to help calm your dog during the journey, making the experience more pleasant for both of you.

Travel-Friendly Gear

Investing in quality travel gear is essential for providing a safe and comfortable experience for your Chihuahua. If you are traveling by car, a well-fitting harness or pet seat belt is important. This gear keeps your dog secure and prevents them from moving too much around the vehicle, reducing the risk of distraction for the driver and potential injury for your dog. Always ensure that the harness is adjusted properly to fit your Chihuahua snugly.

For air travel, you will need a carrier that is approved by the airline. The carrier should be small enough to fit under the seat in front of you while also being spacious enough for your Chihuahua to stand, turn around, and lie down comfortably. Look for a carrier with proper ventilation so your dog can breathe easily.

Pack the Essentials

Once you have the vet visit and travel gear covered, it's time to think about what to pack. Making a comprehensive list of the items your

Chihuahua will need during the trip will help ensure you don't forget anything important. Here are some essentials to consider:

- **Food and Water Bowls**: Collapsible bowls are great for traveling. They are easy to pack and take up minimal space while providing a convenient way for your Chihuahua to eat and drink.
- **Leash and Harness**: Bringing along a leash and harness is essential for keeping control of your dog during stops. Make sure to have a sturdy leash that is comfortable for you to hold.
- **Familiar Blanket or Item**: Consider packing a blanket or another item that smells like home. This can provide comfort to your dog during the trip and help to ease any anxiety they may feel.
- **Treats and Waste Bags**: Pack enough treats to reward your Chihuahua for good behavior during the journey. Additionally, don't forget to bring waste bags for quick clean-ups during outdoor breaks.
- **First-Aid Kit**: Having a small first-aid kit with basic supplies can be helpful. Include items like antiseptic wipes, band-aids, and anything else your Chihuahua may need in case of minor injuries.
- **Favorite Toys**: Bringing along favorite toys can help keep your Chihuahua occupied during travel. Choose toys that are durable and provide mental stimulation, which can be especially useful during long journeys.

Taking the time to prepare your Chihuahua for travel not only enhances their experience but also ensures that both of you can enjoy your time together. By following these steps, you can create a more pleasant and stress-free environment for your furry friend as you embark on your adventures. Remember, a little preparation goes a long way in ensuring a fun-filled journey with your Chihuahua.

Traveling by Car

For many pet owners, taking a road trip with their Chihuahua is a common way to travel. These little dogs often enjoy being in the car, especially when precautions are taken to ensure their safety and comfort. Road trips can be exciting, and there are important tips to remember to make the journey enjoyable for both you and your furry friend.

Car Safety

When it comes to car safety, the first rule is to never allow your Chihuahua to roam freely in the vehicle. This could put them at risk during unexpected stops or accidents. Instead, securing your dog in a well-structured crate or carrier is the best option. A sturdy crate will keep your Chihuahua safe and contained, minimizing the chance of injury. If a crate isn't practical for your trip, consider using a dog seat belt harness. These harnesses attach to the car's seatbelt, providing a safe way for your dog to sit without being able to move around the cabin.

It is crucial to avoid letting your Chihuahua sit in your lap or on the passenger seat. In the case of a sudden stop, having them in those positions can lead to serious injuries. By keeping your Chihuahua secured in the back seat, you help ensure both their safety and your own. Take the time to test the harness or crate before the trip to ensure it's comfortable and secure.

Frequent Breaks

Long road trips can be tiring for both humans and pets. If you're planning to be on the road for an extended period, it's essential to take frequent breaks. Chihuahuas, though small, need opportunities to stretch their legs, relieve themselves, and hydrate. Plan to stop every couple of hours. During these breaks, you can allow your dog to go to the bathroom and take a short walk. This not only gives them the chance to relieve themselves but also helps prevent anxiety from being confined for too long.

Finding pet-friendly rest areas or parks along your route can make these stops more enjoyable. Ideally, choose locations where your Chihuahua can explore a little and enjoy some fresh air. It is also a great time for you to stretch and re-energize. Don't forget to bring water with you so you can hydrate your Chihuahua during these breaks. Having a portable water bowl can be very handy for this purpose.

Temperature Control

Temperature control is another vital aspect of traveling with your Chihuahua. These small dogs are sensitive to extreme temperatures, which can be a concern while on the road. Under no circumstances should you leave your Chihuahua alone in the car, especially on warm days. This can lead to overheating very quickly. Chihuahuas can become uncomfortable or distressed in hot conditions, so it's essential to use your car's air conditioning to keep the environment cool.

Similarly, in cold weather, ensure the car has enough heat to keep your pet warm and comfortable. Dress your Chihuahua in a dog sweater or coat if necessary, especially during the winter months. Pay close attention to how your dog is feeling during the trip. If they seem too hot or too cold, take immediate action to adjust the temperature or take a break to allow them to feel comfortable.

Remember, creating a comfortable environment in the car contributes significantly to your dog's overall travel experience. Ensure that your car is well-ventilated and the temperature is at a comfortable level for both you and your pet. Keep a close eye on your Chihuahua for any signs of discomfort or distress throughout the journey.

In summary, traveling by car with a Chihuahua can be a delightful experience when you take the necessary precautions to ensure their safety and comfort. By adhering to these simple guidelines — securing your dachshund properly, allowing frequent breaks, and controlling the car's temperature — you can create a pleasant road trip for both of you. Whether it's a quick jaunt or a long journey, your Chihuahua will appreciate the careful planning and attention you provide. Enjoy your adventures together!

Flying with a Chihuahua

Flying with a Chihuahua can be an exciting adventure, but it does require some extra planning and care. Many airlines allow small dogs to travel in the cabin, which makes it easier for you to keep your furry friend close. However, there are specific rules and guidelines you need to follow to ensure a smooth journey.

Carrier Requirements

First and foremost, you'll need to consider the carrier requirements set by the airline. Each airline has its own policies about how pets can travel, so it's essential to check these details in advance. Most often, your Chihuahua will need to be in a carrier that fits under the seat in front of you. This means the carrier must be the right size—not too big—and designed for safety and comfort. The carrier should have good ventilation to allow for airflow, and it should be secure to prevent any escape attempts.

Moreover, comfort is key for your Chihuahua. If your dog tends to get anxious, make the carrier a cozy space for them. You can do this by placing a familiar blanket or a favorite toy inside. This small gesture can help alleviate anxiety and make them feel more at home while flying.

Booking Your Flight

When it comes to booking your flight, it's good practice to call the airline ahead of time to confirm their pet policies. Not all airlines have the same rules, and space for pets in the cabin can be limited. It's wise to book early to secure a spot for your Chihuahua. During your call, be sure to inquire about any weight limits for in-cabin pets. Chihuahuas typically meet these requirements, but confirming details will give you peace of mind.

Pre-Flight Preparations

Before heading to the airport, it's important to prepare your Chihuahua for the flight. One way to do this is to acclimate them to their carrier. You can start by taking your Chihuahua on short car rides with the carrier, helping them feel more familiar with the space. This can prevent chaos on the day of your flight when they might feel overwhelmed.

Feeding your Chihuahua a light meal a few hours before traveling is also a good idea. This precaution can help reduce the risk of motion sickness during the flight, allowing for a more pleasant experience for both of you.

During the Flight

Once you're on the plane, it's time to make sure that your Chihuahua remains calm and comfortable. Keep the carrier securely under the seat in front of you for the duration of the flight. It is crucial not to open the carrier during the flight. Opening it might not only cause stress for your dog but could also lead to unexpected situations if your Chihuahua feels the urge to explore the unfamiliar environment.

If your furry friend begins to whine or bark during the flight, try to remain calm. Bring along some calming treats or their favorite chew toy. These items can provide comfort and distraction, easing any anxiety your dog may experience due to the new experience.

Accommodations and Local Regulations

After you land, you'll want to ensure that your Chihuahua is welcome wherever you plan to stay. Many hotels today offer pet-friendly accommodations, but it's always a good idea to call ahead and verify their pet policy. Some places might have breed restrictions or additional fees for having pets in the room.

Pet-Friendly Lodging

When searching for a place to stay, consider hotels that specially cater to pet owners. Look for amenities that will make your stay easier, such as dog parks where your Chihuahua can run and play, pet-friendly restaurants where you can dine together, or even special features like dog beds and bowls provided in your room. These extra touches can enhance the experience and provide comfort for both you and your Chihuahua.

Exploring Your Destination

Once you've settled into your accommodation, take some time to explore pet-friendly activities and locations in the area. Research parks, hiking trails, and beaches that allow dogs. This way, you can plan fun outings that include your Chihuahua. While enjoying these activities, remember to follow local regulations as well, particularly leash laws, to ensure that everyone has a safe and enjoyable experience.

Safety and Comfort

Throughout your travels, always keep your Chihuahua's safety and comfort as a top priority. Make sure they stay hydrated, especially in warmer weather, and avoid overexertion during your explorations. Be mindful of potential hazards in new surroundings, as unfamiliar environments can sometimes present risks that you may not expect. Keeping a watchful eye on your Chihuahua will help ensure that their experience is just as enjoyable as yours.

Conclusion

Traveling with a Chihuahua can be a fun and rewarding experience, but it requires thoughtful preparation and attention to detail. By following the right steps to ensure their safety, comfort, and health, you can enjoy stress-free adventures with your furry companion. Whether it's a road trip or a plane ride, a little planning goes a long way in making sure your Chihuahua enjoys the journey as much as you do.

References:

- American Kennel Club (AKC). (n.d.). *Traveling with Your Dog: Tips and Advice for Safe and Enjoyable Journeys.* Retrieved from https://www.akc.org

- PetMD. (2020). *How to Prepare for Traveling with Your Dog.* Retrieved from https://www.petmd.com

- Veterinary Partner. (2021). *Tips for Traveling with Pets*. Retrieved from https://www.veterinarypartner.com

Living in Small Spaces

Living in small spaces can be challenging for both humans and pets, but it doesn't mean that your Chihuahua can't live comfortably in a cozy environment. Chihuahuas, being small dogs themselves, are actually well-suited for apartment living and other confined spaces. However, ensuring they have a fulfilling and healthy lifestyle in a limited area requires some thoughtful adjustments and planning.

One of the most important things to consider is creating an environment where your Chihuahua has enough room to move around freely. Even though they are tiny, Chihuahuas still need space to stretch their legs, play, and explore. A small apartment or house should not feel restrictive for them if the space is used thoughtfully. Designating an area where they can comfortably sleep, eat, and play is essential to their well-being.

Creating a Dog-Friendly Space

In smaller living environments, it's key to set up a designated space for your Chihuahua where they feel safe and comfortable. Whether it's a cozy dog bed in a quiet corner or a small crate, having their own spot in your home allows them to feel secure. Chihuahuas are known to be sensitive to their surroundings, so creating a familiar space helps reduce anxiety.

You can also maximize vertical space, which is often underutilized in smaller living areas. Shelves, dog gates, or platforms can offer your Chihuahua a spot to perch, mimicking their natural instinct to observe from a higher vantage point. Just make sure that these elevated spots are safe and accessible for your dog.

Exercise and Mental Stimulation

Even though your home might be small, Chihuahuas still need to stay active and mentally stimulated. Regular walks outside are crucial for their physical health, but you can also provide them with indoor play opportunities. Consider interactive toys, puzzle feeders, and games like hide-and-seek that engage your dog's mind. A few minutes of play throughout the day can keep your Chihuahua happy, even if there isn't much space to roam indoors.

Another consideration is providing access to outdoor spaces, such as a dog park, where they can socialize and exercise in a larger area. Socializing with other dogs and experiencing different environments are important for their emotional well-being.

Keeping Things Clean

In small spaces, it's easy for your Chihuahua's belongings to start taking up more room than necessary. One of the key aspects of living with a dog in a small environment is staying organized. Use space-saving furniture that doubles as storage for toys, grooming supplies, and food, and keep their belongings in dedicated areas to minimize clutter. Regular cleaning is also important since Chihuahuas have a tendency to shed, and smaller spaces can accumulate dust or hair quickly.

Managing Noise and Anxiety

Chihuahuas are often sensitive to noise and may become anxious in a bustling environment. In small apartments or homes, noise can sometimes be amplified, which may stress your dog. To minimize anxiety, try to create a calm and quiet environment, especially in the areas where they rest. Using calming music or a white noise machine may help drown out external sounds. Additionally, a consistent routine—especially with feeding and bathroom breaks—can reduce stress and provide your Chihuahua with a sense of security.

Conclusion

Living in small spaces with a Chihuahua can be incredibly rewarding. With a little creativity and planning, you can make your home a comfortable and enriching place for both you and your dog. Ensuring they have enough room to play, rest, and explore, while also keeping their needs for exercise and mental stimulation in mind, will help your Chihuahua thrive in any space. By making small adjustments to your home and daily routine, you'll ensure that your Chihuahua feels happy, secure, and loved, no matter how big or small the space may be.

References

- American Kennel Club (AKC). "Chihuahua Temperament and Characteristics." Retrieved from https://www.akc.org.
- PetMD. "How to Make Your Dog Comfortable in Small Spaces." Retrieved from https://www.petmd.com.
- The Spruce Pets. "Creating a Pet-Friendly Apartment." Retrieved from https://www.thesprucepets.com.

Clothing and Accessories

Chihuahuas are known for their small size and big personalities, but they also come with some special needs when it comes to clothing and accessories. While their charming little outfits might be fun to dress them in, these items also serve a practical purpose. From providing warmth to offering safety, the right clothing and accessories are essential in ensuring your Chihuahua stays comfortable and protected. Here are some of the key clothing and accessories every Chihuahua owner should consider.

1. Dog Sweaters and Jackets

Chihuahuas are prone to getting cold, especially due to their small size and thin coats. In colder weather, it's crucial to have a few well-fitting sweaters or jackets to keep your Chihuahua warm. Sweaters made from soft, stretchy materials like cotton, wool, or fleece are great choices as they allow your dog to move freely while offering insulation. Pay special attention to the fit—too tight can cause discomfort, while too loose can lead to chafing or tripping.

When selecting a coat, look for options that cover not only the chest and back but also protect the neck area. A good-quality winter jacket or coat with a hood can help protect your Chihuahua from harsh winds and snow. Some coats even come with waterproofing, which is particularly helpful for rainy or wet conditions. Always remember that while Chihuahuas love the warmth, they also need a breathable fabric to ensure they don't overheat when indoors.

2. Boots for Protection

Chihuahuas, with their small paws and delicate skin, can easily be harmed by rough terrain, hot pavement, or icy conditions. Booties or protective shoes can provide much-needed protection for their feet. In the summer, the hot pavement can burn your dog's sensitive paw pads, and during the winter, the salt used to melt snow can irritate their paws.

A good set of dog boots will shield them from these elements and keep their paws safe.

Choose boots that are lightweight and flexible, as Chihuahuas need the freedom to move comfortably. Look for options with a secure fit to prevent them from slipping off during walks. Some boots even have anti-slip soles, which is an added bonus when you're out on slick surfaces. When fitting your Chihuahua for boots, ensure the shoes are snug, but not too tight, and allow them to walk naturally.

3. **Harness and Leash Sets**

A harness and leash are essential accessories for any Chihuahua owner. Due to their small size and delicate tracheas, traditional collars can put pressure on their throats, potentially leading to injuries. A harness evenly distributes pressure across their chest and back, making it much safer and more comfortable for walking. Harnesses also help prevent pulling and provide better control, especially when your Chihuahua gets excited and pulls on the leash.

Look for a harness made from soft, breathable material that's gentle on your Chihuahua's skin. Adjustable straps are key for finding the perfect fit, and ensure the harness is snug enough to prevent slipping without restricting movement. Leash sets made specifically for small dogs are also a great investment, as they are lighter and more manageable.

4. **Bowls and Travel Accessories**

While not strictly clothing, travel accessories are essential for a Chihuahua owner. These tiny dogs are often on the go, whether it's to the vet, on a trip, or a short car ride. A travel-friendly water bottle or bowl is a must-have to keep your Chihuahua hydrated during trips. Look for collapsible bowls or compact water bottles that are easy to pack and carry in a bag or car.

Additionally, a comfortable dog carrier or car seat is key for traveling. Chihuahuas are very small and need a secure, comfortable space during car trips. A well-designed dog carrier with a strap to secure it in place or a dog booster seat for the car will help keep your Chihuahua safe and snug. Many of these carriers come with a soft interior lining, giving your dog a familiar and cozy space to relax during travel.

5. Bandanas and Bowties

For owners who love dressing up their Chihuahuas, bandanas and bowties are simple, yet stylish accessories. These can be worn for special occasions or just to add some flair to your dog's everyday look. Bandanas come in a variety of colors and patterns, and they're easy to tie around your dog's neck without causing discomfort. Similarly, a small bowtie collar can make your Chihuahua look extra dapper for parties, photoshoots, or holiday events.

When choosing accessories, make sure they are not too tight or too loose. Comfort is always a priority, and you should ensure that your dog is not bothered by the extra fabric around their neck. Avoid accessories with small parts that can be chewed off and swallowed, as these can pose a choking hazard.

6. Sunglasses and Hats

For the fashion-forward Chihuahua owner, sunglasses and hats can add a touch of flair while also offering some practical protection. Sunglasses can shield your Chihuahua's eyes from the harsh glare of the sun, particularly in bright or snowy environments. Many small dog sunglasses are designed to block UV rays and reduce eye strain. As for hats, a lightweight sun hat or a soft beanie can help protect your Chihuahua's head and ears from the elements.

When selecting sunglasses or hats, it's essential to choose products designed specifically for small dogs. These accessories should fit comfortably on their tiny heads and not obstruct their vision or cause irritation. Always monitor your dog while they wear these items to ensure they're comfortable.

7. Raincoats and Ponchos

Raincoats or ponchos are essential for Chihuahuas who enjoy walks, even when the weather isn't perfect. These coats provide much-needed protection from the rain, keeping your Chihuahua dry and warm. Look for lightweight, water-resistant raincoats that are easy to put on and remove. Ponchos are another option that can cover your Chihuahua from head to tail, providing full protection from wet weather.

8. Personalized Tags

Lastly, personalized tags are a must-have accessory for every Chihuahua. These tags help ensure that if your dog ever gets lost, they can be easily identified. A durable, engraved tag with your Chihuahua's name, your contact information, and any special medical needs is invaluable. Attach the tag to their collar or harness to ensure they are always wearing it, even during outdoor adventures.

References:

- PetMD. (2022). *Best Dog Boots for Your Small Dog.* Retrieved from https://www.petmd.com/dog/care

- American Kennel Club (AKC). (2023). *Chihuahua Health and Care.* Retrieved from https://www.akc.org/dog-breeds/chihuahua/

- The Spruce Pets. (2021). *Essential Dog Gear for Chihuahuas.* Retrieved from https://www.thesprucepets.com

Chapter 10: Chihuahua Myths and Stereotypes

"They're Yappy": Barking Explained, and How to Manage It

Chihuahuas are often misunderstood due to certain myths and stereotypes surrounding their breed. One of the most common misconceptions is that they are excessively yappy. While it's true that Chihuahuas can be vocal, this trait doesn't define the breed entirely. In this chapter, we'll explore the reasons behind a Chihuahua's barking, why they tend to be more vocal than other breeds, and how to manage excessive barking effectively.

Why Do Chihuahuas Bark So Much?

The audible vocalization known as "barking" is a distinctive and frequently discussed characteristic of the Chihuahua breed. Chihuahuas are characterized by their notably loud voices, which is disproportionate to their size. Consequently, they are often described as "yappy," "high-strung," or "overreactive." However, beneath the apparent commotion lies a canine of notable intelligence, emotional sensitivity, and communicative aptitude, utilizing vocalizations as a means of expression. For a breed so profoundly attached to its human companions and so attuned to its surroundings, vocalizing is not merely a behavioral quirk; rather, it is a natural behavior that is underpinned by substantial, genuine reasons. A comprehensive understanding of the underlying causes of barking is paramount to its effective management.

Chihuahuas are known for their alert and observant nature. Their diminutive stature, a trait that is particularly pronounced in the animal kingdom, necessitates the compensation of this deficiency through an augmented state of vigilance. This characteristic renders them highly effective watchdogs, not due to their physical capacity to defend the home, but rather their ability to discern changes in their environment. A novel auditory stimulus, the movement of an individual in proximity to the window, or a subtle disturbance in the environment, such as a rustle, is sufficient to initiate the internal alarm system. This phenomenon, however, does not stem from paranoia but rather from an innate, hardwired instinct. For millennia, these canines have functioned as companions and protectors. While they may not possess an imposing physical stature, these canines are regarded by their owners as being just as adept as any guard dog. Their barking serves as the primary means of communication in the execution of their protective duties.

Beyond the act of guarding, Chihuahuas have been observed to vocalize in order to establish a connection with their owners. They are highly social animals that establish profound, frequently exclusive bonds with their peers. In the context of domestic canines, the barking behavior of a Chihuahua may be indicative of a perceived lack of attention, neglect, or a desire for acknowledgment. This behavior, which can be characterized as attention-seeking, is commonly exhibited by canines that have become habituated to playing an active role in their daily routines. A Chihuahua that is typically the recipient of excessive affection may exhibit vocal tendencies if it perceives itself to be marginalized. These canines exhibit a high degree of emotional responsiveness, which enables them to discern subtle cues that may not be consciously perceived by their owners. It is important to note that reacting to barking, whether positively or negatively, may inadvertently reinforce the behavior.

Another significant cause of incessant barking in Chihuahuas is separation anxiety. The profound bond that can develop between service animals and their owners can render prolonged periods of isolation highly distressing for the animal. This assertion is particularly salient in the context of canines that have not been socialized to function independently. In the context of separation anxiety, the barking of a Chihuahua can be understood as a manifestation of its emotional distress, serving as a cry for reassurance. This behavior is not indicative of misbehavior; rather, it is a manifestation of distress. The audible vocalizations, or barking, may commence immediately following one's departure and persist until one's return. In more severe cases, this type of barking can be accompanied by destructive behavior, pacing, or even self-harm. Comprehension of the emotional underpinnings of this barking is imperative to its resolution in a compassionate manner.

It is important to note that not all instances of barking can be attributed to defensive or emotional responses; occasionally, the barking may simply reflect a state of excitement. Despite their diminutive stature, Chihuahuas possess an abundance of energy. When they are in a state of contentment, they seek to disseminate this information to a global audience. The auditory stimulus of a treat bag, the visual cue of a leash, or the arrival of a favored individual can elicit barking in Chihuahuas, indicative of their anticipation. The barking that is indicative of excitement is typically characterized by its high pitch, brevity, and marked energy. While this phenomenon is not inherently problematic, if left unaddressed, it has the potential to evolve into a habit. Instructing canines to express enthusiasm through alternative means, such as maintaining composure or displaying enthusiastic tail wagging, can assist in mitigating auditory intensity while preserving their capacity to derive pleasure from the experience.

A further challenge that many Chihuahua owners encounter pertains to fear-based barking. Canines of smaller stature tend to exhibit heightened sensitivity to large movements, unfamiliar individuals, and unanticipated environments. In situations where Chihuahuas perceive a threat, whether it be the presence of a large dog, a sudden noise, or an unfamiliar individual, they are known to respond with a distinctive barking pattern that is both audible and persistent. This is an act of self-preservation. From the Chihuahua's perspective, barking functions as a form of communication intended to either deter perceived threats or, at the very least, alert its owner to an anomalous situation. While this behavior can be disconcerting, particularly in social environments, it is imperative to recognize that such vocalizations are indicative of fear rather than aggression. It has been demonstrated that socialization, training, and desensitization are effective methods for reducing fear in Chihuahuas, thereby enhancing their sense of security.

Therefore, what measures can be implemented to address this issue? The solution to this issue is threefold: consistency, patience, and a comprehensive understanding of canine behavior. One of the most effective strategies in this regard is the use of positive reinforcement in training. The training of commands such as "quiet" or "enough" can effectively communicate to the dog that the barking is no longer necessary. Timing is of the essence in this process. It is recommended that the command be issued in a calm and composed manner when the dogs are barking. The moment they cease barking, the appropriate reward should be administered. This could be achieved through the administration of a treat, the provision of a toy, or the utterance of verbal praise. It has been demonstrated that, over time, the domestic dog known as the Chihuahua learns that maintaining a state of silence is often indicative of positive outcomes, whereas the converse is also true, i.e., that excessive noise is often associated with negative consequences.

Another tactic that can be employed is redirection. In the event that a Chihuahua exhibits excessive vocalization, such as barking, with the apparent intent of garnering attention or eliciting excitement from its environment, it is advisable to attempt to redirect its focus. The introduction of a toy, the initiation of a training game, or the navigation to a novel section of the domestic environment can serve as effective strategies. This process facilitates a cognitive reset, effectively mitigating the underlying causes of the barking behavior. Mental stimulation has been demonstrated to be a particularly effective strategy in this regard. Toys such as puzzle toys, snuffle mats, and scent games have been shown to provide cognitive engagement that can alleviate the need for excessive noise.

A frequently overlooked aspect of bark control involves the necessity of avoiding inadvertent reinforcement of the targeted behavior. In the event that a Chihuahua emits a bark, and the owner responds promptly —by picking up the dog, feeding it, or even yelling—this serves as evidence that barking is an effective method of communication. Instead, it is recommended to wait for a moment of quiet and then to offer a reward for the calm behavior exhibited. It is imperative to understand that, over time, canines will establish a correlation between periods of silence and the allocation of attention, as opposed to the expression of vocalizations such as barking.

In the event that a Chihuahua's barking is associated with particular triggers, such as the sound of the doorbell or the sight of other canines, desensitization can serve as an effective intervention. The gradual introduction of the trigger in controlled, low-stress environments, coupled with the use of treats or praise as reinforcers, facilitates the acquisition of a neutral response. For instance, the doorbell can be rung gently while the Chihuahua is in a state of calm, followed by the provision of a reward for its ability to remain silent. The volume and frequency of the auditory stimuli should be gradually increased, with calm behavior being consistently reinforced. Through repetition, the trigger becomes an ordinary aspect of life, no longer eliciting a sense of alarm.

It is imperative to recognize that no efficacious behavioral solution is complete without the incorporation of exercise and enrichment. It has been demonstrated that a Chihuahua that is fatigued will be a less vocal Chihuahua. It is imperative to ensure that canines receive adequate physical activity and mental stimulation on a daily basis. It is important to note that this does not imply engaging in extensive physical activity, such as running long distances, or maintaining a constant level of stimulation. However, a balanced approach that incorporates a variety of activities, including brief walks, structured training, social interaction, and the use of interactive toys, has been shown to be highly effective in promoting well-being in canines. In the absence of adequate outlets, the energy and intellect of the Chihuahua may be redirected into undesirable behaviors, such as barking and chewing.

In instances where barking is rooted in separation anxiety, a more comprehensive approach involving emotional work is necessary to address the underlying issues. The process of habituating a canine to prolonged periods of solitude should be initiated with caution and gradualism. It is recommended that these activities be engaged in for brief periods initially, with the duration gradually increasing over time. It is recommended that a scent be left behind, such as a personal fragrance or a favored toy, to ensure the subject's continued presence. The utilization of ambient sounds, such as white noise, music, or pheromone diffusers, has been demonstrated to facilitate relaxation in canines during the absence of their owners. The utilization of crate training in a manner that does not employ it as a form of punishment but rather as a safe and comforting space has been demonstrated to be effective. It is imperative to maintain composure during the arrival and departure of others. It is imperative to maintain composure, adhere to a routine of a minimalist nature, and assist the canine in comprehending that transitions are to be expected and should not elicit panic.

In the event that an individual has attempted various remedial measures and the barking persists or intensifies, it may be advisable to seek the expertise of a professional. A certified dog trainer or veterinary behaviorist can offer customized strategies based on the specific situation of the animal in question. In some cases, the manifestation of barking may be indicative of underlying medical conditions, particularly if the occurrence is abrupt or deviates from the animal's typical behavior. In such cases, a comprehensive veterinary examination serves as an intelligent preliminary measure.

In conclusion, while Chihuahuas may have a reputation for being vocal, it is possible to train them to reduce their barking. This phenomenon, manifesting as a message, a symptom, and a behavior, is susceptible to comprehension and modification. By identifying the underlying cause of excessive barking—whether it be alertness, attention-seeking, fear, or excitement—and implementing consistent, reward-based strategies, it is possible to reduce this behavior and help the Chihuahua develop greater calm and confidence. Canine communication is a multifaceted phenomenon, with each breed exhibiting distinct vocal tendencies. In the case of Chihuahuas, for instance, the vocalizations tend to be more pronounced. However, with the proper equipment, it is possible to reduce the volume without diminishing the vibrant personality that distinguishes this breed and makes it so exceptional.

While barking is a natural and necessary form of communication for Chihuahuas, it can become a problem when it's excessive or constant. A comprehensive understanding of the underlying causes of Chihuahua barking is paramount to its effective management. Fortunately, there are practical, humane, and effective strategies that can help reduce and control barking while still respecting a dog's need to express itself. Excessive barking does not have to be a permanent trait; with time, consistency, and patience, most barking issues can be significantly reduced or eliminated.

A critical component of mitigating excessive barking is the utilization of positive reinforcement training. Rather than attempting to entirely eliminate barking, it is more effective to focus on teaching the Chihuahua to recognize when it is appropriate to be silent. The objective is not to induce silence in the dog, but rather to provide a clear cue that will assist in managing barking in a manner that is acceptable to all parties. A calm and consistent vocal command, such as "quiet" or "enough," can effectively communicate to the Chihuahua that it is time to desist from its actions. Timing is of the essence in this regard: the moment a barking episode concludes, immediate praise or a treat should be offered. It has been demonstrated that, with sufficient repetition, canines will develop an association between silence and receiving a reward. This association is a powerful motivator that can be used to encourage calm behavior.

In instances where barking is rooted in excitement or a need for attention, redirecting the canine's focus has been demonstrated to be a highly effective strategy. Rather than resorting to scolding or becoming frustrated, consider employing toys, training games, or tricks as effective tools to redirect the dog's energy. For instance, if a dog begins to bark when an individual passes by a window, it is recommended to redirect the dog away from the source of the stimulus. This can be accomplished by offering a toy or a simple command, such as "sit," followed by a reward. These minor adjustments have the potential to disrupt the Chihuahua's barking habit and redirect its attention toward more constructive and productive activities.

It is equally important to avoid unintentionally rewarding barking. In the event that a Chihuahua exhibits barking behavior and the guardian responds by offering food, physically picking up the dog, or even scolding it, the dog may interpret this behavior as a form of attention, which is the precise outcome the guardian was seeking. Instead, it is advisable to wait for a pause in the barking. It is important to offer praise or a treat as soon as your dog becomes quiet, even if only for a moment. This approach instills in them the understanding that maintaining composure and refraining from excessive vocalization are effective strategies for achieving their desired outcomes.

A critical strategy in this regard is desensitization, particularly in cases where barking is elicited by specific stimuli such as the doorbell, traffic, or unfamiliar individuals. The objective is to methodically acclimate the canine subject to the stimulus in a low-intensity manner while incentivizing tranquil behavior. To illustrate, the utilization of a recording of a doorbell at a subdued volume in conjunction with the provision of treats can be effective. The volume should be increased gradually over time, with quiet responses being reinforced. This approach assists in fostering a novel, more composed association with the stimulus in question.

The vocalization known as barking frequently serves as an indication that a canine's physiological or psychological requirements are not being adequately addressed. Despite their diminutive stature, Chihuahuas possess an impressive degree of vitality and acumen. It is imperative to ensure that adequate physical and mental stimulation is provided. It has been demonstrated that canines can be engaged and prevented from barking due to boredom through the implementation of short walks, interactive toys, training exercises, and puzzle games. It has been demonstrated that a fatigued canine is one that is less vocal, and the implementation of a consistent play schedule has been shown to significantly mitigate undesired noise.

In the event that a Chihuahua's incessant barking is indicative of separation anxiety, it is imperative that this issue be addressed in a direct manner. Canines that vocalize excessively in solitude are often exhibiting genuine distress. A helpful approach would be to gradually acclimate the dog to periods of solitude. Initiate brief departures, and ensure a prompt return to avoid causing distress to the canine. It is imperative to gradually extend the duration of the separation, while concurrently recognizing and rewarding calm behavior. The creation of a soothing environment, characterized by the presence of familiar olfactory stimuli, preferred playthings, and a comfortable bedding arrangement, has been demonstrated to play a pivotal role in the alleviation of anxiety. It has been demonstrated that tools such as calming music, white noise, and pheromone diffusers may also offer relief.

In certain instances, despite optimal efforts, excessive barking may persist or even intensify. In such cases, the provision of professional assistance has been demonstrated to be a highly effective measure. A certified dog trainer or behaviorist can evaluate a Chihuahua's specific triggers and behaviors to create a customized training plan. In more extreme cases, particularly when anxiety is the underlying cause, a veterinarian may prescribe medication as part of a comprehensive behavioral modification strategy.

The management of excessive barking in Chihuahuas does not entail the complete abatement of the behavior. Barking is an inherent aspect of their nature, serving as a spontaneous means of conveying their needs, emotions, and environmental perceptions. The objective is to facilitate comprehension regarding the appropriate circumstances, and to provide the necessary tools and a structured framework to foster feelings of security, confidence, and understanding. Through consistent training, the provision of adequate stimulation, and the establishment of a calm and supportive environment, it is possible to teach Chihuahuas to speak exclusively in designated situations, thereby enhancing their overall well-being and reducing stress levels.

Conclusion

Chihuahuas may be known for their vocal tendencies, but excessive barking is not a behavior that has to be accepted as part of the breed. By understanding the underlying reasons for barking and implementing consistent training techniques, you can reduce unwanted noise and help your Chihuahua develop into a well-behaved and content companion. With the right approach, barking can become manageable, allowing you and your Chihuahua to enjoy a peaceful and harmonious home.

References:

- American Kennel Club. "Chihuahua Dog Breed Information." AKC.org.
- PetMD. "Excessive Barking in Dogs." PetMD.com.
- The Spruce Pets. "How to Stop a Dog From Barking." TheSprucePets.com.
- VCA Animal Hospitals. "Behavioral Problems in Chihuahuas." VCAhospitals.com.
- DogTime. "Why Do Chihuahuas Bark?" DogTime.com.

"They're Mean": Root Causes of Aggression and How to Correct It

Chihuahuas are often stereotyped as aggressive or "mean," primarily due to their small size and bold personalities. Many people are surprised to learn that Chihuahuas are not naturally aggressive by nature. However, like any breed, they can develop behavioral issues, including aggression, if not properly socialized or trained. In this chapter, we will explore the root causes of aggression in Chihuahuas and provide strategies to address and correct these behaviors.

Root Causes of Aggression in Chihuahuas

Understanding the underlying reasons for aggression in Chihuahuas is crucial for addressing the behavior effectively. While no two dogs are the same, there are several common factors that can contribute to aggression in this breed:

Fear and Insecurity

Chihuahuas are naturally alert and often reactive to their environment. Small dogs can sometimes feel threatened by larger dogs, unfamiliar people, or new situations, which can lead to fearful aggression. If a Chihuahua perceives a situation as threatening, they may display aggressive behaviors as a means of self-defense. This fear-based aggression is often a result of poor socialization or past negative experiences.

Territorial Behavior

Chihuahuas are known to be protective of their home and their family. Territorial aggression occurs when a Chihuahua perceives intruders—whether people, animals, or even other dogs—as a threat to their territory. This behavior may manifest as growling, barking, or snapping, especially when visitors enter the home or when they encounter other dogs in their space.

Lack of Socialization

Early socialization is essential in shaping a well-adjusted dog. If a Chihuahua is not properly introduced to a variety of people, animals, and environments as a puppy, they may develop aggressive tendencies later in life. Poor socialization can lead to fear, anxiety, and uncertainty, all of which can contribute to aggressive behavior. Chihuahuas that have not been exposed to different situations may react aggressively to new experiences or unfamiliar faces.

Protective Instincts

Chihuahuas are naturally inclined to protect their owners. While this trait is often seen as a positive quality, it can lead to possessiveness or aggression when they feel their loved ones are in danger. If a Chihuahua perceives a threat, even if it's not significant, they may respond aggressively in an attempt to defend their family.

Pain or Discomfort

Aggression can sometimes be the result of physical pain or discomfort. If a Chihuahua is in pain due to an injury, illness, or an undiagnosed health issue, they may become irritable and more prone to aggression. It's essential to rule out any medical problems if your Chihuahua suddenly starts exhibiting aggressive behavior.

Overindulgence and Spoiling

Some Chihuahuas may develop behavioral issues due to overindulgence. If they are treated like "royalty" and never corrected when they display undesirable behavior, they may grow up thinking they are the "alpha" of the household. This can lead to issues with dominance and territorial aggression, as the Chihuahua believes it has the right to control situations and people.

How to Correct Aggression in Chihuahuas

While aggression in Chihuahuas can be concerning, it is a behavior that can often be corrected with proper training, patience, and consistency. Here are some strategies to address aggression in Chihuahuas:

Early Socialization

The best way to prevent aggression in Chihuahuas is by starting socialization as early as possible. Expose your Chihuahua to different people, pets, and environments when they are young, allowing them to experience a variety of situations in a controlled and positive manner. Puppy classes are a great way to introduce your dog to new experiences and build their confidence in social settings.

For adult Chihuahuas, gradual exposure to new people, pets, and places is still essential. Be patient and use positive reinforcement to encourage calm behavior during these experiences. Over time, this will help your Chihuahua feel more comfortable in unfamiliar situations and reduce fear-based aggression.

Positive Reinforcement

Positive reinforcement is one of the most effective ways to correct aggressive behavior. When your Chihuahua behaves calmly and appropriately, reward them with treats, praise, or affection. This helps them associate good behavior with positive outcomes. On the other hand, when they act aggressively, avoid reacting with anger or punishment. Instead, redirect their behavior and reward them when they calm down.

Redirect Aggressive Energy

If your Chihuahua starts to display aggression, such as growling or snapping, try to redirect their attention to something else. Offer them a toy or engage them in a game to distract them from the trigger. This helps to break the cycle of aggressive behavior and refocus their energy in a positive direction.

Set Boundaries and Consistency

Establish clear rules and boundaries for your Chihuahua, and be consistent in enforcing them. If your Chihuahua is allowed to behave aggressively in some situations but not in others, they may become confused and continue to display unwanted behavior. Consistency is key in helping them understand which behaviors are acceptable and which are not.

Desensitize to Triggers

If your Chihuahua becomes aggressive in specific situations—such as when visitors arrive or when encountering other dogs—desensitize them to these triggers in a gradual and controlled manner. For example, you can invite friends over regularly and reward your Chihuahua for staying calm when someone enters the home. Over time, your Chihuahua will learn that there is no need to act aggressively in these situations.

Provide Mental and Physical Stimulation

Aggression can sometimes be the result of pent-up energy. Chihuahuas are small but energetic dogs that require regular exercise and mental stimulation. Ensure that your Chihuahua gets enough physical activity through daily walks and playtime. Puzzle toys and training sessions can also help provide mental stimulation, which can reduce stress and frustration that may lead to aggression.

Seek Professional Help

If your Chihuahua's aggression is severe or if you're unsure how to proceed, consider seeking professional help from a certified dog trainer or behaviorist. They can assess your dog's behavior, identify the root cause of the aggression, and work with you to develop a tailored training plan. In some cases, a veterinarian may also recommend behavior modification techniques or medication if the aggression is linked to anxiety or pain.

Conclusion

While Chihuahuas may have a reputation for being "mean" or aggressive, the truth is that this behavior is often the result of fear, insecurity, poor socialization, or other underlying factors. With patience, proper training, and early socialization, most aggression issues in Chihuahuas can be managed and corrected. By addressing the root causes and using positive reinforcement techniques, you can help your Chihuahua become a well-adjusted and affectionate companion.

References:

- American Kennel Club. "Chihuahua Dog Breed Information." AKC.org.
- PetMD. "Aggressive Behavior in Dogs." PetMD.com.
- The Spruce Pets. "How to Stop Aggressive Behavior in Dogs." TheSprucePets.com.
- VCA Animal Hospitals. "Chihuahua Behavioral Issues." VCAhospitals.com.
- DogTime. "Understanding Aggression in Dogs." DogTime.com.

"Too Fragile for Kids": When It's True and When It's Not

Chihuahuas, often perceived as delicate due to their small size, are frequently labeled as "too fragile for kids." This stereotype leads many potential pet owners to assume that Chihuahuas are unsuitable for families with young children. However, this belief is not always accurate. While Chihuahuas do require careful handling and proper care, they can thrive in family environments under the right conditions. In this chapter, we will explore when the "too fragile for kids" myth is true and when it's not, providing insights into how to ensure a safe and harmonious relationship between Chihuahuas and children.

When the "Too Fragile for Kids" Myth Holds Some Truth

While Chihuahuas can be excellent companions, there are specific factors that make them less suitable for young children in certain situations. Their small size, combined with their sometimes delicate nature, can make them vulnerable in a household where rough play or accidental mishandling is common.

Small Size and Fragility

Chihuahuas are one of the smallest dog breeds, typically weighing between 2 to 6 pounds. Due to their small size, they are physically more fragile compared to larger dogs. This makes them more susceptible to injury, particularly from rough handling, accidental drops, or boisterous play. Children, especially toddlers and young kids who haven't yet learned proper handling techniques, may unintentionally hurt a Chihuahua by grabbing too tightly, dropping them, or startling them. The risk of injury is a valid concern, and this is where the "fragile" aspect of the stereotype holds some truth.

Sensitive Temperament

Chihuahuas are known for their alert, protective nature, and they can sometimes be more anxious and easily startled than other breeds. Children who are loud or overly excitable may cause a Chihuahua to feel threatened or overwhelmed. In these situations, a Chihuahua might react defensively, leading to growling, snapping, or even biting. This can be particularly challenging for families with children who aren't yet old enough to understand how to respect a dog's boundaries.

Unpredictable Behavior

Chihuahuas, like all dogs, can have varying temperaments. Some may be more tolerant of children, while others may not appreciate the attention or handling they receive. If a Chihuahua is not properly socialized or has had negative experiences with children in the past, they might develop a fear of children or exhibit aggressive behavior. This can make the dog seem "fragile" in the sense that they are more likely to react out of fear rather than trust.

When the "Too Fragile for Kids" Myth is Not True

Despite their small stature, Chihuahuas can make wonderful companions for families with children, as long as certain precautions and guidelines are followed. With proper socialization, training, and supervision, Chihuahuas can adapt to family life and enjoy close bonds with kids.

Proper Socialization from a Young Age

The key to having a Chihuahua co-exist peacefully with children is early and consistent socialization. Puppies who are raised around children tend to be more tolerant and adaptable to the energy and behavior of kids. Positive interactions with children—such as gentle petting, play, and teaching respect for the dog's boundaries—will help the Chihuahua develop confidence and trust in kids. The more positive exposure they have, the more likely they will become comfortable in a family setting.

Teaching Children How to Handle a Chihuahua

A crucial factor in ensuring a harmonious relationship between Chihuahuas and children is teaching kids how to handle the dog properly. Children must be taught to approach the dog gently, respect their space, and avoid behaviors that could startle or hurt the dog, such as pulling on ears or tails, grabbing too hard, or picking the dog up without permission. With appropriate guidance, many Chihuahuas are quite tolerant of children, and the bond they develop can be extremely rewarding.

Chihuahuas as Loyal and Protective Companions

Despite their size, Chihuahuas are incredibly loyal and can form strong bonds with family members, including children. They are known for their protective instincts, and some Chihuahuas may even act as "little guardians" of the family, watching over children and alerting parents to any potential dangers. This protective nature can make Chihuahuas a good match for families with older children who understand how to interact with dogs and appreciate their small but mighty protective instincts.

Energy Levels and Playfulness

Chihuahuas may be small, but they are often full of energy and playfulness, which can make them a fun and engaging companion for kids. They enjoy interactive play like fetch, running, and even learning new tricks. Chihuahuas who are adequately exercised and mentally stimulated are less likely to be stressed or anxious, making them more patient and tolerant of children. With proper exercise, Chihuahuas can thrive in a family environment and enjoy spending time with children.

How to Ensure a Positive Relationship Between Chihuahuas and Kids

If you're considering adding a Chihuahua to your family with children, there are steps you can take to ensure that everyone gets along:

Supervision

Always supervise interactions between your Chihuahua and young children, especially during the first few weeks of introducing the dog to the household. This ensures that the dog's boundaries are respected and that children don't accidentally harm or overwhelm the dog.

Training for Both Dog and Children

Invest in training for both your Chihuahua and your children. Teaching your dog basic commands, such as "sit," "stay," and "leave it," can help create a well-behaved pet. Meanwhile, educating your children on how to treat the dog gently and respectfully will foster a positive environment for both parties.

Provide a Safe Space for Your Chihuahua

Chihuahuas, like all dogs, need a space where they can retreat and rest when they feel overwhelmed. Provide your Chihuahua with a comfortable bed or crate where they can go to get away from the hustle and bustle of family life. This gives the dog a sense of security and helps reduce stress.

Conclusion

While it's true that Chihuahuas are small and need to be handled with care, the myth that they are "too fragile for kids" is not entirely accurate. With proper training, socialization, and supervision, Chihuahuas can make wonderful pets for families with children. Their loyalty, playful nature, and protective instincts can create a strong bond with kids, as long as both the dog and children are taught to respect each other's boundaries. The key is to ensure that both the Chihuahua and the children understand how to interact with one another in a safe and positive manner.

References:

- American Kennel Club. "Chihuahua Dog Breed Information." AKC.org.
- PetMD. "Can Small Dogs Be Good with Kids?" PetMD.com.
- The Spruce Pets. "Are Chihuahuas Good Family Dogs?" TheSprucePets.com.
- VCA Animal Hospitals. "Caring for Your Chihuahua." VCAhospitals.com.

- DogTime. "Chihuahua Behavior and Temperament." DogTime.com.

Hollywood vs. Reality: Media Portrayals vs. Real-Life Chihuahuas

Chihuahuas are one of the most recognizable dog breeds, thanks in part to their appearances in Hollywood films and media. From Paris Hilton's famous Chihuahua, Tinkerbell, to the talking Chihuahua in *Beverly Hills Chihuahua*, the breed has been glamorized and turned into a pop culture symbol. However, while the media often depicts Chihuahuas as glamorous, sassy, and full of charm, the reality of living with a Chihuahua is much more nuanced. Understanding the difference between these portrayals and real-life experiences can help potential dog owners decide if a Chihuahua is truly the right breed for them.

1. The Glamorous, High-Maintenance Chihuahua

In Hollywood films and celebrity culture, Chihuahuas are often seen as glamorous accessories. They are carried around in designer handbags, dressed in tiny outfits, and doted on by their owners like royalty. This portrayal has led to a perception that Chihuahuas are primarily fashion statements, beloved for their cute size and high-maintenance nature.

Reality:
While Chihuahuas may indeed enjoy the spotlight, the reality of owning a Chihuahua is far from the glamorous portrayal seen in movies. Yes, they are small, but this comes with unique challenges. Chihuahuas need regular care, including grooming, proper diet, and lots of attention. They are also known for being highly energetic, which may surprise those who expect them to be mere lapdogs. Their small size means they are more vulnerable to injury, so owners need to be extra careful with their safety, especially around other larger pets or small children. In short, they're not just a pretty accessory—they're full of personality and need proper care.

2. The Sassy, Spoiled Chihuahua

The image of a Chihuahua as a feisty, diva-like dog has been cemented by countless media portrayals, where they are shown as demanding and brash. From animated films to commercials, the Chihuahua is often depicted as a small dog with a big attitude. They bark loudly, snap at other animals, and act as if they own the world. This stereotype leads people to believe that Chihuahuas are simply "sassy" and might be difficult to manage.

Reality:
In truth, many Chihuahuas are affectionate and loyal companions. While they do tend to have bold personalities, they are also known for being extremely loving towards their owners. In fact, Chihuahuas often form deep bonds with their human family members and can become quite attached, making them excellent lap dogs. Yes, some Chihuahuas may act protective and be a bit yappy, but this is often a result of their alert nature and desire to keep their loved ones safe. The "sassy" image of Chihuahuas is often overstated in the media, and many are well-mannered and gentle if properly socialized and trained.

3. The Yappy, Uncontrollable Chihuahua

Hollywood movies and shows love to portray Chihuahuas as dogs that bark incessantly and are impossible to control. In *Beverly Hills Chihuahua*, the main character, Chloe, is constantly barking and causing chaos wherever she goes. This perpetuates the stereotype that Chihuahuas are yappy and always on edge. It's a common misconception that these little dogs are always loud and hyperactive.

Reality:
While it's true that Chihuahuas have a tendency to bark more than some other breeds, this behavior is often exaggerated in media portrayals. In reality, a Chihuahua's barking is usually a response to their environment. They are naturally alert and territorial, which means

they may bark at unfamiliar sounds or people. However, with proper training and socialization, Chihuahuas can learn to control their barking. Like any other dog, they benefit from structure, exercise, and positive reinforcement. Many Chihuahuas are calm and well-mannered when in a safe, familiar environment.

4. The Tiny, Fragile Chihuahua

One of the most common portrayals of Chihuahuas in the media is their portrayal as frail, delicate creatures that need constant protection. Movies often show them being carried around in handbags, wrapped in scarves, or bundled up like fragile treasures. This feeds into the idea that Chihuahuas are almost too small and too weak to live the life of an active dog.

Reality:
In reality, Chihuahuas are surprisingly tough for their size. While they are indeed small, they have a strong will and often exhibit the confidence of a much larger dog. Chihuahuas are active and energetic, and they thrive on regular walks, playtime, and mental stimulation. It's true that they are more vulnerable to injuries due to their size, but with proper care and supervision, they can live an active, happy life. Many owners find that Chihuahuas have a brave and even mischievous side, making them excellent companions for those willing to engage with their playful personalities.

5. The Single-Purpose, Fashionable Chihuahua

Media portrayals often paint the Chihuahua as a one-dimensional pet whose main job is to look cute. Whether it's appearing in a movie, strutting down a runway, or being carried around in a designer purse, Chihuahuas seem to be accessories rather than companions.

Reality:
Real-life Chihuahuas are complex, loving dogs with a variety of needs.

While they may look adorable in an outfit or curled up in a purse, they are so much more than just a fashion accessory. They need daily exercise, mental stimulation, and socialization to be happy and healthy. Many Chihuahuas are highly trainable and enjoy participating in activities like agility courses or obedience training. Their intelligence and eagerness to please make them great candidates for more active roles in their owners' lives. Far from being a passive accessory, a Chihuahua is a full-fledged member of the family with its own quirks, personality, and emotional needs.

Conclusion: A Balance Between Hollywood and Reality

While the media has undoubtedly shaped the image of the Chihuahua in fun and sometimes exaggerated ways, the reality of owning one is far richer. Chihuahuas are not just lapdogs or accessories; they are spirited, intelligent, and loving companions who thrive on interaction and affection. The Hollywood portrayal of Chihuahuas may have given them fame, but it's important to recognize that real-life Chihuahuas are full of personality and deserve the same level of care and attention as any other breed. Understanding both the charm and the responsibilities of owning a Chihuahua can ensure a happier, healthier relationship between you and your furry friend.

References:

- American Kennel Club (AKC). (2023). *Chihuahua Health and Care.* Retrieved from https://www.akc.org/dog-breeds/chihuahua/

- PetMD. (2022). *Chihuahua Characteristics and Care.* Retrieved from https://www.petmd.com/dog/breeds/c_dg_chihuahua

- The Spruce Pets. (2021). *Chihuahua Dog Breed Information.* Retrieved from https://www.thesprucepets.com

Chapter 11: The Senior Chihuahua

Signs of Aging

As your Chihuahua ages, their needs and behavior may change, and it's important to recognize the signs of aging so you can provide the proper care for your senior companion. Like all dogs, Chihuahuas experience a natural aging process, and while they can live long and healthy lives, there are some typical signs and symptoms that indicate your dog is becoming a senior. By understanding these signs, you can ensure that your Chihuahua continues to live a comfortable, happy, and healthy life in their golden years.

1. Slower Movement and Reduced Activity

As Chihuahuas get older, their activity levels often change noticeably. This change is usually due to natural aging processes. An older Chihuahua may not run as quickly, play as energetically, or seem as eager to go for walks as they once did. You might see them resting more often or choosing to lie down instead of chasing after a toy.

Several factors contribute to this slower pace. Joint stiffness is one common issue that affects older Chihuahuas. Similar to humans, dogs can experience arthritis, which makes movement painful. When joints do not function as they used to, activities that once brought joy may seem daunting. Additionally, older Chihuahuas can simply have lower energy levels than younger dogs. It can be tiring for them to participate in vigorous play or extended walks.

Adjusting your Chihuahua's exercise routine is essential as they enter their senior years. Although they don't need as much exercise as when they were younger, it is still important they stay active. Gentle movement helps maintain muscle mass and flexibility, supports joint health, and boosts overall well-being. A good starting point is to take shorter, more frequent walks. This approach allows them to enjoy the outdoors without overexerting themselves.

For example, instead of a 30-minute walk at a fast pace, consider breaking it into two 15-minute walks at a leisurely pace. This can make the experience enjoyable while still keeping them active. During these walks, pay attention to your Chihuahua's body language. If they seem tired or reluctant to continue, take a break or head back home. Providing plenty of opportunities for rest is just as vital as the exercise itself.

Gentle playtime can also be beneficial. Use toys that encourage light activity, like soft balls or plush toys that are easy to carry. Engaging in short games of fetch can provide a fun way to keep your Chihuahua moving lightly without the stress of vigorous exercise. This way, you can help them stay mentally stimulated and physically active without pushing their limits.

Monitoring your Chihuahua for any signs of discomfort is crucial. If they seem to be limping, favoring a leg, or exhibiting behaviors like excessive panting or whimpering, these may be indications that they are in pain. In such cases, consult with your veterinarian to address these concerns. Vets can provide guidance on appropriate exercise routines based on your dog's specific health needs.

When it comes to aging, proper nutrition also plays an important role. A balanced diet tailored to senior dogs is essential for maintaining their strength and energy levels. Nutrient-rich foods can help them manage their weight and support joint health. Consult with your vet about the best food options that will match your Chihuahua's age and health requirements.

Another aspect to consider is the environment. Ensure that your living space is comfortable and safe for a senior Chihuahua. Keep their favorite resting spots accessible and ensure they are free of any obstacles that could lead to falls or injuries. Low ramps can be beneficial if your Chihuahua struggles with stairs. Making small changes like these can support their independence while keeping them safe.

Socialization and gentle interactions are other great ways to keep your Chihuahua engaged. Allowing them to meet other calm dogs or people can provide mental stimulation and help combat any feelings of isolation. Be cautious and observant, ensuring interactions are stress-free and enjoyable for your dog.

Incorporating massage or gentle stretching exercises can also benefit an older Chihuahua. This can improve circulation and relieve any stiffness they may have. Lightly massaging their joints or legs can be soothing and can help them relax, making the process of aging a little easier for them.

Lastly, maintaining a regular check-up schedule with your veterinarian is vital for monitoring your senior Chihuahua's health. Regular visits will help catch any emerging health issues early. During these check-ups, your vet can provide advice on modifications to exercise, diet, and general care, making sure your Chihuahua stays healthy and happy in their later years.

These steps form a comprehensive approach to caring for an aging Chihuahua. By being attentive to their needs and adjusting their routines accordingly, you can ensure that they continue to lead a fulfilling life even as they slow down with age.

2. Weight Changes

Senior Chihuahuas may experience changes in their weight. Some may become overweight due to reduced activity levels, while others may lose weight because of decreased appetite or difficulty eating. Both extremes can be problematic for your senior Chihuahua's health.

If your Chihuahua starts to gain weight, it's essential to manage their diet by providing a balanced, age-appropriate food. Senior dogs often require fewer calories but more fiber to prevent obesity. On the other hand, if your Chihuahua is losing weight, it's important to have them checked by a veterinarian to rule out any medical conditions like dental issues, digestive problems, or illness that may be affecting their appetite or ability to eat.

3. Changes in Coat and Skin

As Chihuahuas age, their coat and skin often undergo noticeable changes. One of the first things you may see is a shift in the fur's appearance. It can lose its shine and may become thinner over time. You might also start to notice gray hairs, especially around the muzzle and face areas. This graying is a natural part of aging for dogs, much like how humans can experience silver strands in their hair. While it can be surprising to see, it's usually nothing to worry about.

In addition to changes in the fur, senior Chihuahuas may face drier skin. This dryness can make their skin feel rough or flaky. If you touch their skin and it doesn't feel smooth, this can indicate the need for better skin care. One common issue is the development of lumps or bumps on their skin. While many of these changes are harmless, it's crucial to monitor any new growths or variations. Some bumps can be benign, but others might require medical attention.

Regular grooming plays a significant role in maintaining your Chihuahua's coat and skin. Brushing their fur not only removes loose hair but also helps distribute natural oils that keep their coat healthy and shiny. Using a soft brush is usually best, as it can be gentle on their skin while still providing the necessary care. This routine can also serve as a bonding experience between you and your dog. When you make grooming a regular part of their schedule, it can help both you and your pet feel relaxed and comfortable.

Moisturizing shampoos can be another effective tool in your care routine. These shampoos can help hydrate their skin, making it less prone to dryness. When bathing your Chihuahua, opt for products specifically made for dogs. Human shampoos often contain ingredients that can irritate their skin. Follow the instructions on the bottle, and don't forget to rinse thoroughly to avoid leaving any residue. Aim for a bath every month or as needed based on their activity level and coat condition.

It's also important to keep a close eye on any changes in their skin texture. If you notice sores, swelling, or any abnormal changes in their coat, contacting a veterinarian is always a wise choice. They can provide a professional evaluation and determine whether treatment is necessary. Early detection of skin issues often leads to better outcomes and can prevent more serious health problems down the line.

Aside from their physical appearance, it's essential to consider how these changes might affect your Chihuahua's overall well-being. Older dogs may experience discomfort from their skin changes, which can impact their mood and mobility. Watch for signs that your dog is itchy or uncomfortable, such as excessive scratching or licking. If they seem restless or are adapting their behavior around certain activities, this may indicate they are feeling the effects of skin dryness or irritation.

Nutrition also plays a key role in skin health. A balanced diet rich in nutrients helps support a healthy coat and skin condition. Foods that contain omega-3 and omega-6 fatty acids can be particularly beneficial. These fatty acids assist in maintaining skin hydration and can help reduce inflammation. Consider looking into high-quality dog food that includes these ingredients or consult with your veterinarian about the best dietary options for your aging Chihuahua.

Hydration is equally important. Make sure your Chihuahua always has access to fresh water. Proper hydration can help prevent skin dryness and keep overall health in check. If your dog isn't drinking enough or seems disinterested in water, you might want to consider wet dog food or adding water to their kibble to encourage them to drink more.

Another way to support your Chihuahua during their senior years is through regular check-ups with the veterinarian. Routine appointments can catch potential issues early on and ensure your dog receives the appropriate vaccinations and treatments. These visits create a chance for you to ask questions and address any concerns you have regarding your dog's skin and coat. Your vet can recommend specific products or solutions tailored to your dog's needs.

Creating a comfortable environment at home is also essential for an aging Chihuahua. Soft bedding can ease discomfort from joint issues, while a consistent temperature can prevent skin irritation from extreme heat or cold. Pay attention to how your dog is resting and adjust their sleeping area to ensure they feel safe and relaxed.

Lastly, remember that aging is a natural process that comes with its own set of challenges and changes. Your senior Chihuahua will benefit from your understanding and care as they navigate these new phases in life. Be patient as they adapt, and continue to show them love and support through their changes. A little extra attention during this time can make a significant difference in their quality of life and happiness.

4. Vision and Hearing Decline

Just like humans, Chihuahuas can experience a decline in their vision and hearing as they age. Signs of vision problems in senior Chihuahuas may include squinting, difficulty navigating in low-light environments, or bumping into furniture and obstacles. Cataracts and retinal issues are common among older dogs, and they can lead to partial or complete blindness. If you suspect your Chihuahua's vision is deteriorating, consult your veterinarian, who may recommend an eye exam to check for conditions like cataracts or glaucoma.

Hearing loss is also common in senior Chihuahuas, and it may be more difficult for you to notice at first. Signs of hearing loss include your dog not responding to their name or common sounds (like the doorbell, barking, or commands) or appearing startled when you approach. Although hearing loss is irreversible, it is not a major cause for concern as long as your Chihuahua can still interact with you in other ways.

5. Changes in Behavior and Personality

You may notice that your senior Chihuahua's behavior and personality begin to shift. Some older dogs become more anxious or confused, especially in unfamiliar environments. They may become more clingy and desire more attention or, conversely, may become more withdrawn. If your Chihuahua suddenly exhibits changes in behavior, it could be due to cognitive dysfunction syndrome (CDS), a condition similar to dementia in humans. Symptoms of CDS include disorientation, disrupted sleep patterns, or forgetting previously learned commands.

It's also not uncommon for senior Chihuahuas to become more protective or irritable as they age. This can be due to physical discomfort or a decrease in their overall tolerance for certain stimuli. Understanding that these changes are a normal part of aging can help you address them with patience and compassion.

6. Dental Problems

Dental issues are common in senior Chihuahuas and can significantly affect their health. As they age, they are more likely to develop tartar buildup, gum disease, or tooth decay. These issues can lead to pain, difficulty eating, and even systemic infections if left untreated. It's important to regularly check your Chihuahua's teeth and gums and schedule regular dental checkups with your veterinarian.

Signs of dental issues in senior Chihuahuas include bad breath, difficulty chewing, drooling, or pawing at the mouth. Regular brushing, dental chews, and professional cleanings can help maintain their dental health and prevent painful conditions.

7. Incontinence or Difficulty with Bathroom Habits

Senior Chihuahuas may experience incontinence or have accidents indoors due to weakening bladder control. This is often a result of aging and can be caused by conditions such as urinary tract infections, kidney disease, or hormonal changes. If your Chihuahua is house-trained and begins to have accidents, it's important to consult your veterinarian to rule out any medical issues. In some cases, incontinence can be managed with medication or adjustments to their bathroom routine.

8. Joint and Mobility Issues

Arthritis is common in senior Chihuahuas, and it can affect their mobility. As they age, their joints may become stiff or painful, leading to difficulty walking, jumping, or climbing stairs. If you notice your Chihuahua is limping, having trouble getting up, or seems reluctant to move, it's important to address these symptoms. Pain management, joint supplements like glucosamine, and controlled physical therapy can help your senior Chihuahua remain mobile and comfortable.

Conclusion

Recognizing the signs of aging in your Chihuahua is essential to ensuring they continue to enjoy their later years. By staying attentive to their physical and behavioral changes, you can provide the right care and make adjustments to their lifestyle to enhance their quality of life. Regular veterinary visits, a balanced diet, and appropriate exercise are crucial components of caring for a senior Chihuahua. With the right care and attention, your senior Chihuahua can continue to be a loving and cherished companion well into their golden years.

References:

- American Kennel Club. "Caring for Senior Dogs." AKC.org.
- PetMD. "Senior Dog Care: What to Expect as Your Dog Ages." PetMD.com.
- VCA Animal Hospitals. "Aging in Dogs: Senior Dog Care." VCAhospitals.com.

- The Spruce Pets. "Signs of Aging in Dogs." TheSprucePets.com.
- DogTime. "How to Care for Your Senior Dog." DogTime.com.

Adjusting Their Routine

As your Chihuahua grows older, their needs and routines will inevitably change. Senior Chihuahuas, much like older humans, require more attention and care to ensure they remain comfortable and healthy in their later years. Recognizing and adjusting their daily routines can make a significant difference in their quality of life. In this chapter, we will explore how to adapt to the changing needs of your senior Chihuahua, from their exercise routine to their diet, and everything in between.

Understanding the Aging Process

As your Chihuahua enters their senior years, typically around 7 years of age or older, you may notice physical and behavioral changes. Their energy levels might decrease, and they may begin to slow down, which is completely normal for aging dogs. Joint stiffness, less enthusiasm for play, and more frequent naps are all signs of the natural aging process. However, it's important to note that these changes don't mean your Chihuahua's quality of life has to suffer. With proper care, you can help them maintain a comfortable and happy life as they age.

Adjusting Their Exercise Routine

One of the first things you'll notice as your Chihuahua ages is a shift in their energy levels. While younger Chihuahuas are often full of boundless energy, senior Chihuahuas may tire more quickly. This doesn't mean exercise should be eliminated; instead, it should be adjusted to suit their current abilities.

Shorter Walks: Instead of long walks, consider taking your senior Chihuahua on shorter, more frequent walks. Short walks throughout the day allow them to get some fresh air, stretch their legs, and stay active without overexerting themselves. Pay attention to their pace—if they seem to tire, it's okay to take breaks or cut the walk short.

Low-Impact Activities: Older Chihuahuas can still enjoy playtime, but their play routine may need to shift from high-energy activities to more gentle, low-impact games. Tossing a soft toy, playing with a puzzle feeder, or gently playing tug-of-war are great alternatives that will keep your dog mentally stimulated without taxing their joints.

Consider Joint Health: Senior Chihuahuas are more likely to experience joint stiffness or arthritis. If you notice your dog having difficulty walking or jumping onto furniture, consider investing in orthopedic beds and ramps to make their environment more comfortable. Joint supplements and medications may also be beneficial, but consult your vet to determine what's best for your dog.

Modifying Their Diet

A senior Chihuahua's dietary needs will evolve over time. As they age, their metabolism slows, and their body may not process food the way it used to. Adjusting their diet is crucial to maintaining their health and preventing obesity, which can further stress their joints and organs.

Senior Dog Food: Many brands offer specially formulated food for senior dogs. These foods are often lower in calories but still rich in the nutrients seniors need, such as fiber for digestive health and antioxidants for immune support. Make sure to choose a high-quality senior food that meets the specific needs of your Chihuahua.

Portion Control: Senior Chihuahuas are less active, which means they don't need the same calorie intake as younger dogs. Overfeeding can lead to weight gain, which is particularly harmful to small breeds. Monitor your dog's weight closely, and work with your vet to adjust portions accordingly.

Supplements: Consider adding joint supplements, such as glucosamine and chondroitin, to help support your Chihuahua's joints. Omega-3 fatty acids can also be beneficial for maintaining a healthy coat and reducing inflammation. Always consult your vet before adding new supplements to your dog's diet.

Hydration: Older Chihuahuas may be at greater risk of dehydration, especially if they have any kidney issues or other health concerns. Always provide fresh water, and monitor their drinking habits. Wet food can also help increase their water intake.

Regular Veterinary Check-ups

As your Chihuahua enters their senior years, regular veterinary visits become even more important. Senior dogs are at higher risk for developing health problems such as dental disease, heart disease, kidney failure, and cognitive dysfunction. Routine check-ups allow your vet to catch any potential issues early, giving your Chihuahua the best chance for effective treatment.

During these visits, your vet will likely recommend a senior wellness exam, which includes blood tests, urine tests, and a thorough physical exam. These tests can help detect underlying health issues that may not be immediately apparent. Your vet may also suggest more frequent check-ups—every 6 months instead of once a year—as your dog ages.

Mental Stimulation and Comfort

As your Chihuahua ages, it's just as important to keep their mind sharp as it is to care for their physical health. Cognitive dysfunction syndrome (CDS) is common in senior dogs and is similar to dementia in humans. Symptoms may include confusion, disorientation, disrupted sleep patterns, or a decrease in interest in activities they once enjoyed.

Interactive Toys: Keep your Chihuahua's brain active by providing interactive toys such as puzzle feeders or treat-dispensing toys. These will engage their minds and give them something to focus on, which is especially helpful if they're becoming less physically active.

Routine and Comfort: Senior dogs thrive on routine. Keeping a consistent schedule for feeding, walks, and playtime can help reduce anxiety and confusion. Additionally, make sure your Chihuahua has a comfortable, quiet place to rest. An orthopedic bed can help ease joint pain and improve sleep quality.

Grooming: As Chihuahuas age, they may become less tolerant of grooming sessions, but regular brushing is still essential. Their coat may thin out or become dull with age, and brushing not only keeps them looking their best but also promotes circulation and strengthens your bond with them. Be gentle and patient, especially if they seem more sensitive than before.

Conclusion

Adjusting your senior Chihuahua's routine doesn't just mean slowing down; it's about making small changes that enhance their comfort, health, and happiness. By making adjustments to their exercise, diet, and mental stimulation, you can ensure that your senior Chihuahua continues to lead a fulfilling life. Remember, their golden years are an opportunity to provide extra love and care, showing them the same devotion they've given you throughout their life. With the right care, your Chihuahua will continue to be a joyful companion, filled with love and gratitude, well into their senior years.

References:

- American Kennel Club (AKC). (n.d.). *Caring for Your Senior Dog.* Retrieved from https://www.akc.org
- PetMD. (2020). *How to Care for an Older Dog: Tips for Senior Dog Health.* Retrieved from https://www.petmd.com
- Veterinary Partner. (2021). *Senior Dog Care: Maintaining Your Pet's Health in Their Golden Years.* Retrieved from https://www.veterinarypartner.com

Vet Visits and Medications

As your Chihuahua ages, their health needs evolve, requiring more attention and care. Senior Chihuahuas, typically considered to be over the age of 7, often experience changes in their health and behavior. One of the most important aspects of caring for a senior Chihuahua is ensuring they receive regular vet visits and appropriate medications to help maintain their quality of life.

Regular Vet Visits for Senior Chihuahuas

Annual vet visits are essential for dogs of all ages, but they become even more critical as your Chihuahua enters their senior years. A thorough veterinary checkup helps identify potential health issues early, allowing for quicker intervention and better outcomes. Senior Chihuahuas are prone to a range of health conditions, including dental disease, arthritis, heart disease, and kidney problems. Regular vet visits ensure that any emerging concerns can be addressed before they become serious.

During these visits, your vet will typically perform a physical exam, checking your dog's weight, heart rate, respiration, and overall body condition. Blood tests and urine samples may also be taken to evaluate the function of major organs such as the liver, kidneys, and heart. These tests can help detect conditions like diabetes, liver disease, or hypothyroidism, which are common in older Chihuahuas.

Your vet may also recommend additional screenings such as X-rays to check for arthritis, particularly if your Chihuahua has been showing signs of stiffness or discomfort. This is especially important because Chihuahuas are small dogs with delicate joints, making them more susceptible to joint problems like arthritis as they age.

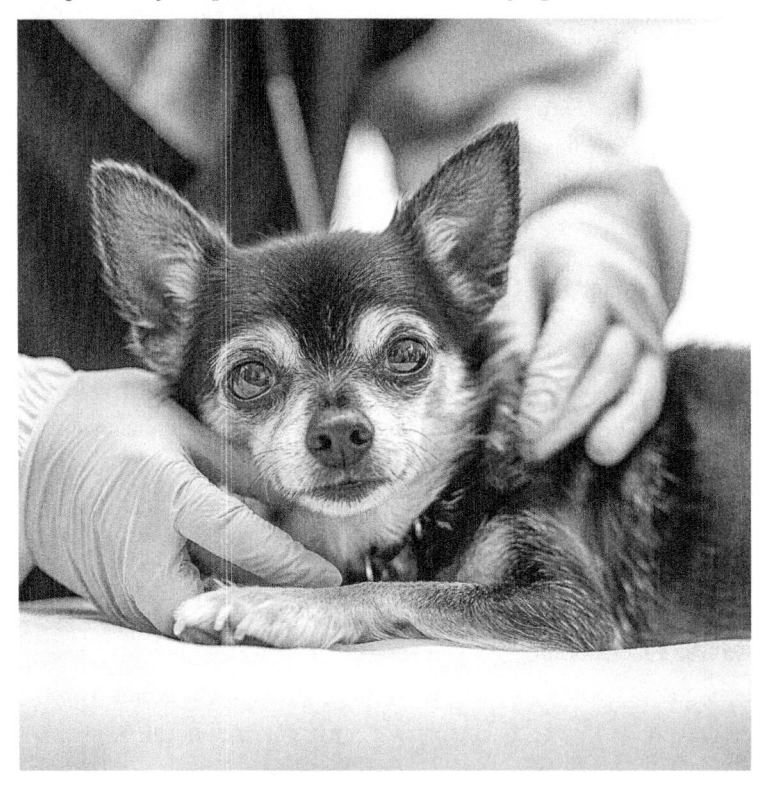

Medications for Senior Chihuahuas

As your Chihuahua ages, they may require medications to manage chronic health conditions or improve their quality of life. The specific medications will depend on the health issues your Chihuahua faces, but common conditions in senior Chihuahuas that often require treatment include arthritis, heart disease, kidney disease, and dental issues.

Arthritis and Joint Pain: Chihuahuas, like many small dog breeds, are prone to developing arthritis, which can lead to pain, stiffness, and difficulty moving. Nonsteroidal anti-inflammatory drugs (NSAIDs) are commonly prescribed to reduce inflammation and provide pain relief. Your vet may also recommend supplements like glucosamine and chondroitin, which support joint health and help manage arthritis symptoms.

Heart Disease: Senior Chihuahuas are prone to heart problems, particularly mitral valve disease, a condition where the heart's mitral valve becomes leaky and inefficient. Medications such as ACE inhibitors or diuretics may be prescribed to help manage this condition, improve heart function, and reduce fluid buildup. Regular vet checkups are critical in managing heart disease to prevent further complications.

Kidney Disease: Kidney function can decline as Chihuahuas age, leading to a condition called chronic kidney disease. Symptoms may include increased thirst, frequent urination, and weight loss. Medications and dietary changes can help manage kidney disease, and in some cases, your vet may recommend supplements like omega-3 fatty acids to support kidney function.

Dental Medications: Dental health is particularly important in senior Chihuahuas. Periodontal disease is common in older dogs and can cause pain, tooth loss, and systemic infections. Medications, along with regular dental cleanings, can help manage this issue. Your vet may also prescribe antibiotics if your Chihuahua is suffering from an infection due to dental disease.

Pain Management and Comfort

As senior Chihuahuas age, they may develop aches and pains, particularly from conditions like arthritis. It's essential to work closely with your vet to manage your Chihuahua's discomfort and ensure they can maintain an active and fulfilling life. Aside from medications, there are other strategies to help manage pain and improve their comfort.

One of the best ways to help a senior Chihuahua with joint pain is by providing a comfortable, supportive bed. Orthopedic dog beds are particularly beneficial, as they provide extra cushioning for sore joints. Additionally, regular, low-impact exercise can help keep your dog's joints moving and prevent stiffness. Short, gentle walks or light indoor play can help maintain mobility.

Consider implementing ramps or stairs to assist your Chihuahua in getting onto furniture or into your car. These small modifications can reduce the strain on their joints and make movement easier for them.

Monitoring Changes and Adjusting Treatment

Senior Chihuahuas may go through subtle but significant changes in their health and behavior. It's essential to closely monitor their day-to-day behavior and notify your vet if you notice anything unusual. Changes such as a decrease in appetite, increased thirst, lethargy, or difficulty moving could indicate an underlying health issue.

It's also important to adjust their medications and treatment plan based on their changing needs. As your Chihuahua ages, their response to certain medications may change, or they may need new medications to manage emerging conditions. Always follow your vet's guidance regarding dosages and treatment regimens to ensure your Chihuahua is getting the best care possible.

Conclusion

Caring for a senior Chihuahua requires dedication and attention to their evolving health needs. Regular vet visits and timely medication can help manage common age-related issues such as arthritis, heart disease, and kidney problems. By staying proactive in your Chihuahua's healthcare, you can help ensure that their senior years are as comfortable and fulfilling as possible. The love and care you provide now will contribute to their well-being for years to come, allowing you to cherish their companionship well into their golden years.

References

- American Veterinary Medical Association (AVMA). "Senior Dog Care." Retrieved from https://www.avma.org.

- PetMD. "Arthritis in Dogs: Causes, Symptoms, and Treatment." Retrieved from https://www.petmd.com.
- American Kennel Club (AKC). "Heart Disease in Dogs." Retrieved from https://www.akc.org.
- Veterinary Partner. "Chronic Kidney Disease in Dogs." Retrieved from https://www.veterinarypartner.com.

End-of-Life Decisions

As Chihuahuas enter their senior years, there is a likelihood that changes in their behavior, health, and energy levels will become apparent. These alterations are an inherent component of the aging process; nevertheless, they have the potential to engender concern among pet owners. As with canines of other breeds, the geriatric years of a Chihuahua's life are accompanied by a series of challenges. It is imperative to be prepared for the inevitable end-of-life decisions that may arise. It is imperative for pet owners to possess the knowledge and skills necessary to provide proper care for their senior Chihuahuas. This includes understanding the signs of aging and making informed decisions about their pets' care during their final days. Being a responsible and compassionate pet owner entails a comprehensive understanding of the needs of aging animals.

1. A study of the Aging Process of the Chihuahua

The average lifespan of the Chihuahua is approximately 12 to 20 years, with proper care enabling them to attain long, healthy lives. However, as individuals age, they are susceptible to physical and cognitive changes. As a Chihuahua reaches its senior years, it may exhibit signs of physical decline, including a reduction in speed, the development of joint ailments, alterations in coat texture or color, and dental changes. These changes can also be accompanied by a decline in sensory abilities, such as reduced vision and hearing. The onset of these signs typically occurs around eight years of age, though individual variability exists based on factors such as health and genetics.

The following are some of the most common signs of aging in Chihuahuas:

Decreased energy levels: It is not uncommon for older Chihuahuas to exhibit increased sleep patterns and a reduction in activity levels when compared to their younger counterparts.

Problems associated with joints: Canines of the Chihuahua breed are predisposed to health problems, including arthritis, which can result in impaired mobility.

Cognitive dysfunction: Canine cognitive dysfunction syndrome (CDS) is a condition that can affect older dogs, causing symptoms such as confusion, disorientation, and changes in behavior.

Dental issues are a concern. Canines of advanced age are predisposed to periodontal disease and dental caries, which can result in impaired mastication and discomfort.

Alterations in appetite and body mass: Canines in their senior years frequently undergo alterations in their appetite, with some exhibiting a loss in body mass despite adequate nourishment.

It is imperative to comprehend these alterations, as it enables one to adapt their care routine and adopt a more patient approach when dealing with their aging canine companion. Regular veterinary checkups are imperative to monitor their health, identify potential issues early, and ensure that their senior years are as comfortable as possible.

2. The Timing of End-of-Life Decisions

One of the most challenging decisions that pet owners must make is determining when it is appropriate to say goodbye to their animal companion. Canines of the Chihuahua breed, like all dogs, will eventually reach a point where their quality of life diminishes due to age-related diseases, injuries, or conditions that cannot be reversed. The recognition of when to make end-of-life decisions for a dog is a deeply personal and emotional process. However, it is imperative to assess the condition of the dog objectively and take their well-being into consideration.

Indications that a Chihuahua may be approaching the end of its life include the following:

The presence of severe pain or discomfort is a key indicator. In the event that a canine companion is persistently in a state of discomfort from which no treatment seems to offer solace, it may be necessary to consider the option of euthanasia. Indications of discomfort manifest through vocalizations such as whining, impaired mobility, or alterations in behavior.

The presence of either anorexia or weight loss of a significant magnitude may be indicative of a underlying medical condition. If a Chihuahua exhibits a cessation of appetite and/or significant weight loss, this may be indicative of a grave health concern that is not amenable to treatment.

The presence of incontinence or the loss of bodily functions is a concern. In the event that a canine patient has lost the capacity to regulate their bladder or bowels, and this loss has occurred despite the administration of medical treatment, it may be indicative of a significant health decline.

The patient exhibited a loss of mobility. If a Chihuahua's mobility is significantly diminished, and its quality of life is adversely affected by its inability to ambulate, jump, or even stand, this may suggest a progressive deterioration in its health condition.

Severe cognitive dysfunction: Canine subjects manifesting signs of confusion, disorientation, or a complete lack of recognition of familiar individuals may be indicative of advanced age-related cognitive issues.

The decision to euthanize a dog is never an easy one, but it is imperative to do so when the animal's suffering outweighs its quality of life. It is imperative to consult with a veterinarian, as they can provide guidance in making this decision. These professionals are able to evaluate the health status of the dog, offer guidance, and facilitate comprehension of the range of available options.

3. A Case for Palliative Care for an Aging Canine of the Chihuahua Breed

In the event that a Chihuahua is in the latter stages of life but is not yet prepared for euthanasia, palliative care can be a viable option to ensure optimal comfort during the final months or years. The primary objective of palliative care is to manage pain, ensure the patient's comfort, and enhance their quality of life, without making the attempt to cure the underlying illness.

A senior Chihuahua may require palliative care, which may include the following key elements:

The management of pain: The administration of pain relief medications, anti-inflammatory drugs, or joint supplements may assist in the management of pain, particularly in canines afflicted with arthritis or other age-related conditions.

The following dietary adjustments have been implemented: A diet that is specifically formulated for senior canines, one that is often characterized by a reduced fat content and an increased fiber content, has been shown to facilitate improved digestion and maintain optimal weight.

Mobility aids: The utilization of joint supplements, ramps, or orthopedic bedding has been demonstrated to facilitate enhanced mobility and promote restful sleep devoid of discomfort for canines.

It is imperative to engage in regular monitoring to ensure optimal outcomes. It is imperative to schedule regular veterinary appointments to monitor the progression of your Chihuahua's health condition and adjust their treatment regimen accordingly.

The provision of mental stimulation and comfort is of paramount importance. It is imperative to provide familiar routines, toys, and activities that can stimulate Chihuahuas mentally and emotionally during their senior years.

4. The practice of euthanasia, which is defined as the act of ending a life to alleviate suffering, involves the implementation of various methods to ensure a dignified farewell for the deceased.

Euthanasia is a difficult decision, but one that is often made in the best interests of the animal when a Chihuahua's suffering becomes unbearable. It is imperative to acknowledge that euthanasia is a painless process, designed to provide canines with a peaceful and dignified end. Prior to arriving at a decision, it may be advisable to allocate time for quality interaction with the dog, thereby fostering enduring memories and articulating a personalized farewell. Some owners elect to be present during the procedure to offer comfort, while others prefer to say their goodbyes before the process begins.

Veterinarians have the capacity to perform euthanasia at their clinic, or in some cases, they may offer home euthanasia services so that your Chihuahua can pass in the comfort of their own space. It is imperative to consult with a veterinarian to thoroughly understand the procedure and to inquire about the available options for post-mortem care, such as cremation or burial.

5. It is imperative to honor the life of a senior Chihuahua.

Following the demise of a Chihuahua, it is imperative to allocate time for the process of grief and to recall the profound love and companionship that the canine provided. One might consider creating a memory box containing the animal's favorite toys, collar, or a lock of fur. Many pet owners also opt for cremation or preservation of their pet in a distinctive manner, such as the creation of a paw print keepsake or the establishment of a memorial.

The Chihuahua, in its advanced years, occupies a unique place in the human-canine bond, and the conscientious and compassionate approach to end-of-life decisions ensures that these animals depart this world with the respect they deserve.

References:

- American Kennel Club (AKC). (2023). *Caring for Your Senior Dog.* Retrieved from https://www.akc.org/expert-advice/health/caring-for-your-senior-dog/
- PetMD. (2022). *End of Life Care for Dogs: Knowing When to Say Goodbye.* Retrieved from https://www.petmd.com/dog/care/end-life-care-dogs-knowing-when-say-goodbye

- The Spruce Pets. (2021). *Euthanasia for Dogs: Making the Decision to Say Goodbye.* Retrieved from https://www.thesprucepets.com

Chapter 12: Heartwarming Chihuahua Stories

Owner Stories

Chihuahuas, with their big personalities and small frames, often leave an indelible mark on the lives of their owners. They have a unique ability to offer both companionship and protection, despite their size, and their antics can bring joy to any household. In this chapter, we'll share some heartwarming stories from Chihuahua owners who have experienced the love, loyalty, and humor that come with having a Chihuahua as a companion.

1. Max, the Fearless Protector

Emily, a single mother living in a quiet suburban neighborhood, had always wanted a small dog to keep her company. She decided to adopt a Chihuahua after hearing how loyal and affectionate they could be. Emily met Max, a three-year-old rescue Chihuahua, at her local shelter. Max immediately stood out—his big brown eyes and bold stance made it clear that he was no ordinary dog.

After adopting Max, Emily quickly learned just how protective and devoted Chihuahuas could be. One evening, as she was walking home from the grocery store with Max by her side, a stranger approached her on the sidewalk. Max, who had never shown any signs of aggression before, suddenly lunged at the stranger, barking fiercely. The man backed away, startled by Max's small but determined stance. Emily was shocked but grateful, realizing that Max had not only become her best friend but also her protector. Since that day, she has felt safe knowing that Max will always have her back, no matter how big or intimidating the situation may be.

2. Bella's Journey of Healing

Mark and Lisa had always been dog lovers, and after the passing of their family's beloved golden retriever, they felt an emptiness that needed to be filled. They decided to adopt a dog from a local shelter, and that's when they met Bella, a timid six-month-old Chihuahua. Bella was shy and withdrawn, unsure of people after being abandoned by her previous owners. She had trouble trusting anyone and would hide under the couch whenever new people came around.

Over time, Mark and Lisa worked patiently with Bella, helping her overcome her fears. They spent hours cuddling, playing, and slowly gaining her trust. Bella's transformation was gradual but remarkable. As weeks passed, Bella started coming out of her shell, her playful and loving personality emerging. Eventually, she became so bonded to Mark and Lisa that she followed them everywhere, never leaving their sides.

But the most heartwarming moment came one winter evening. Lisa was going through a difficult time after a family member's illness. One night, as Lisa sat on the couch, feeling overwhelmed and teary-eyed,

Bella climbed onto her lap and nuzzled her face. For the first time, Bella licked away Lisa's tears, offering comfort in a way no human could. From that moment on, Bella became the emotional support Lisa didn't even know she needed, always offering affection and companionship when times were tough.

3. Chico's Unexpected Fame

Tara, a freelance artist, adopted her Chihuahua, Chico, when he was just a tiny puppy. She instantly fell in love with his curious and fearless nature. As a small dog, Chico had a unique ability to fit into her work environment and keep her company as she painted in her studio. However, one day, Tara took a picture of Chico while he was lounging on her art supplies, and little did she know, this photo would change their lives forever.

Tara shared the picture of Chico on social media, and it quickly went viral. People from all over the world fell in love with the charming little dog with the big, expressive eyes. What started as a cute photo snowballed into an online phenomenon. Tara began receiving messages from people asking for prints of her art featuring Chico, and soon she started posting more pictures of him in different adorable poses.

Before long, Chico had become an internet sensation, with fans following his every move. Tara even started a small business selling artwork, merchandise, and accessories inspired by Chico's adventures. Despite all the attention, Chico remained as lovable and down-to-earth as ever, always by Tara's side. Thanks to Chico's unexpected fame, Tara was able to combine her love for art with her deep bond with her Chihuahua, creating a new chapter in her life.

4. Rosie's Therapy Work

Sam had always been a calm and gentle soul, but after a difficult period in his life involving health struggles and personal losses, he found himself feeling isolated and withdrawn. He had a dog growing up, and he knew that having a companion again would help, so he decided to adopt a Chihuahua. That's when he met Rosie, a spunky, outgoing Chihuahua with a playful personality that instantly lifted Sam's spirits.

As Rosie grew older, Sam noticed something remarkable about her. Rosie had an innate ability to sense when Sam was feeling down or anxious. She would curl up on his lap, nuzzle him, and stay close whenever he was upset. Rosie's comforting presence gave Sam a sense of calm, and he began to feel more connected to the world around him.

Eventually, Sam decided to take Rosie to a therapy dog training program. Rosie passed with flying colors, and soon the two were volunteering at local hospitals, nursing homes, and community centers. Rosie quickly became a favorite of the patients, spreading joy with her gentle demeanor and her love for cuddles. Sam realized that Rosie was not only helping him heal but was also making a significant impact in the lives of others. Rosie's ability to offer comfort and companionship to those in need made her more than just a pet—she was a true therapy dog, touching hearts wherever she went.

5. Peanut's Brave Heart

Kendra and her young daughter, Lily, were looking for a dog to complete their family. They found Peanut, a small Chihuahua with a big heart, at an adoption event. Peanut was shy at first, but Lily's gentle nature helped Peanut warm up to her quickly. From the beginning, Peanut and Lily formed a special bond.

One afternoon, as Kendra was cleaning the kitchen, she heard Peanut barking frantically in the living room. When she rushed to see what was happening, she found that Lily had accidentally knocked over a vase and shattered it on the floor. Lily, startled and afraid, was trying to pick up the broken pieces when Peanut jumped in front of her and barked loudly at Kendra to get her attention.

Kendra realized that Peanut was trying to protect Lily from the glass shards, guiding her away from the dangerous area. Peanut's protective instinct kicked in, and he wasn't afraid to take action. From that day forward, Kendra knew that Peanut was not only a loving companion but also a brave protector of her family.

Conclusion

Chihuahuas, though small in size, have big hearts and even bigger personalities. They show us every day that love comes in all shapes and sizes, and their stories prove just how deeply they impact the lives of their owners. From protectors and healers to internet stars and therapy dogs, Chihuahuas bring joy, comfort, and laughter to everyone they meet. Their loyalty and affection know no bounds, and the bond they share with their families is truly special.

References:

- American Kennel Club. "Chihuahua Dog Breed Information." AKC.org.
- PetMD. "Chihuahua Behavior and Temperament." PetMD.com.
- The Spruce Pets. "Chihuahua Stories of Loyalty." TheSprucePets.com.
- DogTime. "Heartwarming Chihuahua Stories." DogTime.com.

Famous Chihuahuas

Chihuahuas are not only beloved by their owners for their loyalty and feisty personalities, but they've also captured the hearts of millions worldwide through their appearances in pop culture. These tiny dogs have become icons in movies, television, and even the world of fashion. Despite their small stature, they often leave a large imprint on the public's imagination. Here are a few famous Chihuahuas who have made their mark in the spotlight:

1. Taco Bell's Chihuahua (Gidget)

One of the most famous Chihuahuas in pop culture history is the Taco Bell Chihuahua. This adorable dog appeared in a series of commercials for the fast-food chain during the late 1990s and early 2000s. Known for her catchphrase, "Yo quiero Taco Bell" (I want Taco Bell), this Chihuahua became an unforgettable symbol of the brand. Her role in the commercials not only made her a household name but also solidified Chihuahuas as a dog breed with a larger-than-life personality. Gidget, the Chihuahua who played the Taco Bell dog, became a true pop culture icon, and her commercials are still fondly remembered today.

2. Bruiser Woods (Legally Blonde)

In the 2001 hit movie *Legally Blonde*, Reese Witherspoon's character, Elle Woods, is never without her beloved Chihuahua, Bruiser. Bruiser is not just any dog; he's portrayed as a fashion-forward, pampered pooch who accompanies Elle everywhere, even to law school. His role in the film helped highlight Chihuahuas as stylish and spunky companions, contributing to the breed's popularity during the early 2000s. Bruiser's charm and loyalty made him a fan favorite, and his playful character added warmth and humor to the movie's overall feel. Bruiser is so memorable that he even made an appearance in *Legally Blonde 2: Red, White & Blonde*, proving that the bond between a Chihuahua and their owner can be just as important as any legal case.

3. Chloe (Beverly Hills Chihuahua)

Beverly Hills Chihuahua (2008) brought the world of Chihuahuas to the big screen in a fun and heartwarming way. The film's protagonist, Chloe, is a pampered Chihuahua who finds herself lost in Mexico and must rely on her street smarts and newfound friends to find her way home. Chloe, voiced by Drew Barrymore, is a prime example of the breed's feisty and courageous spirit, showing that even the tiniest dog can face big adventures. The movie was a commercial success, and Chloe's character became a symbol of bravery, loyalty, and the importance of friendship. *Beverly Hills Chihuahua* helped introduce Chihuahuas to a new generation of dog lovers, showcasing their charm and unique personalities.

4. Rico (The Secret Life of Pets)

In the animated movie *The Secret Life of Pets* (2016), Rico is a Chihuahua who plays a supporting role in the group of pets who embark on an adventure through the city. While not the main character, Rico's comedic presence and ability to perform tricky tasks made him a memorable part of the film. His character showcases how Chihuahuas, despite their size, can hold their own in a group and be a crucial member of any team. Rico's antics and personality continue to endear him to fans of the movie.

5. Papi (Beverly Hills Chihuahua 2 & 3)

In addition to Chloe, *Beverly Hills Chihuahua* has another famous Chihuahua: Papi. Voiced by George Lopez, Papi is the charming and lovable dog who falls in love with Chloe. His character is a perfect blend of humor and heart, as he is brave and always willing to do whatever it takes to protect those he loves. Papi's appearances in the sequels *Beverly Hills Chihuahua 2* and *Beverly Hills Chihuahua 3* solidified his place in pop culture and demonstrated how these little dogs could have big personalities and hearts. Papi became a role model for loyal and loving Chihuahuas everywhere.

6. Dog (The Mask)

In the 1994 classic *The Mask*, the character of Stanley Ipkiss (played by Jim Carrey) has a sidekick in the form of his adorable Chihuahua, simply named Dog. Though Dog's screen time is limited, the small dog's relationship with Stanley adds a heartwarming touch to the movie. His loyalty to Stanley, even in the face of chaotic adventures, is an example of the unwavering bond between Chihuahuas and their owners.

7. Georgette (Oliver & Company)

Oliver & Company (1988), a Disney animated film, features a sassy and sophisticated Chihuahua named Georgette. Voiced by the legendary Bette Midler, Georgette is a pampered pet who initially seems self-absorbed but eventually proves to be a loyal friend. Her character showcases a more refined, high-society version of the Chihuahua, and she quickly became a favorite for her snarky remarks and glamorous personality. Georgette's role in the movie further cemented the idea of Chihuahuas as small, but full of attitude and flair.

Conclusion

From commercials to Hollywood movies, Chihuahuas have earned their spot in the hearts of millions around the world. These tiny dogs, with their big personalities, have become beloved symbols of loyalty, humor, and courage in popular culture. Whether it's Gidget, Bruiser, Chloe, or Papi, these famous Chihuahuas have proven time and again that size is no measure of heart. As we continue to see more Chihuahuas in the spotlight, it's clear that these little dogs have a lasting impact on the world of entertainment—and in our hearts as well.

References:

- American Kennel Club (AKC). (n.d.). *Famous Dogs in Pop Culture: Chihuahuas.* Retrieved from https://www.akc.org
- PetMD. (2021). *Top Famous Dogs in Movies and TV Shows.* Retrieved from https://www.petmd.com
- IMDb. (n.d.). *Beverly Hills Chihuahua (2008).* Retrieved from https://www.imdb.com

Adoption Transformations

Chihuahuas are small in size, but they have a heart full of love and a spirit that is larger than life. Their resilience, loyalty, and unique personalities have made them a beloved breed for many dog owners. However, not all Chihuahuas come from happy beginnings. For some, their journey begins in a shelter or a rescue center, where they are waiting for the chance to transform into the loving companion they were meant to be. These stories of adoption serve as a powerful reminder of the impact a second chance can have on both a dog's life and that of their human family.

A New Beginning for Bella

Bella was a shy and timid Chihuahua when she was brought to a local shelter. She had been surrendered by her previous owners, who no longer had the time or resources to care for her. At just 5 years old, Bella had already lived through a great deal of uncertainty, but she was about to embark on a life-changing journey.

When Sarah, a first-time dog owner, visited the shelter, Bella was the last dog she expected to connect with. Bella cowered in the corner of her kennel, avoiding eye contact with anyone. However, there was something about her soft brown eyes that pulled Sarah in. After spending some time with Bella, Sarah realized that Bella's hesitation was rooted in fear, not unkindness. With patience, Sarah built a bond with Bella, slowly gaining her trust.

After Bella's adoption, Sarah provided her with a stable home, where she could finally relax. Over time, Bella blossomed into a confident and affectionate companion. Her transformation was remarkable. Bella began to engage more in play, follow Sarah around the house, and even enjoy cuddles. Sarah made sure to maintain a gentle and loving environment that allowed Bella to thrive. Now, Bella's days are filled with joy, and she has become Sarah's loyal best friend. The transformation from a frightened, neglected dog to a happy, loved Chihuahua is a testament to the power of adoption.

Max's Road to Recovery

Max was rescued from an overcrowded puppy mill, where he had spent the first two years of his life in a cage, without the socialization or proper care he needed. The conditions were harsh, and Max had developed severe anxiety, making it difficult for him to trust people. He was afraid of everything – even his own shadow. His tiny body had scars from being kept in cramped, filthy spaces, and his eyes seemed to reflect his troubled past.

When Max was taken in by a rescue organization, they immediately began his rehabilitation. They introduced him to a foster family that had experience with rehabilitating anxious dogs. The first few weeks were challenging as Max had trouble adjusting to his new surroundings. He was scared of people, loud noises, and even the simplest things like walking on a leash.

However, with time and a lot of patience, Max began to open up. His foster family helped him work through his fears, using positive reinforcement to build his confidence. After months of rehabilitation, Max was adopted by Lily, a kind woman who had a special place in her heart for shy dogs. Lily was drawn to Max's gentle spirit and knew that, just like her, he needed a little extra time to adjust to his new life.

Max's transformation was slow but steady. With Lily's constant care, love, and understanding, he learned to trust again. He now enjoys long walks, belly rubs, and playing with his favorite squeaky toys. Max may have had a rough start, but with the love of his new family, he is now a happy and secure Chihuahua who is enjoying the life he always deserved.

Luna's Rescue from the Streets

Luna's story highlights how community support and kindness can change lives. She was discovered roaming the streets of a small town, looking thin and dirty. This stray dog had clearly been left behind, and no one could say how long she had been alone. Fortunately, a nearby rescue group noticed Luna and sprang into action to help her. Their quick response demonstrates the impact that concerned citizens can have on animals in need.

Once rescued, Luna was taken straight to the veterinarian. There, the doctors assessed her condition and found that she was not only underweight but also suffering from mange and a severe ear infection. These health issues were serious, but Luna's gentle nature and eagerness to connect with the volunteers made her story even more compelling. Despite her sad past, Luna showed a strong spirit and a great desire to love and be loved. This highlights how important it is for rescue organizations to provide not just medical care but also emotional support to animals who have faced hardships.

As time went on, Luna began to transform. Her recovery was gradual but remarkable. With proper nutrition and medical treatment, she started to regain her strength. Volunteers at the rescue group worked tirelessly to help Luna learn to trust again. They offered her gentle affection and positive experiences, which slowly brought out her playful personality. It was heartwarming to see how the kindness of the volunteers helped Luna heal, both physically and emotionally. With every passing day, Luna became more and more like the joyful dog she was meant to be.

After several months of recovery in foster care, Luna's big break came when a loving family decided to adopt her. This family had two young children who were excited to welcome a dog into their home. The moment they met Luna, there was an instant connection. The children were thrilled to have a new friend, and Luna sensed their genuine affection. It didn't take long for her to adapt to her new life. The love and care she received in her forever home made a world of difference.

Luna quickly became a loyal companion, joining in the family's daily activities and playtime.

Luna's journey from being an abandoned street dog to a cherished family pet is truly inspiring. Her story serves as a reminder that every animal deserves a chance. It shows how vital it is to support local rescue groups that work tirelessly to save these animals. By raising awareness and contributing to such organizations, people can make a difference in the lives of countless animals like Luna.

Many groups rely on donations and volunteers to carry out their mission. Just a small financial contribution can help provide food, medical care, and shelter for animals in need. Additionally, volunteering time at a local shelter can significantly impact both the animals and the community. It can be a fulfilling experience for those who lend their time to help socialized and care for neglected pets. This kind of involvement not only helps the animals but also strengthens community bonds as people come together for a common cause.

For those considering adopting a pet, it is essential to understand the commitment involved. Owning a pet requires time, effort, and resources. Prospective pet owners should think about their lifestyle and how a pet would fit into it. Researching the breed, understanding their needs, and preparing the home are vital steps in the adoption process. This ensures that the new pet will receive the right care, leading to a happier and healthier life for the animal.

Adopting a rescue dog like Luna can be incredibly rewarding. Many rescue pets come with unique stories that highlight their resilience and capacity for love. While they might have been through tough times, with patience and care, they can thrive in a new environment. It is important to provide them with stability and consistency as they adjust to their new homes.

In the case of Luna, her playful spirit blossomed as she settled into her new family. She became a source of joy and laughter for the children. They taught her tricks, played games, and included her in daily family routines. Each moment spent together further strengthened their bond. Luna's transformation from a frightened, malnourished dog to a vivacious family member serves as a powerful reminder of the healing power of love and attention.

As her story shows, community involvement and compassion can make a difference in the lives of animals in distress. Whether you are volunteering or considering adopting, your actions can have a lasting impact. Every small step contributes to creating a safer environment for animals like Luna, who are in desperate need of love and care. Through collective efforts, many more success stories can emerge, transforming lives and inspiring others to act in kindness.

The Power of Adoption

Adoption is a powerful act that can change lives. When a family chooses to adopt a dog, such as a Chihuahua, they are stepping into a journey filled with love and transformation. Many Chihuahuas arrive at shelters due to various reasons. They could have been abandoned, neglected, or simply surrendered by their previous owners. These dogs are often confused and scared. They show signs of anxiety and fear, which stem from their past experiences. When a Chihuahua is given a second chance, it can lead to remarkable changes.

When a Chihuahua finds a forever home, the transformation can be dramatic. Initially, these dogs may tremble at the sound of a doorbell or flinch at sudden movements. However, with time and patience, they begin to settle into their new environment. It is heartwarming to see them grow more confident and content. An example of this transformation can be seen when a new owner introduces a routine. Simple actions such as regular feeding times, daily walks, and playtime can help create structure for the dog. As the Chihuahua learns to trust their owner, the fear starts to fade.

Adoption is not just providing a dog with a roof over their head. It involves changing their whole life. For many Chihuahuas, adoption means learning what love feels like. In a safe and loving environment, these dogs begin to thrive. They develop a bond with their owners that can be very special. For example, a Chihuahua that once hid at the back of a kennel may start to follow its new owner around the house. This is a sign that the dog feels secure and has begun to trust again.

All dogs, including Chihuahuas, have a remarkable ability to adapt. They may come from troubling pasts, but with the right care, they can blossom into cherished pets. Resilience is a common trait among these furry friends. With enough love, they eventually learn what it means to be part of a family. Adopting a Chihuahua gives them this opportunity, and it can be a rewarding experience for both the dog and the owner.

To help a Chihuahua adjust after adoption, it is important to establish a routine. A predictable schedule can help alleviate anxiety. For instance, feeding the dog at the same time every day helps them feel secure. Regular walks not only provide physical exercise but also mental stimulation. Chihuahuas are curious and enjoy exploring their surroundings. Introducing them to new places gradually can boost their confidence.

Another aspect of helping a Chihuahua is socialization. Exposing them to various experiences, people, and other animals can positively impact their behavior. Starting with quiet, low-stress environments can make a big difference. Gradually introducing them to busier settings allows them to adjust comfortably, building their confidence along the way. This process is crucial for overcoming their initial fears and anxieties.

Training is also a key part of the adoption journey. Simple commands like "sit," "stay," and "come" can be taught using positive reinforcement. Using treats to reward good behavior encourages the dog and helps establish a bond. It is important to be patient during this training process. Chihuahuas may take some time to learn, especially if they are timid. Celebrating small successes can make a huge difference in their training journey.

Emotional health is another important factor post-adoption. Many Chihuahuas may carry emotional scars from their past. Building a loving relationship takes time and effort. Creating a safe space where the dog can retreat when feeling overwhelmed is beneficial. For example, a cozy dog bed in a quiet corner can serve as a comfort zone. This allows them to feel secure when they need it most.

Playtime is essential in enriching the life of an adopted Chihuahua. Engaging them with toys, games, and interaction is crucial for their development. Toys that encourage problem-solving can stimulate their minds. Activities like hide-and-seek or fetch help build trust between owner and pet while keeping the dog active. A happy Chihuahua will show signs of joy, like wagging their tail and being playful with their owners.

The joy of having a Chihuahua as a companion is immense. They often form close bonds with their families and can become very affectionate. Daily cuddles, playtime, and even quiet moments together play a significant role in strengthening this bond. The simple act of petting your dog can release calming hormones for both the dog and the owner.

In addition to physical and emotional benefits, adopting a Chihuahua can also teach important values. It encourages responsibility and compassion. Dog ownership provides lessons about caring for another living being. Children who grow up with pets often develop a greater sense of empathy and understanding. They learn the importance of treating animals with kindness and care, which can lead to a more nurturing attitude towards all living things.

Chihuahuas can also become excellent companions for individuals and families alike. They can adapt to various living conditions, whether it be in a large house or a small apartment. Their small size makes them suitable for different environments. Their playful nature and loyalty can make them wonderful friends. Many owners find that their Chihuahuas provide comfort and joy in their lives every day.

In summary, the adoption journey for a Chihuahua is filled with opportunities for growth and transformation. By providing a safe, loving home, owners can witness a joyful change in their adopted dog. Through routine, socialization, and training, a Chihuahua can flourish and become a beloved member of the family. The impact of adoption is powerful, creating lasting bonds that bring happiness to both the dog and their new owners every single day.

Conclusion

The stories of Bella, Max, and Luna are just a few examples of the incredible transformations that occur when a Chihuahua is adopted. Each of these dogs was given the opportunity to start fresh, and they are now living their best lives with families who cherish them. Adoption is a powerful choice that can make a lasting difference, not only for the dogs but also for the people who open their hearts to them. These transformations remind us that with patience, love, and care, every dog—regardless of their past—deserves a chance to thrive.

References

- American Kennel Club (AKC). "Adopting a Rescue Dog: What to Know." Retrieved from https://www.akc.org.
- Petfinder. "The Benefits of Adopting a Rescue Dog." Retrieved from https://www.petfinder.com.
- The Spruce Pets. "How to Adopt a Dog from a Shelter or Rescue." Retrieved from https://www.thesprucepets.com.

Funny or Surprising Moments

Chihuahuas are small in size but carry huge personalities. Their quirky behaviors, funny antics, and surprising moments are some of the most endearing traits of this little breed. From their fierce loyalty to their unexpected bursts of energy, Chihuahuas never fail to leave their owners with memorable stories to tell. In this chapter, we'll share a few heartwarming and hilarious Chihuahua tales that highlight their unique charm and lovable nature. Whether it's a surprising show of bravery or an unexpected act of mischief, these stories remind us that a Chihuahua's love and personality know no bounds.

1. The Chihuahua Who Took on a Big Dog

One of the most surprising traits of Chihuahuas is their immense bravery despite their tiny size. Often, they act as though they're much bigger than they actually are, and that's exactly what one Chihuahua, named Max, proved when he decided to protect his owner from a much larger dog.

Max's owner, Sarah, was walking through the park one afternoon when a larger dog came charging toward them. The dog was twice the size of Max, and Sarah was immediately concerned that her tiny Chihuahua would be scared and run away. But Max wasn't fazed. As the large dog got closer, Max stood his ground, puffed up his chest, and began barking furiously. The larger dog, confused by Max's boldness, hesitated before backing away, leaving Sarah in awe of her Chihuahua's bravery.

It's these kinds of moments that prove just how fearless Chihuahuas can be. Despite their small size, they often see themselves as protectors, ready to face any challenge head-on, especially when it comes to protecting their beloved human.

2. The Chihuahua Who Loved the Vacuum Cleaner

Most dogs are terrified of vacuum cleaners, running and hiding as soon as they hear the familiar buzzing sound. But not all Chihuahuas are the same, and one in particular, named Bella, took it to a whole new level.

Bella's owner, Laura, was vacuuming the living room one day when Bella, who normally hid under the couch at the sound of the vacuum, surprised everyone. As Laura moved the vacuum closer, Bella started chasing it around the room, barking and wagging her tail excitedly. Every time Laura pushed the vacuum forward, Bella jumped on top of it and tried to "ride" it as if it were some kind of toy. Bella had no fear and was completely fascinated by the vacuum cleaner, much to the amusement of everyone who witnessed the spectacle.

Laura had never seen anything like it—most dogs would run for cover, but Bella seemed to see the vacuum as her new playmate. This funny story highlights just how much Chihuahuas can surprise their owners with their unexpected quirks and behaviors.

3. The Chihuahua Who Was Always the Ringbearer

One of the most heartwarming stories comes from a couple named Kate and Ben, who had a Chihuahua named Oscar. Oscar was a beloved member of their family, and when they decided to get married, they couldn't imagine the big day without him. So, they made Oscar an honorary ringbearer.

On their wedding day, Oscar wore a tiny tuxedo and was responsible for carrying the rings down the aisle. His little suit and bowtie matched perfectly with the wedding theme, and everyone smiled as he proudly trotted down the aisle, his tail wagging with excitement. But the real surprise came during the ceremony.

As the couple exchanged vows, Oscar, who had been sitting quietly next to the best man, suddenly decided it was time to join in. He jumped onto the altar, walked straight up to the bride and groom, and sat beside them as though he was officiating the ceremony. The guests erupted in laughter as Oscar gazed at the couple with wide eyes, clearly pleased with himself for being such an important part of the celebration.

Kate and Ben couldn't stop laughing at the unexpected guest of honor, and they felt that Oscar had truly made their wedding day even more special. Oscar's perfect timing and calm demeanor proved that sometimes, the smallest members of the family can have the biggest impact on the most important moments.

4. The Chihuahua Who Loved to Help in the Kitchen

It's not uncommon for Chihuahuas to want to be close to their owners, especially when food is involved. But one Chihuahua, named Charlie, took his love for the kitchen to a whole new level.

Charlie's owner, Mary, was making cookies one afternoon, and Charlie, as usual, was following her around the kitchen. However, this time, Mary noticed something strange—Charlie was sitting up on his hind legs, staring intently at the countertop, where she had placed a bowl of cookie dough. As she moved around the kitchen, Charlie would carefully climb onto a chair, making sure he stayed as close as possible to the action. He was so focused on the dough that when Mary turned her back for just a moment, Charlie managed to snag a small chunk of dough with his tiny paws.

Mary couldn't help but laugh at Charlie's persistence. He was so eager to be involved that he had managed to sneak some dough when she wasn't looking. From that day on, Charlie became the unofficial kitchen assistant, keeping Mary company during every baking session and occasionally enjoying a small, safe treat (away from the chocolate chips!).

5. The Chihuahua Who Knew How to "Talk"

Chihuahuas can be incredibly vocal, and one particular Chihuahua named Rico became famous in his household for his unique "talking" skills. Rico's owner, Tim, discovered that Rico had an uncanny ability to mimic certain sounds, like the ringing of the doorbell or the microwave timer. However, it wasn't until one day when Tim said, "Do you want to go for a walk?" that Rico really amazed everyone.

To Tim's surprise, Rico let out a series of high-pitched barks that sounded remarkably like "walk" in a Chihuahua voice. Rico's ability to mimic words left everyone laughing and amazed at how quickly he had picked up on the pattern. Tim decided to encourage Rico's talking by asking him questions and rewarding him when he responded. Before long, Rico was not just mimicking sounds, but engaging in what seemed like a conversation with his owner. Rico's "talking" moments became a favorite activity in their household and were always sure to bring smiles to everyone's faces.

Conclusion: The Charm of Chihuahuas

These heartwarming stories showcase just how special and unpredictable Chihuahuas can be. Whether it's their unexpected bravery, hilarious quirks, or their ability to surprise us with their intelligence and charm, Chihuahuas have a way of making life more interesting. Their ability to bring joy, laughter, and heartwarming moments into our lives is one of the many reasons why they hold such a special place in the hearts of their owners.

References:

- American Kennel Club (AKC). (2023). *Chihuahua Characteristics and Care.* Retrieved from https://www.akc.org/dog-breeds/chihuahua/

- PetMD. (2022). *Chihuahua Characteristics and Care.* Retrieved from https://www.petmd.com/dog/breeds/c_dg_chihuahua

- The Spruce Pets. (2021). *Chihuahua Dog Breed Information.* Retrieved from https://www.thesprucepets.com

Epilogue

The Bond Between Chihuahuas and Their Owners

As we come to the end of our exploration into the world of Chihuahuas, we can clearly see the strong connection that these small but fierce dogs have with their owners. Chihuahuas are known for their bright and lively personalities. They are often full of energy and display a range of emotions, from excitement to affection. This spirited nature makes them delightful companions. Their protective instincts are noteworthy. Many Chihuahuas are caring and watchful, often alerting their owners to any unusual sounds or visitors. This behavior illustrates their loyalty and determination to protect those they love. In many ways, Chihuahuas carve a special niche in our lives, creating a bond that goes beyond the ordinary relationship between pets and their owners.

Joys and Challenges of Owning a Chihuahua

In our journey together, we have looked at both the joyful moments and the challenges that come with caring for a Chihuahua. Owning a Chihuahua can be a rewarding experience, filled with laughter and companionship. They are playful and often enjoy interactive games, like fetch or hide and seek. Providing mental stimulation through toys and training can also be enjoyable for both the dog and the owner. Chihuahuas often thrive on attention and affection. However, caring for this breed also comes with its own set of challenges. Their lively nature means they require plenty of exercise and engagement. Understandably, some owners may find it difficult to meet these needs, which can lead to behavioral issues.

Addressing their health needs is crucial. Regular veterinary check-ups ensure that your Chihuahua remains healthy. It's also important to keep an eye on their diet, as weight management is key to preventing health problems later in life. They can also have unique behaviors, as many are known for being stubborn. It requires patience and understanding to train them properly. Every Chihuahua has its quirks, so getting to know your dog's individual personality helps forge a strong bond.

Tales of Connection and Friendship

The stories throughout this book have illustrated just how profoundly Chihuahuas affect the lives they touch. Many families share tales of how their Chihuahua provided comfort during tough times, curled up beside them during moments of sadness. These small dogs, with their big hearts, can brighten your day with a simple wag of their tail. In many cases, they prove that they are not just pets but loyal companions who understand our emotions.

Moreover, Chihuahuas often provide a sense of security. Their natural alertness can make them effective watchdogs, warning owners of any disturbances around the home. This protective nature can offer peace of mind in our daily lives. Some owners have found that their Chihuahuas have a unique knack for detecting changes in their behavior or health, responding with extra cuddles or concern. It's these little moments of connection that remind us of the special relationship we share with them.

Finding Inspiration in Your Relationship

As you reflect on the experiences shared in this book, we hope you feel inspired by your own relationship with your Chihuahua. These dogs have a special way of teaching us about love and patience. The bond deepens in quiet moments spent together, as well as through playful escapades. For those contemplating welcoming a Chihuahua into their lives, consider the joy they bring. They may be small in size, but the love they offer is immense.

Welcoming a Chihuahua might involve preparing your home for their arrival as well. Creating a safe space for them is essential. It's helpful to establish a routine, ensuring they feel secure in their new environment. By doing so, you set the foundation for a loving relationship that can flourish.

A Tribute to Chihuahuas

To the Chihuahuas that enrich our lives with laughter, warmth, and unwavering love, this book serves as a heartfelt tribute. These little dogs are, in many ways, a reflection of their owners, sharing in joy, adventure, and sometimes even sadness. The companionship of a Chihuahua is truly special, reminding us that love knows no bounds.

Whether they curl up on your lap during a lazy afternoon or leap around with excitement during playtime, their presence is a daily reminder of the joy pet ownership brings. It's essential to cherish these moments and learn from the resilience they display. Every bark and wag is a part of their unique personality, reminding us of the power of companionship. Through our shared experiences, we continue to learn from Chihuahuas and appreciate the intangible benefits they bring to our lives, enriching our days with happiness and love.

Printed in Dunstable, United Kingdom